Oxford Paperback English Texts   General Editor **John Buxton**

AF283585

Sir Philip Sidney

Selected Poems

Sir Philip Sidney

Selected Poems

Edited by **Katherine Duncan-Jones**

Clarendon Press · Oxford

Oxford University Press, Walton Street, Oxford OX2 6DP

Oxford New York Toronto
Delhi Bombay Calcutta Madras Karachi
Petaling Jaya Singapore Hong Kong Tokyo
Nairobi Dar es Salaam Cape Town
Melbourne Auckland

and associated companies in
Beirut Berlin Ibadan Nicosia

ISBN 0 19 871053 4

Oxford is a trade mark of Oxford University Press

Published in the United States by
Oxford University Press, New York

© Oxford University Press, 1973

First published 1973
Reprinted 1979, 1982, 1984, 1986

Printed in Great Britain
at the University Printing House, Oxford
by David Stanford
Printer to the University

Contents

POEMS FROM CERTAIN SONNETS

Introduction

Sidney has given an account of his own youth and education in the *Old Arcadia*, where he presents himself in the figure of the melancholy shepherd Philisides:

The name of Samothea is so famous that, telling you I am of that, I shall not need to extend myself further in telling you what that country is. But there I was born, of such parentage as neither left me so great that I was a mark for envy nor so base that I was subject to contempt; brought up from my cradle age with such care as parents are wont to bestow upon their children whom they mean to make the maintainers of their name. And as soon as my memory grew strong enough to receive what might be delivered unto it by my senses, they offered learning unto me, especially that kind that teacheth what in truth, and not in opinion, is to be embraced, and what to be eschewed. Neither was I barred from seeking the natural knowledge of things, so far as the narrow sight of man hath pierced into it; and because the mind's commandment is vain without the body be enabled to obey it, my strength was exercised with horsemanship, weapons, and suchlike other qualities as, besides the practice, carried in themselves some serviceable use; wherein I so profited that, as I was not excellent, so was I accompanable. After that by my years, or perchance by a sooner privilege than years commonly grant, I was thought able to be mine own master, I was suffered to spend some time in travel, that by the comparison of many things I might ripen my judgement: since greatness, power, riches and suchlike standing in relation to another, who doth know none but his own, doth not know his own. Then, being home returned, and thought of good hope (for the world rarely bestows a better title upon youth) I continued to use the benefits of a quiet mind, in truth (I call him to witness that knoweth hearts) even in the secret of my soul bent to honesty. Thus far you see, as no pompous spectacle of an untroubled tenor of a well guided life. But alas, what should I make pathetical exclamations to a most true event? So it happened that love (which what it is, your own feeling can best tell you) diverted this course of tranquillity, which though I did with so much covering hide, that I was thought void of it as any man; yet my wound, which smarted to myself, brought me in fine to this change, much in state, but more in mind.[1]

As far as it goes, this account seems to be accurate, except that we do not (and probably cannot ever) know whether Sidney really fell in love soon after his three years of foreign travel. Certainly he soon began to write love poetry. His comment in the *Defence of Poetry* that 'overmastered by some thoughts, I yielded an inky tribute unto them',[2] suggests that it was under the pressure of *some* experience

---

[1] *Old Arcadia*, pp. 334–5.
[2] *Misc. Prose*, p. 109.

that Sidney became a poet; but the experience may to a large extent
have been that of failing to find worthy employment.

The life of Sidney is remarkable for a great number of potentialities
unrealized. Unhappily for him, though happily for us, he turned to
imaginative writing when outlets for action failed to present them-
selves. His father, Sir Henry Sidney, in whose arms the young Edward
VI is said to have died, achieved high office under Elizabeth. He was
three times Lord Deputy Governor of Ireland, at the same time as
being Lord President of the Marches of Wales. But his long and
faithful service, in which he spent most of his fortune, left him un-
rewarded except by esteem; when he was offered a peerage, he had
to refuse it, being too poor to maintain a suitable style of life.[1] Sidney
described his father's family as 'ancient and always well-esteemed
and well-matched gentry';[2] his mother's family, the Dudleys, were
much better matched, but perhaps less well esteemed. For most of
his life Sidney was heir to his maternal uncle, the Earl of Leicester,
the favourite of the Queen in her youth, and one of the most powerful
men in the country. As well as being Leicester's heir, Philip was
looked to by his parents as the glory of his family; by his friends as
a great English politician; and by much of Protestant Europe as
possible leader of a Protestant League against Spain. His three years
on the Continent, from 1572 to 1575, were a *succès fou* in terms of the
impression Sidney made on leading scholars and statesmen in every
country that he went to. Young though he was (eighteen to twenty-
two), what Matthew Roydon called his 'sweet attractive kind of
grace'[3] seems to have enchanted everyone whom he met. His return
to England must have been something of a disappointment, however,
as he had no official employment, except the trivial sinecure of royal
cup-bearer, for the next year and a half. Early in 1577 he was sent
as an ambassador to the Emperor's court at Prague, and stood god-
father to one of William of Orange's children. This important
mission—a remarkable one for the Queen to entrust to such a young
man—was not followed up by any other; and though he took an
active interest in the political affairs of his father and uncle, Sidney
must have felt cramped and depressed by his lack of opportunities
for action. In a letter to his uncle in 1580, written when a heavy cold
kept him from court, he says with a comic bitterness, 'my only
service is speech, and that is stopped'.[4] It was in these years of com-

[1] Wallace, *Life*, p. 114 and *passim*.
[2] *Misc. Prose*, p. 132.
[3] Matthew Roydon, 'An elegy or friend's passion for his Astrophil', in the
poems after Spenser's *Astrophel*.
[4] *Works*, iii. 129.

parative idleness, however, between 1577 and 1584, that Sidney wrote his major poetry. In 1585 he seems to have begun to turn, after the traditional pattern of a Christian poet's career, from secular to sacred writing, beginning translations of the Psalms and of his Huguenot friend Duplessis-Mornay's demonstration of the truth of the Christian religion.[1] But in the summer of this year he also began to take more energetic steps towards a life of action, attempting to sail to the West Indies with Drake. He was recalled at Plymouth by a letter sent at the Queen's command, and was shortly after appointed Lord Governor of Flushing. This was a somewhat equivocal post, though Sidney seems to have made more of a success of it than Leicester did of his post as Governor-General of the United Provinces.[2] Sidney never returned to England, and the circumstances of his death, a year later, were such as to underline its waste and futility. Arming for a skirmish with the Spanish near Zutphen, he left off his thigh-pieces, either out of a heroic determination not to be better armed than any of the other officers,[3] or, as seems equally likely, out of a fashionable distaste for traditional heavy armour.[4] A stray musket-ball splintered his thigh; infection set in, and Sidney died nearly four weeks later. He was almost the only Englishman of rank to die at enemy hands during Elizabeth's reign, Sir Richard Grenville, of the *Revenge*, being another. In spite of Sidney's habitual affectation of modesty, there is probably some truth in his assertion in *Astrophil and Stella*:

> In truth I swear, I wish not there should be
> Graved in mine epitaph a poet's name.   (AS 90.8–9.)

—not because he thought poorly of poetry, or of his own poetry, but because he had hoped to have graved in his epitaph a great politician's name.

When we turn to the poetry itself, it is surprising, and refreshing, to find how little it directly reflects Sidney's great political ambitions. Though the central idea of the *Defence of Poetry* is that poetry is to be valued as the most effective spur and guide to heroic action, the body of Sidney's writing shows a concern with moral and emotional dilemmas of a personal kind, and with bringing into English the sophistications of French and Italian poetry. His first piece of imaginative writing, the royal entertainment *The Lady of May*, does

---

[1] *Misc. Prose*, pp. 153–5.
[2] Cf. Roy Strong and J. A. van Dorsten, *Leicester's Triumph* (Leiden, 1962).
[3] Greville, *Life*, p. 128.
[4] Sir John Smythe, *Certain discourses concerning the forms and effects of divers sorts of weapons* (1590), fol. 3.

show Sidney primarily in his role as a courtier, in that it was written to entertain the Queen when she came to stay with Leicester at Wanstead House, in Essex, in 1578 or 1579. It is also unusual in that it is in a native tradition, deriving from such entertainments as the magnificent displays at Kenilworth in 1570, also presented to the Queen by Leicester. It is already characteristic of Sidney in the inventiveness of the comic language of the rustics, and in the light way in which it touches on his favourite theme, the debate between contemplation and action. These qualities do not as yet show clearly in the three poems in the piece, which are not included in the present collection. Probably about the same time that Sidney wrote *The Lady of May*—a year or so after his return from the Continent— he began the first version of his pastoral romance, known, to distinguish it from the second version, as the *Old Arcadia*. It was written for the amusement of Sidney's sister, the young Countess of Pembroke, and her friends. He describes it, in his dedicatory letter to her, as 'being done in loose sheets of paper, most of it in your presence, the rest by sheets sent unto you, as fast as they were done'.[1] The three main models for it were the *Aethiopica* of Heliodorus, which Sidney was to describe in the *Defence* as 'an absolute heroical poem', the *Arcadia* of Sannazaro, and the *Diana* of Montemayor. The last two are 'Menippean romances', with a large number of inset poems, some closely related to the story, some forming poetic *divertissements*. Sidney's romance has a much stronger and more varied prose narrative than either of these, but none the less, in the first version, provides occasions for a great many poems and songs. The inhabitants of Arcadia (as in Sannazaro) are described as naturally gifted in poetry, and songs displaying appropriately varied degrees and kinds of poetic skill are ascribed to all the main characters. The Eclogues appended to the first four books are evenings of pastoral entertainment consisting largely of songs and recitations; the first two miscellaneous, and the second two each with a single theme—marriage in the Third Eclogues, which are included whole in this volume, and melancholy and death in the Fourth. The singing competitions and displays of poetic skill in the Eclogues provide an obvious pretext for metrical complexity and experiment. In the former, for instance, each singer introduces fresh complexities of rhyme and line-length, in the hope that his rival will be unable to follow him; double and triple rhymes, for which Sidney in the *Defence* praised the English language,[2] are one of the obvious diffi-

[1] *Works*, i. 3.
[2] *Misc. Prose*, p. 118.

culties employed in this way. There are many experiments in classical metres. Sidney was one of the leaders of the movement to establish classical measures in English verse—others, less successful in terms of the poems they produced, were Spenser, Gabriel Harvey, and Sidney's protégé Abraham Fraunce.[1] Various theories of how quantitative verse could be written in English were evolved; Campion, perhaps the only other poet to do it successfully, had his own scheme. Sidney's rules, based on those of Thomas Drant, are preserved in a passage in an early version of the *Old Arcadia*.[2] In the *Defence of Poetry* Sidney praised the 'ancient' mode of versifying, as 'more fit for music, both words and time observing quantity, and more fit lively to express diverse passions, by the low or lofty sound of the well-weighed syllable'.[3] The most successful uses of technical complexity come not in the formal displays and exercises, such as the singing-contests, but in poems where characters from the romance are hammering out their own concerns—where, in fact, the element of technical experiment either is or appears to be subsidiary to the exploration of a theme. Such poems are Pyrocles's Sapphics, in which he covertly addresses Philoclea in 'eyes' language' (vii); the debate on providence in *terza rima* (xv); and the hyperbolical double sestina in which Strephon and Klaius lament the departure from Arcadia of their mistress Urania (xxxii). None of Sidney's many imitators, in the flowering of the Elizabethan lyric which was to follow in the next two decades, approached either the depth of thought or the astonishing metrical virtuosity displayed by poems such as these.

The *Certain Sonnets*, a 'loose' collection of translations, metrical experiments, and Petrarchan love poems, probably includes some very early work, but was written over a longer period. The poems are variable in quality and in form, including among other metrical experiments half a dozen poems written 'to the tune of' Italian and Spanish art songs. The poems are arranged to form a miniature sequence, opening with two sonnets of submission to love, and closing with two of renunciation; the same rather crude structuring device, a division into love and anti-love poems, was used by Thomas Watson in his *Hekatompathia* (1582), the first English sonnet-sequence to be published.

The uniqueness of Sidney's poetic achievement is only fully displayed in *Astrophil and Stella*, probably written in 1581–2, the

---

[1] For an account of the movement, see John Thompson, *The Founding of English Metre* (1962), pp. 128–38, and Derek Attridge, *Well-weighed Syllables* (1974).

[2] Quoted by Ringler, pp. 389–90.

[3] *Misc. Prose*, pp. 117–18.

whole of which is included in the present volume. It has no single model, and not a single sonnet in it is a direct translation or imitation of an earlier one. It belongs broadly to the tradition of Petrarch's *Canzoniere*, and derives many stylistic and thematic devices from poets such as Serafino, Ronsard, and Desportes. Most of these, however, such as the Anacreontic anecdotes about Cupid, are given a fresh and individual quality; and the most remarkable elements are wholly original.

These elements, in which none of Sidney's successors, even Shakespeare, were to match him, might broadly be described as dramatic coherence, humour, and, in a specialized sense, realism. Astrophil, if not fully a 'character', is undoubtedly a dramatic 'voice', comparable with the speakers in some of Browning's dramatic monologues. It is a voice with a very wide range of tones, moving between jest and earnest as subtly and unexpectedly as that of Chaucer the pilgrim. The realism of the sequence does not lie in the fact that Sidney uses biographical material, though he certainly does this. Astrophil is given the parentage, position at Court, and coat of arms of Philip Sidney (Sonnets 30, 41, 65, 70); and Stella, in so far as she appears, is undoubtedly 'meant for' Penelope Devereux, daughter of the Earl of Essex, and unhappily married late in 1581 to Lord Rich. What reality lay behind the sequence—whether a courtly game, a pretext for writing poetry, an intense personal experience, or some mixture of all three—we shall never know. The important thing is that, whether or not he was to any extent transcribing his own experience, Sidney gave to Astrophil's love that 'forcibleness' which he felt was lacking in most contemporary English love poetry.[1] By colloquial diction, strongly compressed imagery, lifelike shifts of tone, and above all by a comic self-awareness, Sidney gives Astrophil an arresting and convincing voice which no other 'Petrarchan' lover possesses. This is partly because Astrophil is only in a very general sense a 'Petrarchan' lover at all. The realism of the sequence lies in the way Sidney presents a love which is in no way an elevating spiritual experience, like Petrarch's; nor even a painful means of learning profound truths, like Shakespeare's. Astrophil learns nothing from his experience except what he already knew from his education: that to submit to sensual desire is to find moral degradation and unhappiness. Much of the sequence consists, not of attempts to persuade Stella to return his love (as in the sequences of Ronsard), but of attempts to persuade himself that 'all is well'. Sidney gives us a vivid picture of Astrophil's progress into self-deception, and in so

[1] *Misc. Prose*, p. 115.

doing gives the sonnet-sequence a moral quality which the 'melodious doodlings' of the later Elizabethan sonneteers wholly lack.[1]

In form, too, the sequence is more adventurous than its successors. Sidney uses Petrarchan rhyme schemes throughout, rather than the much simpler 'English' or Surreyan form. Like some of the Pléiade poets, he also included variants on the sonnet form, such as sonnets in alexandrines (1, 6, 8, 76, 77) and a sonnet with only two rhyme words (89). The songs interspersed among the later sonnets are also a traditional element, giving formal variety and rather different insights into the lovers' relationship. They too include metrical innovations new in English, such as the trochaic metre of the second, fourth, eighth, and ninth songs.[2] Like so many of Sidney's technical innovations, these are so subtly handled that it is hard to realize that they are new; and the fact that *Astrophil and Stella* was not printed till almost a decade later (two editions in 1591) makes it seem a later example of the sonnet-sequence vogue than it really is.

Sidney wrote virtually no more original poetry after *Astrophil and Stella*, or at least none that survives. At about the same time as *Astrophil and Stella* he wrote *The Defence of Poetry*; and in 1584 he began to revise his *Arcadia*, producing the long but unfinished fragment—almost twice the length of the original version—known as the *New Arcadia*. In the revised romance, which is far more complex in its plot and overtly serious in its themes, the *Arcadia* poems do not blend so well into the narrative. Not all of them reappear; and the scope of the romance has been so much enlarged and deepened that some of the elements from the *Old Arcadia* that do appear seem like fossils. By Book 3 of the revised version Sidney has moved far from the world of singing contests and pastoral games and into a darker one of human cruelty and muddle. Later editions of the *Arcadia*, up to 1613, had a few more 'Arcadian' poems added to them, such as the 'Additional Poem' in the present volume, but these were probably written early rather than late.

The rest of Sidney's works are translations, and all show, like the *New Arcadia*, the increased seriousness of his interests. At some time in the last three or four years of his life he translated Du Bartas's *La Semaine*, a translation which has completely disappeared;[3] probably in 1584 he began to translate Duplessis-Mornay's *De la verité de la religion chrestienne*, a translation so heavily rewritten by

---

[1] F. T. Prince, 'The Sonnet from Wyatt to Shakespeare', in *Stratford-upon-Avon Studies* 2: *Elizabethan Poetry* (1960), p. 21.

[2] The 'trochaic' metres can alternatively be read as iambics lacking the first syllable.

[3] Ringler, p. 339.

Golding, who completed it, that none of it can be clearly recognized
as Sidney's; and perhaps about the same time he translated the first
forty-three Psalms, which were later completed by his sister, the
Countess of Pembroke, but not published until 1823. On stylistic
grounds they have been dated very early;[1] but according to Thomas
Moffett, who was the Countess of Pembroke's doctor, Sidney began
his translation after *Astrophil and Stella* and the *Arcadia*.[2] If this
dating is right, Sidney's short poetical career satisfyingly shows the
traditional progress from secular to sacred verse.

[1] Cf. Theodore Spencer, 'The Poetry of Sir Philip Sidney', *ELH* xii (1945), 254.
Neil L. Rudenstine, *Sidney's Poetic Development* (Cambridge, Mass., 1967),
pp. 284–7.

[2] Thomas Moffett, *Nobilis*, edd. Virgil B. Heltzel and Hoyt H. Hudson (San
Marino, Calif., 1940), p. 74.

Chronological Table

1554   Philip Sidney born at Penshurst in Kent, 29 November, and named after Philip of Spain.

1564   Philip Sidney and Fulke Greville enter Shrewsbury School.

1568   At Christ Church, Oxford.

1572   Sets out, in the train of the Earl of Lincoln, for continental travel; witnesses the Massacre of St. Bartholomew's Day in Paris, 24 August.

1573   Travels to Heidelburg and Frankfurt, where he meets Hubert Languet, and to Vienna, Hungary, and Italy. Studies in Padua and Venice.

1575   Returns to England by way of Vienna, Poland, and the Netherlands. Sir Henry Sidney begins his third term of office as Lord Deputy Governor of Ireland.

1577   Defends his father's policy in Ireland. Is sent as ambassador to the Imperial Court; discusses Protestant League; meets William of Orange.

1578   Perhaps writes *The Lady of May*. Begins to write the *Arcadia* at Wilton, the house of his sister, the Countess of Pembroke.

1580   Writes to the Queen to dissuade her from marrying the Duke of Anjou. Completes the *Old Arcadia*.

1581   Begins to write *Astrophil and Stella*; perhaps writes *The Defence of Poetry*. Penelope Devereux marries Lord Rich.

1582   Escorts the Duke of Anjou back to the Netherlands. Finishes *Astrophil and Stella*.

1583   Knighted for reasons of protocol. Marries Frances, daughter of Sir Francis Walsingham.

1584   Begins to revise the *Arcadia*. Writes the *Defence of the Earl of Leicester*.

1585   Begins to translate Duplessis-Mornay's *De la verité de la religion chrestienne*; perhaps translates Du Bartas's *La Semaine* and begins translation of the *Psalms*, later completed by the Countess of Pembroke. Attempts to sail to the West Indies with Drake. Appointed Governor of Flushing.

1586   Travels in the northern Netherlands. Is actively involved in politics. Wounded in a skirmish near Zutphen, 22 September; dies at Arnhem, 17 October.

1587   Buried in St. Paul's at the expense of Sir Francis Walsingham, his father-in-law, 16 February. Golding's completed version of *The Trueness of the Christian Religion* published.

1590   The *New Arcadia* published.

1591   *Astrophil and Stella* published.

1593   The *New Arcadia* with Books 3–5 of the *Old Arcadia* published.

1595   The *Defence of Poetry* published.

1598   The composite *Arcadia* published with *Astrophil and Stella* and *Certain Sonnets*.

Note on the Text

The present edition is based on Professor Ringler's *Poems of Sir Philip Sidney* (Oxford, 1962), which should be consulted for detailed information about the text. The half dozen places where the text of Ringler's edition has been emended are noted in the commentary. Ringler's numbering of the poems, which has become the standard form of reference, is given in square brackets on the right of the titles of the present edition. In the case of *Astrophil and Stella*, which is included in its entirety, the numbering is identical to Ringler's. For ease of reference, descriptive titles have been given to the *Arcadia* poems and *Certain Sonnets*; it should be stressed that, apart from thirteen titles in *Certain Sonnets*, noted in the commentary, these titles have no claim to being Sidney's. Spelling has been modernized throughout. As none of Sidney's poetry survives in holograph, Ringler's text gives us only the spelling patterns of contemporary scribes and compositors. The aim here has been to modernize the spelling without modernizing the language. In poems such as OA xxviii [64] and xxx [66], where some degree of archaism was clearly intended, editorial decisions about modernization were particularly difficult; and in many places they have inevitably depended on the editor's interpretation of Sidney's syntax. Where he is in doubt, the reader should consult Ringler's edition, whose spelling, though not Sidney's, is at least close to his in time.

A superior 'n' after a word or line in the text indicates that a note is to be found in the commentary, pp. 203 ff.

The prose of the *Old Arcadia* Third Eclogues is based on Jean Robertson's edition of the *Old Arcadia* (1973), pp. 244–63, a text which is modernized. I am grateful to Miss Robertson for her unfailing help and kindness.

Abbreviations

AS	Sidney, *Astrophil and Stella.*
Correspondence	Pears, Steuart A. (ed.), *The Correspondence of Sir Philip Sidney and Hubert Languet* (1845).
CS	Sidney, *Certain Sonnets.*
Diana	Kennedy, J. M. (ed.), *Yonge's translation of George of Montemayor's 'Diana' and Gil Polo's 'Enamoured Diana'* (1968).
Misc. Prose	Duncan-Jones, K. D., and van Dorsten, J. A. (edd.), *Miscellaneous Prose of Sir Philip Sidney* (1973).
OA	Sidney, *Old Arcadia*, poems.
Old Arcadia	Robertson, Jean (ed.), Sidney, *The Countess of Pembroke's Arcadia* (*The Old Arcadia*) (1973).
Tilley, *Proverbs*	Tilley, Morris Palmer, *A Dictionary of Proverbs in England in the Sixteenth and Seventeenth Centuries* (Ann Arbor, Mich., 1960).
Wallace, *Life*	Wallace, Malcom W., *The Life of Sir Philip Sidney* (1915).
Works	Feuillerat, A. (ed.), *The Works of Sir Philip Sidney* (1912–26; repr. 1962).

Reading List

Items marked with an asterisk * are of particular importance. Books are published in the British Isles unless otherwise stated.

1. EDITIONS OF SIDNEY

The Countess of Pembroke's Arcadia (1590). The *New Arcadia*, divided into chapters by Fulke Greville.

The Countess of Pembroke's Arcadia (1593). The *New Arcadia* without the chapter divisions, but with Books 3–5 of the *Old Arcadia* added.

The Countess of Pembroke's Arcadia (1598). As above, with *Astrophil and Stella* and *Certain Sonnets* added.

**The Countess of Pembroke's Arcadia* (*The Old Arcadia*), ed. Jean Robertson (1973).

Astrophil and Stella (1591). Two editions in the same year, the first the pirated one printed by Thomas Newman.

Astrophil and Stella, ed. Vanna Gentili (Bari, 1965). Italian; useful bibliography.

The Defence of Poetry (printed by William Ponsonby, 1595).

An Apology for Poetry (printed by Henry Olney, 1595). A slightly different text of the same work.

**An Apology for Poetry*, ed. Geoffrey Shepherd (1965). Learned introduction and commentary.

The Defence of Poetry, ed. J. van Dorsten (1966).

The Psalms of David, ed. Samuel Weller Singer (1823).

The Psalms of Sir Philip Sidney and the Countess of Pembroke, ed. J. C. Rathmell (New York, 1963).

**The Correspondence of Sir Philip Sidney and Hubert Languet*, edited and translated by S. A. Pears (1845).

**The Works of Sir Philip Sidney*, ed. A. Feuillerat (4 vols., 1912–26); repr. without *Astrophil and Stella* and *Certain Sonnets* (1962).

**The Poems of Sir Philip Sidney*, ed. W. A. Ringler (1962). The basis of the present edition.

**Miscellaneous Prose of Sir Philip Sidney*, ed. K. Duncan-Jones and J. van Dorsten (1973). Includes *The Lady of May* and *The Defence of Poetry*.

2. BOOKS ON SIDNEY

BUXTON, JOHN, *Sir Philip Sidney and the English Renaissance* (1954).

*GREVILLE, FULKE, *The Life of Sir Philip Sidney* [*1652*], ed. Nowell Smith (1907).

KALSTONE, DAVID, *Sidney's Poetry: Contexts and Interpretations* (Cambridge, Mass., 1965).

MOFFET, THOMAS, *Nobilis, or a view of the life and death of a Sidney*, edd. VIRGIL B. HELTZEL and HOYT H. HUDSON (San Marino, Calif., 1940).

MYRICK, K. O., *Sir Philip Sidney as a Literary Craftsman* (Cambridge, Mass., 1935; repr. 1965).

*WALLACE, M. W., *The Life of Sir Philip Sidney* (1915). The standard biography.

WILSON, MONA, *Sir Philip Sidney* (1931; repr. 1950).

ZANDVOORT, R. W., *Sidney's 'Arcadia': A comparison of the two versions* (Amsterdam, 1929).

3. OTHER BOOKS

BUXTON, JOHN, *Elizabethan Taste* (1963).

FRAUNCE, ABRAHAM, *The Arcadian Rhetorike* [*1588*], ed. ETHEL SEATON (1950).

HOSKYNS, JOHN, *Directions for Speech and Style* [*1599*], ed. HOYT H. HUDSON (Princeton, N.J., 1935).

*MONTEMAYOR, JORGE DE, *Yong's translation of George of Montemayor's 'Diana' and Gil Polo's 'Enamoured Diana'*, ed. J. M. KENNEDY (1968).

*PETRARCH, FRANCESCO, *Il Canzoniere*.

PUTTENHAM, GEORGE (?), *The Arte of English Poesie* [*1589*], edd. G. W. WILLCOCK and ALICE WALKER (1936).

RONSARD, PIERRE, *Les Amours*, edd. H. and C. WEBER (Paris, 1963).

*SANNAZARO, JACOPO, *Opere*, ed. ENRICO CARRARA (Turin, 1952).

4. ARTICLES

DOBELL, BERTRAM, 'New Light on Sidney's *Arcadia*', *Quarterly Review*, ccxi (1909), 74–100. The discovery of the complete *Old Arcadia* in MS.

JUEL-JENSEN, BENT, 'Some Uncollected Authors xxiv: Sir Philip Sidney', *The Book-collector*, xi (1962), 468–79. Exhaustive bibliography of early editions.

LAMB, CHARLES, 'Some Sonnets of Sir Philip Sidney', in *Last Essays of Elia*.

LEWIS, C. S., 'Sidney and Spenser', chapter in *English Literature in the Sixteenth Century* (1954), pp. 318–93.

ROBERTSON, JEAN, 'Sir Philip Sidney and his poetry', in *Stratford-upon-Avon Studies 2: Elizabethan Poetry* (1960), pp. 111–29.

SPENCER, THEODORE, 'The Poetry of Sidney', xii (1945), pp. 251–78.

YOUNG, RICHARD B., 'English Petrarke', in *Three Studies in the Renaissance* (New Haven, Conn., 1958).

Addenda

BOOKS ON SIDNEY

CONNELL, DOROTHY, *Sir Philip Sidney: The Maker's Mind* (1977).

NICHOLS, J. G., *The poetry of Sir Philip Sidney* (1974).

ARTICLES

DUNCAN-JONES, KATHERINE, 'Philip Sidney's Toys', Chatterton Lecture 1980 (1982).

Poems from the Old Arcadia

i. Pyrocles's song as an Amazon
[2]

Transformed in show, but more transformed in mind,
I cease to strive, with double conquest foiled:
For (woe is me) my powers all I find
With outward force and inward treason spoiled.
For from without came to mine eyes the blow   5
Whereto mine inward thoughts did faintly yield;
Both these conspired poor reason's overthrow;
False in myself, thus have I lost the field.
Thus are mine eyes still captive to one sight;
Thus all my thoughts are slaves to one thought still;   10
Thus reason to his servants yields his right;
Thus is my power transformed to your will.
    What marvel then I take a woman's hue,
    Since what I see, think, know, is all but you?

ii. A contreblason
[3]

What length of verse can serve brave Mopsa's good to show,
Whose virtues strange, and beauties such, as no man may them
    know?
Thus shrewdly burdened then, how can my muse escape?
The gods must help, and precious things must serve to show her
    shape.
    Like great god Saturn fair, and like fair Venus chaste;   5
As smooth as Pan, as Juno mild, like goddess Iris fast;
With Cupid she foresees, and goes god Vulcan's pace;
And for a taste of all these gifts, she borrows Momus' grace
    Her forehead jacinth-like, her cheeks of opal hue,
Her twinkling eyes bedecked with pearl, her lips of sapphire
    blue,   10

[3] 6 *smooth as Pan*: rough-haired and goat-legged.
    6 *Juno mild*: famous for her jealous rages.
    6 *like goddess Iris fast*: as steadfast as the ephemeral rainbow.
    7 *Cupid*: blind.
    7 *Vulcan*: lame.
    8 *Momus*: the type of censoriousness.
    9 *jacinth*: a blue gem, perhaps sapphire.

Her hair pure crapal-stone, her mouth, O heavenly-wide,
Her skin like burnished gold, her hands like silver ure untried:
  As for those parts unknown, which hidden sure are best,
  Happy be they which well believe, and never seek the rest.

iii. A singing competition[n]   [7]

Lalus:
  Come Dorus, come, let songs thy sorrow signify;
And if for want of use thy mind ashamed is,
That very shame with love's high title dignify.
  No style is held for base, where love well named is;
Each ear sucks up the words a true love scattereth;   5
And plain speech oft than quaint phrase better framed is.

Dorus:
  Nightingales seldom sing, the pie still chattereth;[n]
The wood cries most, before it throughly kindled be;
Deadly wounds inward bleed, each slight sore mattereth.
  Hardly they herd, which by good hunters singled be;   10
Shallow brooks murmur most, deep silent slide away;
Nor true love loves those loves with others mingled be.

Lalus:
  If thou wilt not be seen, thy face go hide away:
Be none of us, or else maintain our fashion.
Who frowns at others' feasts, doth better bide away.   15
  But if thou hast a love, in that love's passion,
I challenge thee, by show of her perfection,
Which of us two deserveth most compassion.

[3]   11 *crapal-stone*: the jewel believed to be found in the forehead of toads.
      12 *silver ure*: silver ore, which is black.
      12 *untried*: unrefined.

[7]   7 *pie*: magpie.

Dorus:

Thy challenge great, but greater my protection:
Sing then, and see (for now thou hast inflamed me) 20
Thy health too mean a match for my infection.

No, though the heavens for high attempts have blamed me,
Yet high is my attempt. O muse, historify
Her praise, whose praise to learn your skill hath framed me.

Lalus:

Muse, hold your peace; but thou, my god Pan, glorify 25
My Kala's gifts, who with all good gifts filled is.
Thy pipe, O Pan, shall help, though I sing sorrily.

A heap of sweets she is, where nothing spilled is,
Who though she be no bee, yet full of honey is;
A lily field, with plough of rose which tilled is; 30
Mild as a lamb, more dainty than a cony is.

Her eyes my eyesight is, her conversation
More glad to me than to a miser money is.

What coy account she makes of estimation!
How nice to touch! How all her speeches peized be! 35
A nymph thus turned, but mended in translation.

Dorus:

Such Kala is: but ah, my fancies raised be
In one, whose name to name were high presumption,
Since virtues all to make her title pleased be.

O happy gods, which by inward assumption 40
Enjoy her soul, in body's fair possession,
And keep it joined, fearing your seat's consumption,

How oft with rain of tears skies make confession,
Their dwellers rapt with sight of her perfection,
From heavenly throne to her heaven use digression. 45

Of best things then what world can yield confection
To liken her? Deck yourselves with comparison:
She is herself of best things the collection.

31 *cony*: rabbit.
35 *nice to touch*: squeamish about being touched.
35 *peized*: carefully deliberated, pondered.

Lalus:

How oft my doleful sire cried to me, 'tarry, son',
When first he spied my love! How oft he said to me   50
'Thou art no soldier fit for Cupid's garrison.

My son, keep this, that my long toil hath laid to me:
Love well thine own; wool's whiteness passeth all;
I never found long love such wealth hath paid to me.'

This wind he spent; but when my Kala glasseth all   55
My sight in her fair limbs, I then assure myself,
Not rotten sheep, but high crowns she surpasseth all.

Can I be poor, that her gold hair procure myself?
Want I white wool, whose eyes her white skin garnished?
Till I get her, shall I to sheep enure myself?   60

Dorus:

How oft, when reason saw love of her harnished
With armour of my heart, he cried: 'O vanity,
To set a pearl in steel so meanly varnished!ⁿ

Look to thyself; reach not beyond humanity;
Her mind, beams, state far from thy weak wings banished;   65
And love which lover hurts is inhumanity.'

Thus reason said; but she came, reason vanished;
Her eyes so mastering me, that such objection
Seemed but to spoíl the food of thoughts long famished.

Her peerless height my mind to high erection   70
Draws up; and if, hope failing, end life's pleasure,
Of fairer death how can I make election?ⁿ

Lalus:

Once my well-waiting eyes espied my treasure,
With sleeves turned up, loose hair, and breasts enlarged,
Her father's corn (moving her fair limbs) measure.   75

'O,' cried I, 'of so mean work be discharged;
Measure my case, how by thy beauty's filling
With seed of woes my heart brim-full is charged.

Thy father bids thee save, and chides for spilling;
Save then my soul, spill not my thoughts well heaped;   80
No lovely praise was ever got with killing.'

55 *glasseth*: reflects, attracts.
60 *enure*: accustom.
61 *harnished*: harnessed, armed.
74 *enlarged*: set at large, uncovered.

These bold words she did hear, this fruit I reaped:
That she, whose look alone might make me blessed,
Did smile on me, and then away she leaped.

Dorus:

Once, O sweet once, I saw, with dread oppressed,   85
Her whom I dread: so that with prostrate lying
Her length the earth in love's chief clothing dressed.[n]
    I saw that riches fall, and fell a-crying:
'Let not dead earth enjoy so rich a cover,
But deck therewith my soul, for your sake dying.   90
    Lay all your fear upon your fearful lover,
Shine eyes on me, that both our lives be guarded:
So I your sight, you shall yourselves recover.'
    I cried, and was with open rays rewarded;
But straight they fled, summoned by cruel honour;   95
Honour, the cause desert is not regarded.

Lalus:

This maid, thus made for joys, O Pan bemoan her,
That without love she spends her years of love:
So fair a field would well become an owner.
    And if enchantment can a hard heart move,   100
Teach me what circle may acquaint her sprite,
Affection's charms in my behalf to prove.[n]
    The circle is my round-about-her sight;
The power I will invoke dwells in her eyes;
My charm should be, she haunt me day and night.   105

Dorus:

Far other care, O muse, my sorrow tries,
Bent to such one in whom myself must say,
Nothing can mend one point that in her lies.
    What circle then in so rare force bears sway,
Whose sprite all sprites can spoil, raise, damn or save?   110
No charm hold her, but well possess she may,
    Possess she doth, and makes my soul her slave,
My eyes the bands, my thoughts the fatal knot:
No thralls like them, that inward bondage have.

---

93 *your sight*: the sight of you.
96 *the cause*: the reason why.

Lalus:

Kala, at length conclude my lingering lot;[n]   115
Disdain me not, although I be not fair.
Who is an heir of many hundred sheep
Doth beauties keep, which never sun can burn,
Nor storms do turn; fairness serves oft to wealth.
Yet all my health I place in your good-will,   120
Which if you will (O do) bestow on me,
Such as you see, such still you shall me find,
Constant and kind; my sheep your food shall breed,
Their wool your weed; I will you music yield
In flowery field; and as the day begins   125
With twenty gins we will the small birds take,
And pastimes make, as nature things hath made.
But when in shade we meet of myrtle boughs,
Then love allows our pleasure to enrich,
The thought of which doth pass all worldly pelf.   130

Dorus:

Lady, yourself, whom neither name I dare,
And titles are but spots to such a worth,
Hear plaints come forth from dungeon of my mind.
The noblest kind rejects not others' woes.
I have no shows of wealth; my wealth is you,   135
My beauty's hue your beams, my health your deeds,
My mind for weeds your virtue's livery wears;
My food is tears; my tunes waymenting yield;
Despair my field; the flowers spirit's wars;
My day new cares; my gins my daily sight,   140
In which do light small birds of thoughts o'erthrown;
My pastimes none; time passeth on my fall;
Nature made all, but me of dolours made;
I find no shade but where my sun doth burn;
No place to turn; without, within, it fries;   145
Nor help by life or death who living dies.

126 *gins*: traps.
138 *waymenting*: lamenting, complaint.

Lalus:
But if my Kala this my suit denies,[n]
    Which so much reason bears,
Let crows pick out mine eyes, which saw too much:
    If still her mind be such,   150
My earthy mould doth melt in watery tears.

Dorus:
My earthy mould doth melt in watery tears,
    And they again resolve
To air of sighs, sighs to the heart's fire turn,
    Which doth to ashes burn;   155
So doth my life within itself dissolve.[n]

Lalus:
So doth my life within myself dissolve
    That I am like the flower
New plucked from the place where it did breed:
    Life showing, dead indeed.   160
Such force hath love above poor nature's power.

Dorus:
Such force hath love above poor nature's power,
    That I grow like a shade
Which, being nought, seems somewhat to the eyne,
    While that one body shine.   165
O, he is marred, that is for others made.[n]

Lalus:
    O, he is marred, that is for others made.
Which thought doth mar my piping declaration,
Thinking how it hath marred my shepherd's trade.
    Now my hoarse voice doth fail this occupation,   170
And others long to tell their love's condition:
Of singing take to thee the reputation.

Dorus:
    Of singing take to thee the reputation,
New friend of mine; I yield to thy ability;
My heart doth seek another estimation.   175
    But ah, my muse, I would thou hadst facility
To work my goddess so by thine invention
On me to cast those eyes, where shine nobility.
    Seen and unknown; heard, but without attention.

iv. A picture of Cupid[n]   [8]

Poor painters oft with silly poets join
To fill the world with strange but vain conceits;
One brings the stuff, the other stamps the coin,
Which breeds nought else but gloses of deceits.
  Thus painters Cupid paint, thus poets do: 5
  A naked god, young, blind, with arrows two.

Is he a god, that ever flies the light?
Or naked he, disguised in all untruth?
If he be blind, how hitteth he so right?
How is he young, that tamed old Phoebus' youth? 10
  But arrows two, and tipped with gold or lead?
  Some hurt accuse a third with horny head.

No, nothing so; an old false knave he is,
By Argus got on Io, then a cow,
What time for her Juno her Jove did miss,   15
And charge of her to Argus did allow.
  Mercury killed his false sire for this act;
  His dam, a beast, was pardoned beastly fact.

With father's death, and mother's guilty shame,
With Jove's disdain at such a rival's seed,   20
The wretch compelled a runagate became,
And learned what ill a miser state doth breed:
  To lie, feign, glose, to steal, pry and accuse,
  Nought in himself, each other to accuse.

Yet bears he still his parent's stately gifts,   25
A horned head, cloven foot, and thousand eyes,
Some gazing still, some winking wily shifts,
With large long ears where never rumour dies.
  His horned head doth seem the heaven to spite;
  His cloven foot doth never tread aright.   30

4 *gloses*: pretences, disguises.
14 *Argus*: the many-eyed dog set by Juno to guard Jove's mistress, Io.
21 *runagate*: vagabond.
23 *glose*: flatter, deceive.

Thus half a man, with man he eas'ly haunts,
Clothed in the shape which soonest may deceive;
Thus half a beast, each beastly vice he plants,
In those weak hearts that his advice receive.
  He prowls each place still in new colours decked,   35
  Sucking one's ill, another to infect.

To narrow breasts he comes all wrapped in gain;
To swelling hearts he shines in honour's fire;
To open eyes all beauties he doth rain;
Creeping to each with flattering of desire: 40
  But for that love's desire most rules the eyes,
  Therein his name, there his chief triumph lies.

Millions of years this old drivel Cupid lives,
While still more wretch, more wicked he doth prove;
Till now at length that Jove him office gives,   45
At Juno's suit, who much did Argus love,
  In this our world a hangman for to be
  Of all those fools, that will have all they see.

v. Advice of age to youth[n]   [9]

Geron:
Up, up, Philisides, let sorrows go;
Who yields to woe, doth but increase his smart.
Do not thy heart to plaintful custom bring,
But let us sing; sweet tunes do passions ease;
An old man hear, who would thy fancies raise.   5

Philisides:
Who minds to please the mind drowned in annoys
With outward joys, which inward cannot sink,
As well may think with oil to cool the fire,
Or with desire to make such foe a friend,
Who doth his soul to endless malice bend.   10

---

43 *drivel*: fool, wretch.

Geron:
Yet sure an end to each thing time doth give;
Though woes now live, at length thy woes must die.
Then virtue try, if she can work in thee
That which we see in many time hath wrought,
And weakest hearts to constant temper brought.   15

Philisides:
Who ever taught a skilless man to teach,
Or stop a breach, that never cannon saw?
Sweet virtue's law bars not a causeful moan.
Time shall in one my life and sorrows end,
And me perchance your constant temper lend.   20

Geron:
What can amend where physic is refused?
The wits abused with will no counsel take.
Yet for my sake discover us thy grief:
Oft comes relief when most we seem in trap;
The stars thy state, fortune may change thy hap.   25

Philisides:
If fortune's lap became my dwelling place,
And all the stars conspired to my good,
Still were I one, this still should be my case:
Ruin's relique, care's web and sorrow's food,
Since she, fair fierce, to such a state me calls,   30
Whose wit the stars, whose fortune fortune thralls.

Geron:
Alas, what falls are fallen unto thy mind,
That there, where thou confessed thy mischief lies,
Thy wit dost use still still more harms to find?
Whom wit makes vain, or blinded with his eyes,   35
What counsel can prevail, or light give light,
Since all his force against himself he tries?
Then each conceit that enters in by sight
Is made, forsooth, a jurate of his woes:
Earth, sea, air, fire, heaven, hell and ghastly sprite; 40

32 *falls*: happenings, events; fallings-off.
39 *jurate*: an officer who has taken an oath, or stands as surety.

Then cries to senseless things, which neither knows
What aileth thee, and if they knew thy mind
Would scorn in man, their king, such feeble shows.
Rebel, rebel, in golden fetters bind
This tyrant love; or rather, do suppress   45
Those rebel thoughts, which are thy slaves by kind.
Let not a glittering name thy fancy dress
In painted clothes, because they call it love:
There is no hate that can thee more oppress.
Begin, and half the work is done, to prove   50
By raising up, upon thyself to stand:
And think, she is a she, that doth thee move.
He water ploughs, and soweth in the sand,
And hopes the flickering wind with net to hold,
Who hath his hopes laid up in woman's hand.[n]   55
What man is he, that hath his freedom sold?
Is he a manlike man, that doth not know man
Hath power that sex with bridle to withhold?
A fickle sex, and true in trust to no man;
A servant sex, soon proud if they be coyed;   60
And, to conclude, thy mistress is a woman.

Histor:

Those words did once the loveliest shepherd use
That erst I knew, and with most plainful muse;
Yet not of women judging, as he said,
But forced with rage, his rage on them upbraid.[n]   65

Philisides:

O gods, how long this old fool hath annoyed
My wearied ears! O gods, yet grant me this,
That soon the world of his false tongue be void.
O noble age, who place their only bliss
In being heard, until the hearer die,   70
Uttering a serpent's mind with serpent's hiss.
Then who will hear a well-authorized lie,
And patience hath, let him go learn of him
What swarms of virtues did in his youth fly;
Such hearts of brass, wise heads, and garments trim   75
Were in his days; which heard, one nothing hears,
If from his words the falsehood he do skim.

60 *coyed*: coaxed, appeased.

And herein most their folly vain appears,
That since they still allege, 'when they were young',
It shows they fetch their wit from youthful years.   80
Like beast for sacrifice, where, save the tongue
And belly, nought is left, such sure is he:
This life-dead man, in this old dungeon flung.
Old houses are thrown down for new, we see;
The oldest rams are culled from the flock;   85
No man doth wish his horse should aged be;[n]
The ancient oak well makes a fired block;
Old men themselves do love young wives to choose;
Only fond youth admires a rotten stock.
Who once a white long beard well handle does   90
(As his beard him, not he his beard, did bear)
Though cradle-witted, must not honour lose.
O, when will men leave off to judge by hair,
And think them old, that have the oldest mind,
With virtue fraught, and full of holy fear?   95

Geron:
If that thy face were hid, or I were blind,
I yet should know a young man speaketh now,
Such wandering reasons in thy speech I find.
He is a beast, that beast's use will allow
For proof of man, who, sprung of heavenly fire,   100
Hath strongest soul, when most his reins do bow.
But fondlings fond, know not your own desire,
Loath to die young, and then you must be old,
Fondly blame that, to which yourselves aspire.
But this light choler that doth make you bold,   105
Rather to wrong than unto just defence,
Is past with me; my blood is waxen cold.
Thy words, though full of malapert offence,
I weigh them not, but still will thee advise
How thou from foolish love may'st purge thy sense.   110

---

85 *culled*: chosen out for slaughter.
100 *for proof of*: as an analogy to.
101 *reins*: loins.
102 *fondlings fond*: silly fools.
108 *malapert*: presumptuous, impertinent.

First think they err, that think them gaily wise
Who well can set a passion out to show:
Such sight have they, that see with goggling eyes.
Passion bears high when puffing wit doth blow,
But is indeed a toy; if not a toy,   115
True cause of evils, and cause of causeless woe.
If once thou may'st that fancy gloss destroy
Within thyself, thou soon wilt be ashamed
To be a player of thine own annoy.
Then let thy mind with better books be tamed;   120
Seek to espy her faults, as well as praise,
And let thine eyes to other sports be framed.
In hunting fearful beasts do spend some days,[n]
Or catch the birds with pit-falls, or with lime,
Or train the fox, that trains so crafty lays;   125
Lie but to sleep, and in the early prime
Seek skill of herbs in hills; haunt brooks near night,
And try with bait how fish will bite sometime;
Go graft again, and seek to graft them right,
Those pleasant plants, those sweet and fruitful trees,   130
Which both the palate and the eyes delight;
Cherish the hives of wisely painful bees;
Let special care upon thy flock be laid.
Such active mind but seldom passion sees.

Philisides:
Hath any heard what this old man hath said?   135
Truly not I, who did my thoughts engage,
Where all my pains one look of hers hath paid.

Histor:
Thus may you see, how youth esteemeth age,
And never hath thereof arightly deemed;
While hot desires do reign in fancy's rage,   140
Till age itself do make itself esteemed.

125 *train*: entice, decoy.
125 *trains*: tricks, wiles.
132 *painful*: painstaking, industrious.

vi. Musidorus's Elegiacs[n]   [11]

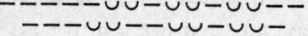

Fortune, nature, love, long have contended about me,
  Which should most miseries cast on a worm that I am.
Fortune thus gan say: 'Misery and misfortune is all one,
  And of misfortune, fortune hath only the gift;
With strong foes on land, on seas with contrary tempests,   5
  Still do I cross this wretch, what so he taketh in hand.'
'Tush, tush,' said nature, 'this is all but a trifle; a man's self
  Gives haps or mishaps, even as he ord'reth his heart.
But so his humour I frame, in a mould of choler adusted,
  That the delights of life shall be to him dolorous.'   10
Love smiled, and thus said: 'Want joined to desire is unhappy;
  But if he nought do desire, what can Heraclitus ail?
None but I works by desire; by desire have I kindled in his soul
  Infernal agonies into a beauty divine,
Where thou, poor nature, left'st all thy due glory; to fortune   15
  Her virtue is sovereign, fortune a vassal of hers.'
Nature abashed went back; fortune blushed; yet she replied thus:
  'And even in that love, shall I reserve him a spite.'
Thus, thus, alas, woeful in nature, unhappy by fortune,
  But most wretched I am, now love awakes my desire.   20

vii. Pyrocles's Sapphics[n]   [12]

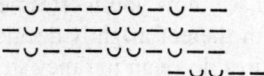

    If mine eyes can speak, to do hearty errand;
    Or mine eyes' language she do hap to judge of,
    So that eyes' message be of her received;
        Hope, we do live yet.

[11]   9 *choler adusted*: black choler, the secretion believed to cause melancholy.
     12 *Heraclitus*: the weeping philosopher, who bewailed the weakness of
     mankind.
[12]   1 *hearty errand*: errand of the heart.

But if eyes fail then, when I most do need them;   5
Or if eyes' language be not unto her known,
So that eyes' message do return rejected,
     Hope, we do both die.

Yet dying and dead do we sing her honour;
So become our tombs monuments of her praise;   10
So becomes our loss the triumph of her gain;
     Hers be the glory.

If the spheres senseless do yet hold a music,
If the swan's sweet voice be not heard, but at death,
If the mute timber when it hath the life lost   15
     Yieldeth a lute's tune;

Are then human minds privileged so meanly
As that hateful death can abridge them of power,
With the voice of truth to record to all worlds
     That we be her spoils?   20

Thus not ending ends the due praise of her praise;
Fleshly veil consumes; but a soul hath his life,
Which is held in love; love it is that hath joined
     Life to this our soul.

But if eyes can speak to do hearty errand,   25
Or mine eyes' language she do hap to judge of,
So that eyes' message be of her received,
     Hope, we do live yet.

viii. Hexameters of Musidorus and Pyrocles (Cleophila)[n]   [13]

         − ∪∪ − ∪∪ − ∪∪ − − ∪∪ − −

Dorus:
Lady, reserved by the heavens to do pastors' company honour,
Joining your sweet voice to the rural muse of a desert,
Here you fully do find this strange operation of love,
How to the woods love runs, as well as rides to the palace;

[13] 2 *desert*: deserted, solitary place.

Neither he bears reverence to a prince, nor pity to a beggar,   5
But, like a point in midst of a circle, is still of a nearness;
All to a lesson he draws, nor hills nor caves can avoid him.

Cleophila:
Worthy shepherd, by my song to myself all favour is happened,
That to the sacred muse my annoys somewhat be revealed;
Sacred muse, who in one contains what nine do in all them.   10
But, O happy be you, which safe from fiery reflection
Of Phoebus' violence, in shade of stately cypress tree,
Or pleasant myrtle, may teach the unfortunate echo
In these woods to resound the renowned name of a goddess:
Happy be you that may to the saint, your only idea,   15
(Although simply attired) your manly affection utter.
Happy be those mishaps which, justly proportion holding,
Give right sound to the ears, and enter aright to the judgement;
But wretched be the souls which, veiled in a contrary subject,
How much more we do love, so the less our loves be believed.   20
What skill serveth the sore of a wrong infirmity judged?
What can justice avail, to a man that tells not his own case?
You, though fears do abash, in you still possible hopes be;
Nature against we do seem to rebel, seem fools in a vain suit;
But so unheard, condemned, kept thence we do seek to abide in,   25
Self-lost and wandering, banished that place we do come from,
What mean is there, alas, we can hope our loss to recover?
What place is there left, we may hope our woes to recomfort?
Unto the heavens? Our wings be too short; the earth thinks us
    a burden;
Air we do still with sighs increase. To the fire? We do want
    none;   30
And yet his outward heat our tears would quench, but an
    inward
Fire no liquor can cool; Neptune's seat would be dried up there.
Happy shepherd, with thanks to the gods, still think to be
    thankful,
That to thy advancement their wisdoms have thee abased.

15 *idea*: the Platonic Idea, or ideal absolute.
19 *veiled in a contrary subject*: a reference to Pyrocles's disguise as an Amazon,
    Cleophila.

Dorus :

Unto the gods with a thankful heart all thanks I do render,   35
That to my advancement their wisdoms have me abased.
But yet, alas, O but yet, alas, our haps be but hard haps,
Which must frame contempt to the fittest purchase of honour.
Well may a pastor plain, but alas, his plaints be not esteemed.
Silly shepherd's poor pipe, when his harsh sound testifies our
        woes   40
Into the fair looker-on pastime, not passion, enters.
And to the woods or brooks who do make such dreary recital
What be the pangs they bear, and whence those pangs be derived,
Pleased to receive that name by rebounding answer of echo,
And hope thereby to ease their inward horrible anguish;   45
Then shall those things ease their inward horrible anguish,
When trees dance to the pipe, and swift streams stay by the
        music,
Or when an echo begins unmoved to sing them a love song.
Say then, what vantage do we get by the trade of a pastor,
Since no estates be so base, but love vouchsafeth his arrow,   50
Since no refuge doth serve from wounds we do carry about us,
Since outward pleasures be but halting helps to decayed souls,
Save that daily we may discern what fire we do burn in?
Far more happy be you, whose greatness gets a free access,
Whose fair bodily gifts are framed most lovely to each eye.   55
Virtue you have; of virtue you have left proofs to the whole
        world,[n]
And virtue is grateful with beauty and richness adorned;
Neither doubt you a whit, time will your passion utter.
Hardly remains fire hid, where skill is bent to the hiding;
But in a mind that would his flames should not be repressed,   60
Nature worketh enough with a small help for the revealing.
Give therefore to the muse great praise, in whose very likeness
You do approach to the fruit your only desires be to gather.

Cleophila :

First shall fertile grounds not yield increase of a good seed,
First the rivers shall cease to repay their floods to the ocean,   65
First may a trusty greyhound transform himself to a tiger,
First shall virtue be vice, and beauty be counted a blemish,

39 *plain*: complain.
57 *grateful*: pleasing.

Ere that I leave with song of praise her praise to solemnize:
Her praise, whence to the world all praise had his only beginning;
But yet well do I find each man most wise in his own case.　　　70
None can speak of a wound with skill, if he have not a wound
　　felt.[n]
Great to thee my estate seems, thy estate is blest by my judge-
　　ment;
And yet neither of us great or blest deemeth his own self;
For yet (weigh this, alas!) great is not great to a greater.
What judge you doth a hillock show by the lofty Olympus?　　75
Such this small greatness doth seem compared to the greatest.
When cedars to the ground be oppressed by the weight of an
　　emmet,
Or when a rich ruby's just price be the worth of a walnut,
Or to the sun for wonders seem small sparks of a candle,
Then by my high cedar, rich ruby, and only shining sun,　　80
Virtue, riches, beauties of mine shall great be reputed.
O no, no, hardy shepherd; worth can never enter a title
Where proofs justly do teach, thus matched, such worth to be
　　nought worth.
Let not a puppet abuse thy spirit; kings' crowns do not help them
From the cruel headache, nor shoes of gold do the gout heal;　　85
And precious couches full oft are shaked with a fever.
If then a bodily evil in a bodily glose be not hidden,
Shall such morning dews be an ease to the heat of a love's fire?

Dorus:
O glittering miseries of man, if this be the fortune
Of those fortune lulls, so small rest in a kingdom,　　90
What marvel though a prince transform himself to a pastor,
Come from the marble bowers, many times the gay arbour of
　　anguish,[n]
Unto a silly caban, though weak, yet stronger against woes?
Now by thy words I begin, most famous lady, to gather
Comfort into my soul. I do find, I do find what a blessing　　95
Is chanced to my life, that from such muddy abundance
Of carking agonies, to estates which still be adherent,

77　*emmet*: ant.
87　*glose*: gloss, outward adornment.
97　*carking*: grievous, fretting.
97　*estates*: high estates.

Destiny keeps me aloof. For if all thy estate to thy virtue
Joined, by thy beauty adorned, be no means these griefs to
   abolish,
If neither by that help thou canst climb up to thy fancy,   100
Nor yet fancy so dressed do receive more plausible hearing,
Then do I think indeed, that better it is to be private
In sorrow's torments, than, tied to the pomps of a palace,
Nurse inward maladies, which have not the scope to be breathed
   out,
But perforce digest all bitter juices of horror   105
In silence, from a man's own self with company robbed.
Better yet do I live, that though by my thoughts I be plunged
Into my life's bondage, yet may disburden a passion,
Oppressed with ruinous conceits, by the help of an outcry;
Not limited to a whispering note, the lament of a courtier,   110
But sometimes to the woods, sometimes to the heavens do
   decipher
With bold clamour unheard, unmarked, what I seek, what I
   suffer.
And when I meet these trees, in the earth's fair livery clothed,
Ease do I feel—such ease, as falls to one wholly diseased—
For that I find in them part of my estate represented.[n]   115
Laurel shows what I seek; by the myrrh is shown how I seek it;
Olive paints me the peace that I must aspire to by conquest;
Myrtle makes my request; my request is crowned with a willow;
Cypress promiseth help, but a help where comes no recomfort;
Sweet Juniper saith this: 'Though I burn, I burn in a sweet fire';   120
Yew doth make me bethink what kind of bow the boy holdeth,
Which shoots strongly without any noise, and deadly without
   smart.
Fir trees great and green, fixed on a high hill, but barren,
Like to my noble thoughts, still new, well-placed, to me fruitless.
Fig that yields most pleasant fruit, his shadow is hurtful,   125
Thus be her gifts most sweet, thus more danger to be near her.
But in a palm when I mark how he doth rise under a burden,
And may I not, say I then, get up, though griefs be so weighty?

116 *Laurel*: victory. This and the following five glosses are Sidney's own.
116 *myrrh*: lamentation.
117 *Olive*: quietness.
118 *Myrtle*: love.
118 *willow*: refusal.
119 *Cypress*: death.

Pine is a mast to a ship; to my ship shall hope for a mast serve?
Pine is high; hope is as high; sharp-leaved, sharp yet be my hope's
    buds.   130
Elm embraced by a vine, embracing fancy reviveth.
Poplar changeth his hue from a rising sun to a setting;
Thus to my sun do I yield, such looks her beams do afford me.
Old aged oak cut down of new works serves to the building;
So my desires by my fear cut down be the frames of her honour. 135
Ash makes spears which shields do resist; her force no repulse
    takes;
Palms do rejoice to be joined by the match of a male to a female,
And shall sensive things be so senseless as to resist sense?[n]
Thus be my thoughts dispersed; thus thinking nurseth a thinking;
Thus both trees and all things else be the books of a fancy.   140
But to the cedar, queen of woods, when I lift my beteared eyes,
Then do I shape to myself that form which reigns so within me,
And think there she do dwell and hear what plaints I do utter.[n]
When that noble top doth nod, I believe she salutes me;
When by the wind it maketh a noise, I do think she doth answer; 145
Then kneeling to the ground, oft thus I do speak to that image:
'Only jewel, O only jewel, which only deservest
That men's hearts be thy seat, and endless fame by thy servant,
O descend for a while, from this great height to behold me:
But nought else do behold (else is nought worth the beholding)   150
Save what a work by thyself is wrought; and since I am altered
Thus by thy work, disdain not that which is by thyself done.
In mean caves oft treasure abides; to an host'ry a king comes;
And so behind foul clouds full oft fair stars do lie hidden.'

Cleophila:
Hardy shepherd, such as thy merits, such may be her insight,   155
Justly to grant thy reward; such envy I bear to thy fortune.
But to myself what wish can I make for a salve to my sorrows,
Whom both nature seems to debar from means to be helped,
And if a mean were found, fortune the whole course of it
    hinders?
Thus plagued, how can I frame to my sore any hope of amend-
    ment?   160
Whence may I show to my mind any light of a possible escape?

---

138 *sensive*: sensitive, having sense.
153 *host'ry*: hostelry.

Bound, and bound by so noble bands, as loath to be unbound;
Jailor am I to myself, prison and prisoner to mine own self.
Yet be hopes thus placed, here fixed lies my recomfort:
That that dear diamond, where wisdom holdeth a sure seat,   165
Whose force had such force so to transform, nay, to reform me,
Will at length perceive these flames by her beams to be kindled,
And will pity the wound festered so strangely within me.
O be it so! Grant such an event, O gods, that event give!
And for a sure sacrifice I do daily oblation offer   170
Of mine heart, where thoughts be the temple, sight is an altar.
But cease we, worthy shepherd; now cease we to weary the
    hearers
With moanful melodies, for enough our griefs be revealed
If by the parties meant our meanings rightly be marked;
And sorrows do require some respite unto the senses.   175

ix. Pyrocles's love-song[n]   [14]

In vain, mine eyes, you labour to amend
With flowing tears your fault of hasty sight,
Since to my heart her shape you so did send
That her I see, though you did lose your light.
In vain, my heart, now you with sight are burned,   5
With sighs you seek to cool your hot desire,
Since sighs, into mine inward furnace turned,
For bellows serve to kindle more the fire.
Reason, in vain, now you have lost my heart,
My head you seek, as to your strongest fort,   10
Since there mine eyes have played so false a part
That to your strength your foes have sure resort:
    And since in vain I find were all my strife,
    To this strange death I vainly yield my life.

x. Old Basilius's love-song   [15]

Let not old age disgrace my high desire,
O heavenly soul, in human shape contained:
Old wood inflamed doth yield the bravest fire,
When younger doth in smoke his virtue spend.
Ne let white hairs, which on my face do grow,   5
Seem to your eyes of a disgraceful hue,
Since whiteness doth present the sweetest show
Which makes all eyes do honour unto you.
Old age is wise, and full of constant truth;
Old age well stayed from ranging humour lives;   10
Old age hath known whatever was in youth;
Old age o'ercome the greater honour gives:
   And to old age since you yourself aspire,
   Let not old age disgrace my high desire.

xi. Musidorus's love-song   [17]

My sheep are thoughts, which I both guide and serve;
Their pasture is fair hills of fruitless love;
On barren sweets they feed, and feeding starve;
I wail their lot, but will not other prove.
My sheephook is wanhope, which all upholds;   5
My weeds, desire, cut out in endless folds.[n]
   What wool my sheep shall bear, while thus they live,
   In you it is, you must the judgement give.

[17] 5 *wanhope*: despair.

xii. Pyrocles's love-complaint[n] [20]

Loved I am, and yet complain of love;
As loving not, accused, in love I die.
When pity most I crave, I cruel prove;
Still seeking love, love found, as much I fly.
Burnt in myself, I muse at others' fire;   5
What I call wrong, I do the same, and more;
Barred of my will, I have beyond desire;
I wail for want, and yet am choked with store.
This is thy work, thou god for ever blind,
Though thousands old, a boy entitled still.   10
Thus children do the silly birds they find
With stroking hurt, and too much cramming kill.
   Yet thus much love, O love, I crave of thee:
   Let me be loved, or else not loved be.

xiii. Pyrocles seeks a refuge from love [21]

Over these brooks trusting to ease mine eyes,
Mine eyes, even great in labour with their tears,
I laid my face; my face, wherein there lies
Clusters of clouds, which no sun ever clears.
   In wat'ry glass my wat'ry eyes I see;   5
   Sorrows ill eased, where sorrows painted be.

My thoughts imprisoned in my secret woes
With flamy breath do issue oft in sound;
The sound to this strange air no sooner goes,
But that it doth with echo's force rebound,   10
   And make me hear the plaints I would refrain:
   Thus outward helps my inward griefs maintain.

[20] 14 *loved*: by Philoclea.
      14 *not loved*: by Basilius and Gynecia.

Now in this sand I would discharge my mind,
And cast from me part of my burdenous cares;
But in the sands my pains foretold I find,   15
And see therein how well the writer fares.ⁿ
    Since stream, air, sand, mine eyes and ears conspire,
    What hope to quench, since each thing blows the fire?

xiv. A rustic singing competitionⁿ   [29]

Nico:

And are you there, old Pas? In troth, I ever thought,
Among us all we should find out some thing of nought.

Pas:

And I am here the same, so mote I thrive and thee,
Despaired in all this flock to find a knave, but thee.

Nico:

Ah, now I see why thou art in thyself so blind: 5
Thy grey hood hides the thing, that thou despair'st to find.

Pas:

My grey hood is mine own, all be it be but grey;
Not as the scrip thou stal'st, while Dorcas sleeping lay.

Nico:

Mine was the scrip; but thou, that seeming raged with love,
Did'st snatch from Cosma's hand her green y-wroughten glove. 10

Pas:

Ah, fool; so courtiers do. But who did lively skip,
When for a treen-dish stol'n thy father did thee whip?

[29] 3 *thee*: prosper.
     10 *y-wroughten*: embroidered.
     12 *treen*: wooden.

Nico:

Indeed, the witch thy dam her crutch from shoulder spread,
For pilfering Lalus' lamb, with crutch to bless thy head.

Pas:

My voice the lamb did win; Menalcas was our judge,   15
Of singing match we made, whence he with shame did trudge.

Nico:

Could'st thou make Lalus fly? So nightingales avoid,
When with the cawing crows their music is annoyed.

Pas:

Nay, like to nightingales the other birds give ear;
My pipe and song made him both song and pipe forswear.   20

Nico:

I think it well; such voice would make one music hate;
But if I had been there, thou'd'st met another mate.

Pas:

Another sure, as is a gander from a goose;
But still when thou dost sing, methinks a colt is loose.

Nico:

Well aimed, by my hat;[n] for as thou sang'st last day,   25
The neighbours all did cry, 'Alas, what ass doth bray?'

Pas:

But here is Dicus old; let him then speak the word,
To whether with best cause the nymphs fair flowers afford.

Nico:

Content; but I will lay a wager hereunto,
That profit may ensue to him that best can do.   30
I have (and long shall have) a white great nimble cat,
A king upon a mouse, a strong foe to a rat,
Fine ears, long tail he hath, with lion's curbed claw,
Which oft he lifteth up, and stays his lifted paw,

17 *avoid*: depart.
28 *whether*: which.
33 *curbed*: bent, curved.

Deep musing to himself, which after mewing shows,   35
Till with licked beard his eye of fire espy his foes.
If thou (alas, poor if) do win, then win thou this:
And if I better sing, let me thy Cosma kiss.

Pas:
Kiss her? Now may'st thou kiss. I have a fitter match;
A pretty cur it is; his name i-wis is Catch.   40
No ear nor tail he hath, lest they should him disgrace;
A ruddy hair his coat, with fine long speckled face;
He never musing stands, but with himself will play,
Leaping at every fly, and angry with a flea;
He eft would kill a mouse, but he disdains the fight,   45
And makes our home good sport with dancing bolt upright.
This is my pawn; the price let Dicus' judgement show:
Such odds I willing lay; for him, and you, I know.

Dicus:
Sing then, my lads; but sing with better vein than yet,
Or else who singeth worse, my skill will hardly hit.   50

Nico:
Who doubts but Pas' fine pipe again will bring
The ancient praise to Arcad shepherds' skill?
Pan is not dead, since Pas begins to sing.

Pas:
Who ever more will love Apollo's quill,
Since Nico doth to sing so widely gape?   55
Nico his place far better furnish will.

Nico:
Was this not he, who for Syringa's 'scape,
Raging in woes first pastors taught to plain?
Do you not hear his voice, and see his shape?

Pas:
This is not he that failed her to gain,   60
Which, made a bay, made bay a holy tree:
But this is one that doth his music stain.

45 *eft*: even, also.
57 *he*: Pan, who pursued the nymph Syriax.
60 *he*: Apollo, who pursued the nymph Daphne.

Nico:
O fauns, O fairies all, and do you see,
And suffer such a wrong? A wrong, I trow,
That Nico must with Pas compared be. 65

Pas:
O nymphs, I tell you news, for Pas you know:
While I was warbling out your wonted praise,
Nico would needs with Pas his bagpipe blow.

Nico:
If never I did fail your holy-days,
With dances, carols, or with barley-break, 70
Let Pas now know, how Nico maketh lays.

Pas:
If each day hath been holy for your sake,
Unto my pipe, O nymphs, now help my pipe:
For Pas well knows what lays can Nico make.

Nico:
Alas, how oft I look on cherries ripe, 75
Methinks I see the lips my Leuca hath,
And wanting her, my weeping eyes I wipe.

Pas:
Alas, when I in spring meet roses rathe,
And think from Cosma's sweet red lips I live,
I leave mine eyes unwiped my cheeks to bathe. 80

Nico:
As I of late near bushes used my sieve,
I spied a thrush where she did make her nest:
That will I take, and to my Leuca give.

Pas:
But long have I a sparrow gaily dressed,
As white as milk, and coming to the call, 85
To put it with my hand in Cosma's breast.[n]

70 *barley-break*: a country game.
75 *how oft*: as often as.
78 *rathe*: early.
81 *sieve*: net for catching birds.

Nico:
I oft do sue, and Leuca saith, 'I shall';
But when I did come near with heat and hope,
She ran away, and threw at me a ball.

Pas:
Cosma once said, she left the wicket ope   90
For me to come; and so she did; I came,
But in the place found nothing but a rope.[n]

Nico:
When Leuca doth appear, the sun for shame
Doth hide himself; for to himself he says,
'If Leuca live, she darken will my fame.'   95

Pas:
When Cosma doth come forth, the sun displays
His utmost wit; for well his wit doth know,
Cosma's fair beams emblemish much his rays.

Nico:
Leuca to me did yester-morning show
In perfect light, which could not me deceive,   100
Her naked leg, more white than whitest snow.

Pas:
But yesternight by light I did receive
From Cosma's eyes, which full in darkness shine,
I saw her arm, where purest lilies cleave.

Nico:
She once stark nak'd did bathe a little time;   105
But still (methought) with beauties from her fell[n]
She did the water wash, and make more fine.

Pas:
She once, to cool herself, stood in a well;
But ever since that well is well-besought,
And for rose-water sold of rarest smell.   110

Nico:
To river's bank, being a-walking brought,
She bid me spy her baby in the brook:
'Alas,' said I, 'this babe doth nurse my thought.'

Pas:
As in a glass I held she once did look,
I said my hands well paid her for mine eyes, 115
Since in my hands' self goodly sight she took.[n]

Nico:
O if I had a ladder for the skies,
I would climb up, and bring a pretty star
To wear upon her neck, that open lies.

Pas:
O, if I had Apollo's golden car, 120
I would come down, and yield to her my place,
That (shining now) she then might shine more far.

Nico:
Nothing, O Leuca, shall thy fame deface,
While shepherds' tunes be heard, or rhymes be read,
Or while that shepherds love a lovely face. 125

Pas:
Thy name, O Cosma, shall with praise be spread,
As far as any shepherds piping be,
As far as love possesseth any head.

Nico:
Thy monument is laid in many a tree,
With name engraved; so though thy body die, 130
The after-folks shall wonder still at thee.

Pas:
So oft these woods have heard me 'Cosma!' cry,
That after death, to heaven in woods' resound,
With echo's help, shall 'Cosma, Cosma', fly.

112 *baby*: reflection.

Nico:
Peace, peace, good Pas; thou weariest even the ground   135
With sluttish song; I pray thee learn to blay,
For good thou may'st yet prove in sheepish sound.

Pas:
My father hath at home a pretty jay;
Go win of him, for chattering, praise or shame,
For so yet of a conquest speak thou may.   140

Nico:
Tell me (and be my Pan) the monster's name,
That hath four legs, and with two only goes;
That hath four eyes, and only two can frame.

Pas:
Tell this (and Phoebus be) what monster grows
With so strong lives, that body cannot rest   145
In ease, until that body life foregoes.[n]

Dicus:
Enough, enough; so ill hath done the best,
That since the having them to neither's due,
Let cat and dog fight which shall have both you.

xv. A debate on providence and human suffering[n]   [30]

Plangus:
Alas, how long this pilgrimage doth last!
    What greater ills have now the heavens in store
    To couple coming harms with sorrows past?
Long since, my voice is hoarse, and throat is sore,
    With cries to skies, and curses to the ground;   5
    But more I plain, I feel my woes the more.

136 *blay*: bleat.

Ah, where was first that cruel cunning found,
 To frame of earth a vessel of the mind,
 Where it should be to self-destruction bound?
What needed so high spirits such mansions blind?   10
 Or wrapped in flesh, what do they here obtain
 But glorious name of wretched human-kind?
Balls to the stars, and thralls to fortune's reign;
 Turned from themselves, infected with their cage,
 Where death is feared, and life is held with pain;   15
Like players placed to fill a filthy stage,
 Where change of thoughts one fool to other shows,
 And all but jests, save only sorrow's rage.
The child feels that; the man that feeling knows,
 With cries first born, the presage of his life;   20
 Where wit but serves to have true taste of woes.
A shop of shame, a book where blots be rife,
 This body is; this body, so composed
 As in itself to nourish mortal strife.
So divers be the elements disposed   25
 In this weak work, that it can never be
 Made uniform to any state reposed.
Grief only makes his wretched state to see;
 (Even like a top, which nought but whipping moves)
 This man, this talking beast, this walking tree;   30
Grief is the stone which finest judgement proves;
 For who grieves not, hath but a blockish brain,
 Since cause of grief no cause from life removes.

Boulon:

How long wilt thou with moanful music stain
 The cheerful notes these pleasant places yield,   35
 Where all good haps a perfect state maintain?

Plangus:

Cursed be good haps, and cursed be they that build
 Their hopes on haps, and do not make despair
 For all these certain blows the surest shield.
Shall I, that saw Erona's shining hair   40
 Torn with her hands, and those same hands of snow
 With loss of purest blood themselves to tear;
Shall I, that saw those breasts, whence beauties flow,

Swelling with sighs, made pale with mind's disease,
   And saw those eyes (those suns) such showers to show;   45
Shall I, whose ears her mournful words did seize,
   Her words in syrup laid of sweetest breath,
   Relent those thoughts, which then did so displease?
No, no; despair my daily lesson saith;
   And saith, although I seek my life to fly,   50
   Plangus must live, to see Erona's death.
Erona die? O heaven—if heaven there be—
   Hath all thy whirling course so small effect?
   Serve all thy starry eyes this shame to see?
Let dolts in haste some altars fair erect   55
   To those high powers, which idly sit above,
   And virtue do in greatest need neglect.

Boulon:

O man, take heed how thou the gods do move
   To causeful wrath, which thou canst not resist.
   Blasphemous words the speaker vain do prove.   60
Alas, while we are wrapped in foggy mist
   Of our self-love (so passions do deceive)
   We think they hurt, when most they do assist.
To harm us worms should that high justice leave
   His nature? Nay, himself? For so it is: 65
   What glory from our loss can he receive?
But still our dazzled eyes their way do miss,
   While that we do at his sweet scourge repine,
   The kindly way to beat us on to bliss.
If she must die, then hath she passed the line   70
   Of loathsome days. Whose loss how canst thou moan,
   That dost so well their miseries define?
But such are we, with inward tempest blown
   Of winds quite contrary, in waves of will;
   We moan that lost, which had we did bemoan.   75

Plangus:

And shall she die? Shall cruel fire spill
   Those beams that set so many hearts on fire?
   Hath she not force even death with love to kill?
Nay, even cold death, enflamed with hot desire

76 *spill*: destroy.

Her to enjoy, where joy itself is thrall,   80
    Will spoil the earth of his most rich attire;
Thus death becomes a rival to us all,
    And hopes with foul embracements her to get,
    In whose decay virtue's fair shrine must fall.
O virtue weak, shall death his triumph set   85
    Upon thy spoils, which never should lie waste?
    Let death first die; be thou his worthy let.
By what eclipse shall that sun be defaced?
    What mine hath erst thrown down so fair a tower?
    What sacrilege hath such a saint disgraced?   90
The world the garden is; she is the flower
    That sweetens all the place; she is the guest
    Of rarest price, both heaven and earth her bower.
And shall (O me) all this in ashes rest?
    Alas, if you a phoenix new will have,   95
    Burnt by the sun, she first must build her nest.
But well you know, the gentle sun would save
    Such beams, so like his own, which might have might
    In him the thoughts of Phaethon's dam to grave.
Therefore, alas, you use vile Vulcan's spite,   100
    Which nothing spares to melt that virgin wax
    Which, while it is, it is all Asia's light.
O Mars, for what doth serve thy armed axe,
    To let that witold beast consume in flames,
    Thy Venus' child, whose beauty Venus lacks?   105
O Venus—if her praise no envy frames
    In thy high mind—get her thy husband's grace;
    Sweet speaking oft a currish heart reclaims.
O eyes of mine, where once she saw her face;
    Her face, which was more lively in my heart;   110
    O brain, where thought of her hath only place:
O hand, which touched her hand when we did part;
    O lips, that kissed that hand with my tears sprent;
    O tongue, then dumb, not daring tell my smart;
O soul, whose love in her is only spent;   115
    What e'er you see, think, touch, kiss, speak or love,
    Let all for her, and unto her, be bent.

87 *let*: prevention, hindrance.
99 *Phaethon's dam*: Clymene, who bore Phaethon to Phoebus.
100 *Vulcan's spite*: fire, since Vulcan was a smith.
102 *all Asia's light*: Erona is imprisoned in Persia.
104 *witold*: cuckold.

Boulon:
Thy wailing words do much my spirits move;
   They uttered are in such a feeling fashion
   That sorrow's work against my will I prove.   120
Methinks I am partaker of thy passion,
   And in thy case do glass my own debility;
   Self-guilty folk must prove to feel compassion.
Yet reason saith, reason should have ability
   To hold these worldly things in such proportion   125
   As let them come or go with even facility.
But our desire's tyrannical extortion
   Doth force us there to set our chief delightfulness,
   Where but a baiting-place is all our portion.[n]
But still, although we fail of perfect rightfulness,   130
   Seek we to tame these childish superfluities;
   Let us not wink, though void of purest sightfulness.
For what can breed more peevish incongruities
   Than man to yield to female lamentations?
   Let us some grammar learn of more congruities.   135

Plangus:
If through mine ears pierce any consolations,
   By wise discourse, sweet tunes, or poet's fiction;
   If aught I cease these hideous exclamations,
While that my soul, she, she, lives in affliction,
   Then let my life long time on earth maintained be,   140
   To wretched me, the last worst malediction.
Can I, that know her sacred parts, restrained be
   From any joy, know fortune's vile displacing her
   In moral rules let raging woes contained be?
Can I forget, when they in prison placing her,   145
   With swelling heart, in spite and due disdainfulness,
   She lay for dead, till I helped with unlacing her?
Can I forget, from how much mourning plainfulness,
   With diamond in window-glass she graved,
   'Erona die, and end this ugly painfulness'?   150

122 *glass*: perceive as in a glass.
123 *must prove to feel*: must have experienced in order to understand.
129 *baiting-place*: resting place, such as an inn.
132 *wink*: close our eyes completely.
135 *grammar*: appropriate order, discipline.

Can I forget in how strange phrase she craved
   That quickly they would her burn, drown, or smother,
   As if by death she only might be saved?
Then let me eke forget one hand from other;
   Let me forget that Plangus I am called;   155
   Let me forget I am son to my mother;
But if my memory thus must be thralled
   To that strange stroke which conquered all my senses,
   Can thoughts, still thinking so, rest unappalled?

Boulon:

Who still doth seek against himself offences   160
   What pardon can avail? Or who employs him
   To hurt himself, what shields can be defences?
Woe to poor man; each outward thing annoys him
   In divers kinds; yet as he were not filled,
   He heaps in inward grief, that most destroys him.   165
Thus is our thought with pain for thistles tilled;
   Thus be our noblest parts dried up with sorrow;
   Thus is our mind with too much minding spilled.
One day lays up stuff of grief for the morrow;
   And whose good hap doth leave him unprovided,   170
   Condoling cause of friendship he will borrow.
Betwixt the good and shade of good divided
   We pity deem that which but weakness is:
   So are we from our high creation slided.
But Plangus, lest I may your sickness miss,
   Or rubbing hurt the sore, I here do end;
   The ass did hurt, when he did think to kiss.[n]

xvi. An echo song in hexameters[n]   [31]

          — — — ◡◡ — — — ◡◡ — ◡◡ — —

Philisides: *Echo:*
Fair rocks, goodly rivers, sweet woods, when shall
   I see peace?   Peace.
Peace? What bars me my tongue? Who is it that
   comes me so nigh?   I.

O, I do know what guest I have met: it is Echo.   'Tis Echo.

Well met, Echo; approach; then tell me thy will
    too.   I will too.

Echo, what do I get yielding my sprite to my
    grieves?   Grieves.   5

What medicine may I find for a pain that draws
    me to death?   Death.

O poisonous medicine! What worse to me can be
    than it?   It.

In what state was I then, when I took this deadly
    disease?   Ease.

And what manner a mind, which had to that
    humour a vein?   Vain.

Hath not reason enough vehemence the desire to
    reprove?   Prove.   10

Oft prove I: but what salve, when reason seeks to
    be gone?   One.

O, what is it, what is it, that may be a salve to my
    love?   Love.

What do lovers seek for, long seeking for to
    enjoy?   Joy.

What be the joys for which to enjoy they went to
    the pains?   Pains.

Then to an earnest love, what doth best victory
    lend?   End.   15

End? But I never can end; love will not give me
    the leave.   Leave.

How be the minds disposed that can not taste thy
    physic?   Sick.

Yet say again thy advice for the ills that I told
    thee.   I told thee.

Doth the infected wretch of his ill the extremity
    know?   No.

But if he know not his harms, what guides hath
    he whilst he be blind?   Blind.   20

What blind guides can he have, that leans to a
    fancy?   A fancy.

Can fancy want eyes, or he fall that steppeth
    aloft?   Oft.

What causes first made these torments on me to
    light?   Light.

Can then a cause be so light, that forceth a man to
    go die?   Aye.

Yet tell what light thing I had in me to draw me to
    die?   Eye.   25

Eyesight made me to yield, but what first pierced
    to mine eyes?   Eyes.

Eyes hurters, eyes hurt: but what from them to me
    falls?   Falls.

But when I first did fall, what brought most fall to
    my heart?   Art.

Art? What can be that art which thou dost mean
    by thy speech?   Speech.

What be the fruits of speaking art? What grows by
    the words?   Words.   30

O much more than words; those words served
    more me to bless.   Less.

O when shall I be known, where most to be known
    I do long?   Long.

Long be thy woes for such news: but how recks
    she my thoughts?   Orts.

Then what do I gain, since unto her will I do
    wind?   Wind.

Wind, tempest and storms; yet in end what gives
    she desire?   Ire.   35

Silly reward! Yet among women hath she of virtue
    the most.   Most.

What great name may I give to so heavenly a
    woman?   A woe-man.

Woe but seems to me joy, that agrees to my
    thought so.   I thought so.

Think so, for of my desired bliss it is only the
    course.   Curse.

Cursed be thyself, for cursing that which leads me
    to joys.   Toys.   40

What be the sweet creatures, where lowly demands
    be not heard?   Hard.

Hard to be got, but got, constant, to be held like
    steels.   Eels.

How can they be unkind? Speak, for th'hast
    narrowly pried.   Pride.

33 *orts*: trifles, fragments.

Whence can pride come there, since springs of
   beauty be thence?   Thence.
Horrible is this blasphemy unto the most holy.   O lie.   45
Thou liest, false Echo; their minds as virtue be
   just.   Just.
Mock'st thou those diamonds, which only be
   matched by the gods?   Odds.
Odds? What odds is there, since them to the
   heavens I prefer?   Err.
Tell yet again me the names of these, fair formed
   to do evils.   Devils.
Devils? If in hell such devils do abide, to the hells
   I do go.   Go.   50

xvii. Anacreontics[n]   [32]

∪ – ∪ – ∪ – –

My muse, what ails this ardour,
To blaze my only secrets?
Alas, it is no glory
To sing my own decayed state;
Alas, it is no comfort   5
To speak without an answer;
Alas, it is no wisdom
To show the wound without cure.

My muse, what ails this ardour?
My eyes be dim, my limbs shake,   10
My voice is hoarse, my throat scorched,
My tongue to this my roof cleaves,
My fancy amazed, my thoughts dulled,
My heart doth ache, my life faints,
My soul begins to take leave: 15
So great a passion all feel
To think a sore so deadly
I should so rashly rip up.

[32] 2 *blaze*: display, advertise.

My muse, what ails this ardour?
If that to sing thou art bent   20
Go sing the fall of old Thebes,
The wars of ugly Centaurs,
The life, the death of Hector,
So may thy song be famous:
Or if to love thou art bent,   25
Recount the rape of Europe,
Adonis' end, Venus' net,
The sleepy kiss the moon stale:
So may thy song be pleasant.

My muse, what ails this ardour,   30
To blaze my only secrets?
Wherein do only flourish
The sorry fruits of anguish;
The song thereof a last will,
The tunes be cries, the words plaints,   35
The singer is the song's theme,
Wherein no ear can have joy,
Nor eye receives due object,
Ne pleasure here, ne fame got.

My muse, what ails this ardour?   40
'Alas,' she saith, 'I am thine,
So are thy pains my pains too;
Thy heated heart my seat is,
Wherein I burn; thy breath is
My voice, too hot to keep in.   45
Besides, lo here the author
Of all thy harms; lo here she,
That only can redress thee:
Of her I will demand help.

My muse, I yield; my muse, sing: 50
But all thy song herein knit:
The life we lead is all love,
The love we hold is all death,
Nor ought I crave to feed life,
Nor ought I seek to shun death,   55
But only that my goddess
My life, my death, do count hers.

28 *The sleepy kiss*: when Diana loved the shepherd Endymion.

xviii. Phaleuciacs[n]   [33]

— — — ∪ ∪ — ∪ — ∪ — ∪

Reason, tell me thy mind, if here be reason,
In this strange violence to make resistance,
Where strange graces erect the shining banner
Of virtue's regiment, shining in harness
Of fortune's diadems, by beauty mustered.   5
Say then, reason, I say, what is thy counsel?

Her loose hair be the shot, the breasts the pikes be,
Scouts each motion is, the hands the horsemen;
Her lips are the riches the wars to maintain,
Where well couched abides a coffer of pearl;   10
Her legs' carriage is of all the sweet camp.
Say then reason, I say, what is thy reason?

Her cannons be her eyes; mine eyes the walls be,
Which at first volley gave too open entry,
Nor rampier did abide; my brain was up blown,   15
Undetermined with a speech, the piercer of thoughts:
Thus weakened by myself, no help remaineth.
Say then reason, I say, what is thy counsel?

And now fame, the herald of her true honour,
Doth proclaim with a sound made by all men's mouths   20
That nature, sovereign of earthly dwellers,
Commands all creatures to yield obeisance
Under this, her own, her only darling.
Say then reason, I say, what is thy counsel?

Reason sighs; but in end he thus doth answer: 25
'Nought can reason avail in heavenly matters.'
Thus, nature's diamond, receive thy conquest;
Thus, pure pearl, I do yield my senses and soul;
Thus, sweet pain, I do yield, what e'er I can yield.
Reason look to thyself; I serve a goddess.   30

15 *rampier*: rampart, barrier.

xix. Asclepiadics[n]   [34]

—— — — ᴗᴗ — — ᴗᴗ — ᴗᴗ

O sweet woods, the delight of solitariness,
O how much I do like your solitariness!
Where man's mind hath a freed consideration
Of goodness to receive lovely direction;
Where senses do behold th'order of the heavenly host,   5
And wise thoughts do behold what the creator is.
Contemplation here holdeth his only seat,
Bounded with no limits, borne with a wing of hope,
Climbs even to the stars; nature is under it.
Nought disturbs thy quiet; all to thy service yield;   10
Each sight draws on a thought, thought mother of science;
Sweet birds kindly do grant harmony unto thee;
Fair trees' shade is enough fortification,
Nor danger to thyself, if it be not in thyself.

O sweet woods, the delight of solitariness,   15
O how much I do like your solitariness!
Here no treason is hid, veiled in innocence,
Nor envy's snaky eye finds any harbour here,
Nor flatterers' venomous insinuations,
Nor cunning humorists' puddled opinions,   20
Nor courteous ruin of proffered usury,
Nor time prattled away, cradle of ignorance,
Nor causeless duty, nor cumber of arrogance,
Nor trifling title of vanity dazzleth us,
Nor golden manacles, stand for a paradise: 25
Here wrong's name is unheard; slander a monster is.
Keep thy sprite from abuse, here no abuse doth haunt.
What man grafts in a tree dissimulation?

O sweet woods, the delight of solitariness,
O how well I do like your solitariness!   30
Yet dear soil, if a soul enclosed in a mansion
As sweet as violets, fair as a lily is,
Straight as a cedar, a voice stains the canary birds,

20 *humorists*: men of disturbed temperament, or humour.

Whose shade safety doth hold, danger avoideth her;
Such wisdom, that in her lives speculation;   35
Such goodness, that in her simplicity triumphs;
Where envy's snaky eye, winketh or else dieth;
Slander wants a pretext, flattery gone beyond;
O, if such one have bent to a lonely life
Her steps, glad we receive, glad we receive her eyes,   40
And think not she doth hurt our solitariness:
For such company decks such solitariness.

xx. Basilius falls in love with the disguised Pyrocles[n]   [38]

Phoebus, farewell, a sweeter saint I serve;
The high conceits thy heavenly wisdoms breed
My thoughts forget; my thoughts, which never swerve
From her in whom is sown their freedom's seed,
And in whose eyes my daily doom I read.   5

Phoebus, farewell, a sweeter saint I serve;
Thou art far off, thy kingdom is above;
She heaven on earth with beauties doth preserve.
Thy beams I like, but her clear rays I love;
Thy force I fear, her force I still do prove.   10

Phoebus, yield up thy title in my mind:
She doth possess, thy image is defaced.
But if thy rage some brave revenge will find
On her, who hath in me thy temple razed,
Employ thy might, that she my fires may taste: 15
    And how much more her worth surmounteth thee,
    Make her as much more base by loving me.

[38] 10 *still do prove*: continually experience.
     11 *title in*: claim to.

xxi. Gynecia falls in love with Pyrocles[n]   [42]

How is my sun, whose beams are shining bright,
Become the cause of my dark ugly night?
Or how do I, captived in this dark plight,
Bewail the cause, and in the cause delight?
My mangled mind huge horrors still do fright,   5
With sense possessed, and claimed by reason's right,
Betwixt which two in me I have this fight,
Where, who so wins, I put myself to flight.
Come, cloudy fears, close up my dazzled sight;
Sorrow, suck up the marrow of my might;   10
Due sighs, blow out all sparks of joyful light;
Tire on, despair, upon my tired sprite.
 An end, an end, my dulled pen cannot write,
 Nor mazed head think, nor faltering tongue recite.

xxii. A shepherdess in love[n]   [45]

My true love hath my heart, and I have his,
By just exchange one for the other given.
I hold his dear, and mine he cannot miss:
There never was a better bargain driven.
His heart in me keeps me and him in one;   5
My heart in him his thoughts and senses guides;
He loves my heart, for once it was his own;
I cherish his, because in me it bides.
His heart his wound received from my sight;
My heart was wounded with his wounded heart;   10
For as from me on him his hurt did light,
So still, methought, in me his hurt did smart;
 Both equal hurt, in this change sought our bliss:
 My true love hath my heart, and I have his.

[42] 12 *Tire*: prey, feed.

xxiii. The reply: a herdsman in love[n]   [46]

O words which fall like summer dew on me,
O breath more sweet than is the growing bean,
O tongue in which all honeyed liquors be,
O voice that doth the thrush in shrillness stain:
   Do you say still, this is her promise due,   5
   That she is mine, as I to her am true.

Gay hair, more gay than straw when harvest lies,
Lips red and plum, as cherry's ruddy side,
Eyes fair and great, like two fair ox's eyes,
O breast, in which two white sheep swell in pride: 10
   Join you with me, to seal this promise due,
   That she be mine, as I to her am true.

But thou, white skin, as white as curds well pressed,
So smooth as, sleek-stone like, it smoothes each part;
And thou dear flesh, as soft as wool new dressed,   15
And yet as hard as brawn made hard by art:
   First four but say, next four their saying seal:
   But you must pay the gage of promised weal.

xxiv. An evening madrigal[n]   [52]

Why dost thou haste away,
O Titan fair, the giver of the day?
Is it to carry news
To Western wights, what stars in East appear?
Or dost thou think that here   5
Is left a sun, whose beams thy place may use?
Yet stay, and well peruse

[46] 8 *plum*: plump.
    14 *sleek-stone*: stone used for smoothing or polishing.
    18 *you*: skin and flesh.

What be her gifts, that make her equal thee;
Bend all thy light to see
In earthly clothes enclosed a heavenly spark.   10
Thy running course cannot such beauties mark;
No, no, thy motions be
Hastened from us with bar of shadow dark,
Because that thou, the author of our sight,
Disdain'st we see thee stained with other's light.   15

xxv. A night-time madrigal[n]   [55]

When two suns do appear
Some say it doth betoken wonders near,
As prince's loss, or change;
Two gleaming suns of splendour like I see,
And seeing, feel in me   5
Of prince's heart quite lost the ruin strange.
But now each where doth range
With ugly cloak the dark envious night,
Who, full of guilty spite
Such living beams should her black seat assail,   10
Too weak for them our weaker sight doth veil.
'No', says fair moon, 'my light
Shall bar that wrong; and though it not prevail
Like to my brother's rays, yet those I send
Hurt not the face, which nothing can amend.'   15

xxvi. Pyrocles praises Philoclea[n]   [62]

What tongue can her perfections tell
In whose each part all tongues may dwell?
Her hair fine threads of finest gold
In curled knots man's thought to hold,

But that her forehead says, 'In me   5
A whiter beauty you may see.'
Whiter indeed; more white than snow
Which on cold winter's face doth grow;
That doth present those even brows
Whose equal lines their angle bows,   10
Like to the moon when, after change,
Her horned head abroad doth range,
And arches be to heavenly lids,
Whose wink each bold attempt forbids.
For the black stars those spheres contain,   15
The matchless pair even praise doth stain:
No lamp whose light by art is got,
No sun which shines and seeth not,
Can liken them, without all peer
Save one as much as other clear,   20
Which only thus unhappy be,
Because themselves they cannot see.
Her cheeks with kindly claret spread,
Aurora-like new out of bed;
Or like the fresh queen-apple's side,   25
Blushing at sight of Phoebus' pride.[n]
Her nose, her chin, pure ivory wears,
No purer than the pretty ears,
So that therein appears some blood,
Like wine and milk that mingled stood;   30
In whose incirclets if you gaze
Your eyes may tread a lover's maze,
But with such turns the voice to stray
No talk untaught can find the way.
The tip no jewel needs to wear: 35
The tip is jewel of the ear.
But who those ruddy lips can miss,
Which blessed still themselves do kiss?
Rubies, cherries, roses new,
In worth, in taste, in perfect hue;   40
Which never part, but that they show
Of precious pearl the double row,

23 *kindly*: natural.
25 *queen-apple*: an old variety of apple.
31 *incirclets*: spirals, convolutions.

The second sweetly-fenced ward
Her heavenly-dewed tongue to guard,
Whence never word in vain did flow.   45
Fair under these doth stately grow
The handle of this pleasant work,
The neck, in which strange graces lurk:
Such be, I think, the sumptuous towers
Which skill doth make in princes' bowers.   50
So good a say invites the eye
A little downward to espy
The lovely clusters of her breasts,
Of Venus' babe the wanton nests,
Like pommels round of marble clear   55
Where azured veins well mixed appear,
With dearest tops of porphyry.
Betwixt these two a way doth lie,
A way more worthy beauty's fame
Than that which bears the milken name: 60
This leads unto the joyous field
Which only still doth lilies yield,
But lilies such, whose native smell
The Indian odours doth excel.
Waist it is called, for it doth waste   65
Men's lives, until it be embraced.
There may one see, and yet not see,
Her ribs in white well armed be,
More white than Neptune's foamy face
When struggling rocks he would embrace.   70
In these delights the wandering thought
Might of each side astray be brought,
But that her navel doth unite,
In curious circle, busy sight;
A dainty seal of virgin-wax   75
Where nothing but impression lacks.
The belly there glad sight doth fill,
Justly entitled Cupid's hill;
A hill most fit for such a master,
A spotless mine of alabaster;   80
Like alabaster fair and sleek,
But soft and supple, satin-like.

51 *a say*: aphetic form of assay, = trial, experience.
55 *pommels*: round bosses.

In that sweet seat the boy doth sport;
Loth, I must leave his chief resort;
For such an use the world hath gotten   85
The best things still must be forgotten.
Yet never shall my song omit
Those thighs, for Ovid's song more fit,
Which flanked with two sugared flanks
Lift up their stately swelling banks,   90
That Albion cleeves in whiteness pass,
With haunches smooth as looking glass.
But bow all knees; now of her knees
My tongue doth tell that fancy sees:
The knots of joy, the gems of love,   95
Whose motion makes all graces move,
Whose bought incaved doth yield such sight,
Like cunning painter shadowing white.[n]
The gartering place with child-like sign
Shows easy print in metal fine;   100
But there again the flesh doth rise
In her brave calves, like crystal skies,
Whose Atlas is a smallest small
More white than whitest bone of whale.
There oft steals out that round clean foot,   105
This noble cedar's precious root,
In show and scent pale violets,
Whose step on earth all beauty sets.
But back unto her back, my muse,
Where Leda's swan his feathers mews,   110
Along whose ridge such bones are met
Like comfits round in marchpane set.
Her shoulders be like two white doves
Perching within square royal rooves,
Which leaded are with silver skin,   115
Passing the hate-spot ermelin;[n]
And thence those arms derived are;
The Phoenix' wings be not so rare,

91 *Albion cleeves*: white cliffs of Dover.
97 *bought*: curve behind the knee.
103 *Atlas*: the ankle, holding up the sky of her calves.
110 *mews*: moults, sheds.
112 *marchpane*: marzipan.
116 *ermelin*: ermine.

For faultless length, and stainless hue.
Ah, woe is me, my woes renew,   120
Now course doth lead me to her hand,
Of my first love the fatal band,
Where whiteness doth for ever sit.
Nature herself enamelled it,
For there, with strange compact, doth lie   125
Warm snow, moist pearl, soft ivory.
There fall those sapphire-coloured brooks
Which conduit-like with curious crooks
Sweet islands make in that sweet land.
As for the fingers of the hand,   130
The bloody shafts of Cupid's war,
With amethysts they headed are.
   Thus hath each part his beauty's part:
But how the graces do impart
To all her limbs a special grace   135
Becoming every time and place,
Which doth even beauty beautify,
And most bewitch the wretched eye;
How all this is but a fair inn
Of fairer guest, which dwells within;   140
Of whose high praise, and praiseful bliss,
Goodness the pen, heaven paper is,
The ink immortal fame doth lend;
As I began, so must I end:
No tongue can her perfections tell   145
In whose each part all pens may dwell.

The Third Eclogues

The Third Eclogues

Lalus, not with many painted words, nor false-hearted promises, had won the consent of his beloved Kala, but with a true and simple making her know he loved her; not forcing himself beyond his reach to buy her affection, but giving her such pretty presents as neither could weary him with the giving nor shame her for the taking. Thus, the first strawberries he could find were ever in a clean washed dish sent to Kala. Thus posies of the spring flowers were wrapped up in a little green silk and dedicated to Kala's breasts. Thus sometimes his sweetest cream, sometimes the best cake-bread his mother made, were reserved for Kala's taste. Neither would he stick to kill a lamb when she would be content to come over the way unto him. But then lo, how the house was swept, and rather no fire, than any smoke left to trouble her. Then love songs were not dainty, when she would hear them, and as much mannerly silence when she would not. In going to church, great worship to Kala, so that all the parish said never a maid they knew so well waited on; and when dancing was about the maypole, nobody taken out but she, and he, after a leap or two to show her his own activity, would frame all the rest of his dancing only to grace her. As for her father's sheep, he had no less care of them than his own; so that she might play her as she would, warranted with honest Lalus's carefulness. But if he spied Kala favoured any one of the flock more than his fellows, then that was cherished, shearing him so (when shorn he must be) as might most become him; but while the wool was on, wrapping within it some verses (wherein Lalus had a special gift), and making the innocent beast his unwitting messenger. Thus constantly continuing, though he were none of the fairest, at length he won Kala's heart, the honestest wench in all those quarters. And so, with consent of both parents (without which neither Lalus would ask nor Kala grant), their marriage day was appointed; which, because it fell out in this time, I think it shall not be impertinent to remember a little our shepherds while the other greater persons are either sleeping or otherwise occupied. Lalus's marriage time once known, there needed no inviting of the neighbours in that valley; for so well was Lalus beloved that they were all ready to do him credit. Neither yet came they like harpies to devour him, but one brought a fat pig, the other a tender kid, a third a great goose; as for cheese, milk and butter were the gossips' presents. Thither came of stranger shepherds only the melancholy Philisides; for the virtuous Coredens had long since left off all joyful solemnities, and as for Strephon and Klaius,

they had lost their mistress, which put them into such extreme
sorrows as they could scarcely abide the light of day, much less the
eyes of men. But of the Arcadian-born shepherds, thither came good
old Geron, young Histor (though unwilling), and upright Dicus,
merry Pas, and jolly Nico; as for Dametas, they durst not presume,
his pride was such, to invite him; and Dorus they found might not be
spared. And there under a bower was made of boughs (for Lalus's
house was not able to receive them), they were entertained with hearty
welcome, and every one placed according to his age. The women
(for such was the manner of that country) kept together to make good
cheer among themselves, from which otherwise a certain painful
modesty restrains them. And there might the sadder matrons give
good counsel to Kala, who, poor soul, wept for fear of that she
desired. But among the shepherds was all honest liberty; no fear
of dangerous telltales (who hunt greater preys), nor indeed minds
in them to give telltales any occasion; but one questioning with
another of the manuring his ground, and governing his flock. The
highest point they reached to was to talk of the holiness of marriage;
to which purpose, as soon as their sober dinner was ended, Dicus
instead of thanks sang this song with a clear voice and cheerful
countenance:

xxvii. An epithalamium[n]   [63]

Let mother earth now deck herself in flowers,
To see her offspring seek a good increase,
Where justest love doth vanquish Cupid's powers[n]
And war of thoughts is swallowed up in peace,
    Which never may decrease   5
    But like the turtles fair
    Live one in two, a well united pair:
    Which, that no chance may stain,
    O Hymen, long their coupled joys maintain.

O heaven awake, show forth thy stately face,   10
Let not these slumbering clouds thy beauties hide,
But with thy cheerful presence help to grace
The honest bridegroom, and the bashful bride,
    Whose loves may ever bide

Like to the elm and vine,   15
With mutual embracements them to twine:[n]
In which delightful pain
O Hymen, long their coupled joys maintain.

Ye muses all, which chaste affects allow,
And have to Lalus showed your secret skill,   20
To his chaste love your sacred favours bow,
And so to him and her your gifts distil
    That they all vice may kill,
    And like to lilies pure
    Do please all eyes, and spotless do endure;   25
    Where, that all bliss may reign,
    O Hymen, long their coupled joys maintain.

Ye nymphs, which in the water empire have,
Since Lalus' music oft doth yield you praise,
Grant too the thing which we for Lalus crave: 30
Let one time (but long first) close up their days,
    One grave their bodies seize;
    And like two rivers sweet,
    When they, though diverse, do together meet,
    One stream both streams contain:
    O Hymen, long their coupled joys maintain.   35

Pan, father Pan, the god of silly sheep,
Whose care is cause that they in number grow,
Have much more care of them that do them keep,
Since from these good the others' good doth flow,   40
    And make their issue show
    In number like the herd
    Of younglings, which thyself with love hast reared;
    Or like the drops of rain:
    O Hymen, long their coupled joys maintain.   45

Virtue, if not a god, yet God's chief part,
Be thou the knot of this their open vow,
That still he be the head, she be his heart;
He lean to her, she unto him do bow,
    Each other still allow

19 *affects*: affections.
40 *these good*: the good of these.

Like oak and mistletoe,
Her strength from him, his praise from her do grow:
In which most lovely train,
O Hymen, long their coupled joys maintain.

But thou, foul Cupid, sire to lawless lust,   55
Be thou far hence with thy empoisoned dart,
Which, though of glittering gold, shall here take rust,ⁿ
Where simple love, which chasteness doth impart,
    Avoids thy hurtful art,
    Not needing charming skill   60
    Such minds with sweet affections for to fill:
    Which, being pure and plain,
    O Hymen, long their coupled joys maintain.

All churlish words, shrewd answers, crabbed looks,
All privateness, self-seeking, inward spite,   65
All waywardness, which nothing kindly brooks,
All strife for toys, and claiming master's right,
    Be hence aye put to flight;
    All stirring husband's hate
    'Gainst neighbours' good for womanish debate   70
    Be fled as things most vain:
    O Hymen, long their coupled joys maintain.

All peacock pride, and fruits of peacock's pride,
Longing to be with loss of substance gay,
With recklessness what may thy house betide,   75
So that you may on higher slippers stay,
    For ever hence away;
    Yet let not sluttery,
    The sink of filth, be counted housewifery:
    But keeping wholesome mean,   80
    O Hymen, long their coupled joys maintain.

But above all, away vile jealousy,
The ill of ills, just cause to be unjust:
How can he love, suspecting treachery?
How can she love, where love can not win trust?   85
    Go snake, hide thee in dust,

66 *kindly brooks*: takes in good part, accepts amiably.
76 *So that*: provided that.

Ne dare once show thy face,
Where open hearts do hold so constant place
That they thy sting restrain:
O Hymen, long their coupled joys maintain.   90

The earth is decked with flowers, the heavens displayed,
Muses grant gifts, nymphs long and joined life,
Pan store of babes, virtue their thoughts well-stayed,
Cupid's lust gone, and gone is bitter strife:
Happy man, happy wife.   95
No pride shall them oppress,
Nor yet shall yield to loathsome sluttishness,
And jealousy is slain:
For Hymen will their coupled joys maintain.

'Truly, Dicus,' said Nico, 'although thou didst not grant me the prize the last day, when undoubtedly I wan it, yet must I needs say thou for thy part hast sung well and thriftily.'

Pas straight desired all the company they would bear witness that Nico had once in his life spoken wisely: 'For,' said he, 'I will tell it to his father, who will be a glad man when he hears such news.'

'Very true,' said Nico, 'but, indeed, so would not thine in like case, for he would look thou shouldst live but one hour longer, that a discreet word wandered out of thy mouth.'

'And I pray thee,' said Pas, 'gentle Nico, tell me what mischance it was that brought thee to taste so fine a meat?'

'Marry, goodman blockhead,' said Nico, 'because he speaks against jealousy, the filthy traitor to true affection, and yet disguising itself in the raiment of love.'

'Sentences, sentences,' cried Pas, 'alas, how ripe-witted these young folks be nowadays! But well counselled shall that husband be when this man comes to exhort him not to be jealous.'

'And so shall he,' answered Nico, 'for I have seen a fresh example, though it be not very fit to be known.'

'Come, come,' said Pas, 'be not so squeamish. I know thou longest more to tell it than we to hear it.'

But for all his words, Nico would not bestow his voice till he

---

Sentences: Clever sayings, aphorisms.

was generally entreated of the rest; and then with a merry marriage
look he sang this following discourse—for with a better grace he
could sing than tell:

xxviii. Nico's fabliau[n]   [64]

A neighbour mine not long ago there was
(But nameless he, for blameless, he shall be)
That married had a trick and bonny lass
As in a summer day a man might see;
    But he himself a foul unhandsome groom,   5
    And far unfit to hold so good a room.

Now, whether moved with self-unworthiness,
Or with her beauty, fit to make a prey,
Fell jealousy did so his brain oppress
That if he were but absent half a day,   10
    He guessed the worst (you wot what is the worst)
    And in himself new doubting curses nursed.

While thus he feared the silly innocent,
Who yet was good, because she knew none ill,[n]
Unto his house a jolly shepherd went,   15
To whom our prince did bear a great good will
    Because in wrestling and in pastoral
    He far did pass the rest of shepherds all.

And therefore he a courtier was benamed,
And as a courtier was with cheer received,   20
(For they have tongues to make a poor man blamed,
If he to them his duty misconceived):
    And for the courtier should well like his table,
    The goodman bade his wife be serviceable.

3 *trick*: fine, neat.

And so she was, and all with good intent,   25
But few days passed while she good manner used
But that her husband thought her service bent
To such an end as he might be abused:
    Yet like a coward, fearing stranger's pride,
    He made the simple wench his wrath abide.   30

With chumpish looks, hard words, and secret nips,
Grumbling at her when she his kindness sought,
Asking her how she tasted courtier's lips,
He forced her think that which she never thought.
    In fine, he made her guess there was some sweet   35
    In that which he so feared that she should meet.

When once this entered was in woman's heart,
And that it had enflamed a new desire,
There rested then, to play a woman's part,
Fuel to seek, and not to quench the fire: 40
    But, for his jealous eye she well did find,
    She studied cunning how the same to blind.

And thus she did: one day to him she came,
And, though against his will, on him she leaned,
And out gan cry: 'Ah, wellaway for shame,   45
If you help not, our wedlock will be stained!'
    The goodman, starting, asked what did her move;
    She sighed, and said the bad guest sought her love.

He, little looking that she should complain
Of that whereto he feared she was inclined,   50
Bussing her oft, and in his heart full fain,
He did demand what remedy to find,
    How they might get the guest from them to wend
    And yet the prince, that loved him, not offend.

'Husband', quoth she, 'go to him by and by,   55
And tell him that you find I do him love,
And therefore pray him that of courtesy
He will absent himself, lest he should move
    A young girl's heart, to that were shame for both,
    Whereto you know his honest heart were loath.   60

31 *chumpish*: sullen.
51 *bussing*: kissing.

'Thus shall you show that him you do not doubt;
And as for me (sweet husband) I must bear.'
Glad was the man when he had heard her out,
And did the same, although with mickle fear;
    For fear he did, lest he the young man might   65
    In choler put, with whom he would not fight.

The courtly shepherd, much aghast at this,
Not seeing erst such token in the wife,
Though full of scorn, would not his duty miss,
Knowing that ill becomes a household strife,   70
    Did go his way, but sojourned near thereby,
    That yet the ground hereof he might espy.

The wife, thus having settled husband's brain,
Who would have sworn his spouse Diana was,
Watched when she a further point might gain,   75
Which little time did fitly bring to pass:
    For to the court her man was called by name,
    Whither he needs must go, for fear of blame.

Three days before that he must sure depart,
She written had (but in a hand disguised)   80
A letter such, which might from either part
Seem to proceed, so well it was devised:
    She sealed it first, then she the sealing brake,
    And to her jealous husband did it take.

With weeping eyes (her eyes she taught to weep)   85
She told him that the courtier had it sent:
'Alas,' quoth she, 'thus women's shame doth creep.'
The goodman read on both sides the content:
    It title had, 'Unto my only love',
    Subscription was, 'Yours most, if you will prove.'   90

The 'pistle self such kind of words it had:
'My sweetest joy, the comfort of my sprite,
So may thy flocks increase, thy dear heart glad,
So may each thing, even as thou wishest, light,
    As thou wilt deign to read, and gently read,   95
    This mourning ink, in which my heart doth bleed.

68 *erst*: previously, hitherto.

'Long have I loved (alas, thou worthy art)
Long have I loved (alas, love craveth love)
Long have I loved thyself—alas, my heart
Doth break, now tongue unto thy name doth move; 100
   And think not that thy answer answer is,
   But that it is my doom of bale or bliss.

'The jealous wretch must now to court be gone;
Ne can he fail, for prince hath for him sent;
Now is the time we may be here alone, 105
And give a long desire a sweet content:
   Thus shall you both reward a lover true,
   And eke revenge his wrong suspecting you.'

And this was all, and this the husband read
With chafe enough, till she him pacified; 110
Desiring that no grief in him he bred,
Now that he had her words so truly tried,
   But that he would to him the letter show,
   That with his fault he might her goodness know.

That straight was done, with many a boisterous threat 115
That to the duke he would his sin declare;
But now the courtier gan to smell the feat,
And with some words, which showed little care,
   He stayed until the goodman was departed,
   Then gave he him the blow which never smarted. 120

Thus may you see, the jealous wretch was made
The pandar of the thing he most did fear:
Take heed therefore, how you ensue that trade,
Lest that some marks of jealousy you bear.
   For sure, no jealousy can that prevent 125
   Whereto two parties once be full content.

'Behold,' said Pas, 'a whole dicker of wit! He hath picked out such a tale, with intention to keep a husband from jealousy, which were enough to make a sanctified husband jealous, to see subtleties so

102 *bale*: woe.
117 *feat*: trick.

much in the feminine gender. But', said he, 'I will strike Nico dead
with the wise words shall flow out of my gorge'; and without
further entreaty thus sang:

xxix. Advice to husbands   [65]

> Who doth desire that chaste his wife should be,
> First be he true, for truth doth truth deserve:
> Then such be he, as she his worth may see,
> And one man still credit with her preserve.
> Not toying kind, nor causelessly unkind,   5
> Not stirring thoughts, nor yet denying right,
> Not spying faults, nor in plain errors blind,
> Never hard hand, nor ever reins too light:
> As far from want, as far from vain expense
> (The one doth force, the latter doth entice):   10
> Allow good company, but keep from thence
> All filthy mouths, that glory in their vice.
>   This done, thou hast no more; but leave the rest
>   To virtue, fortune, time, and woman's breast.

'Well concluded', said Nico, 'when he hath done all, he leaves the
matter to his wife's discretion. Now whensoever thou marriest, let
her discretion deck thy head with Actaeon's ornament!'

Pas was so angry with his wish, being indeed towards marriage,
that they might perchance have fallen to buffets, but that Dicus
(who knew it more wisdom to let a fray than part a fray) de-
sired Philisides (who as a stranger sat among them, revolving in
his mind all the tempests of evil fortune he had passed) that he would
do so much grace to the company as to sing one of his country
songs. Philisides knew it no good manners to be squeamish of his
cunning, having put himself in their company, and yet loath either
in time of marriage to sing his sorrows, more fit for funerals, or by
any outward matter to be drawn to such mirth as to betray (as it were)
that passion to which he had given over himself, he took a mean way

Actaeon's ornament: horns, badge of the cuckold.

betwixt both, and sang this song he had learned before he had ever
subjected his thoughts to acknowledge no master but a mistress:

xxx. Philisides's beast fable[n]   [66]

As I my little flock on Ister bank
(A little flock, but well my pipe they couth)
Did piping lead, the sun already sank
Beyond our world, and ere I gat my booth
Each thing with mantle black the night doth soothe,   5
    Saving the glow-worm, which would courteous be
    Of that small light oft watching shepherds see.

The welkin had full niggardly enclosed
In coffer of dim clouds his silver groats
Y-cleped stars; each thing to rest disposed;   10
The caves were full, the mountains void of goats;
The birds' eyes closed, closed their chirping notes;
    As for the nightingale, wood-music's king,
    It August was, he deigned not then to sing.

Amid my sheep, though I saw nought to fear,   15
Yet, for I nothing saw, I feared sore:
Then found I which thing is a charge to bear,
For for my sheep I dreaded mickle more
Than ever for myself since I was bore.
    I sate me down, for see to go ne could,   20
    And sang unto my sheep lest stray they should.

The song I sang old Languet had me taught,
Languet, the shepherd best swift Ister knew,
For clerkly rede, and hating what is nought,
For faithful heart, clean hands, and mouth as true;   25
With his sweet skill my skilless youth he drew
    To have a feeling taste of him that sits
    Beyond the heaven, far more beyond our[n] wits.

1 *Ister*: the river Danube.
2 *couth*: knew, understood.
4 *gat my booth*: reached my shelter.
17 *charge*: responsibility.
24 *clerkly rede*: learned counsel, advice.

He said, the music best thilk powers pleased
Was jump concord between our wit and will,   30
Where highest notes to godliness are raised,
And lowest sink not down to jot of ill:
With old true tales he wont mine ears to fill,
   How shepherds did of yore, how now they thrive,
   Spoiling their flock, or while 'twixt them they strive.   35

He liked me, but pitied lustful youth;
His good strong staff my slippery years upbore;
He still hoped well, because I loved truth;
Till forced to part, with heart and eyes even sore,
To worthy Coredens he gave me o'er.[n]   40
   But thus in oak's true shade recounted he,
   Which now in night's deep shade sheep heard of me.

Such manner time there was (what time, I not)
When all this earth, this dam or mould of ours,
Was only woned with such as beasts begot;   45
Unknown as then were they that builden towers;
The cattle wild or tame, in nature's bowers
   Might freely roam or rest, as seemed them;
   Man was not man, their dwellings in to hem.

The beasts had sure some beastly policy: 50
For nothing can endure where order n'is;
For once the lion by the lamb did lie;
The fearful hind the leopard did kiss;
Hurtless was tiger's paw and serpent's hiss.
   This think I well, the beasts with courage clad   55
   Like senators, a harmless empire had.

At which, whether the others did repine,
(For envy harboureth most in feeble hearts)[n]
Or that they all to changing did incline,
(As even in beasts their dams leave changing parts)   60

29 *thilk*: those.
30 *jump*: exact, precise.
43 *not*: know not.
45 *woned*: inhabited.
50 *policy*: order of government.

The multitude to Jove a suit imparts,
　With neighing, blaying, braying and barking,
　Roaring and howling, for to have a king.

A king, in language theirs they said they would;
(For then their language was a perfect speech)　　　65
The birds likewise with chirps and pewing could,
Cackling and chattering, that of Jove beseech.
Only the owl still warned them not to seech
　So hastily that which they would repent:
　But saw they would, and he to deserts went.　　　70

Jove wisely said (for wisdom wisely says):
'O beasts, take heed what you of me desire;
Rulers will think all things made them to please,
And soon forget the swink due to their hire.
But since you will, part of my heavenly fire　　　75
　I will you lend; the rest yourselves must give,
　That it both seen and felt may with you live.'

Full glad they were, and took the naked sprite,
Which straight the earth y-clothed in his clay;
The lion, heart; the ounce gave active might;　　　80
The horse, good shape; the sparrow, lust to play;
Nightingale, voice, enticing songs to say;
　Elephant gave a perfect memory;
　And parrot, ready tongue that to apply.

The fox gave craft; the dog gave flattery;　　　85
Ass, patience; the mole, a working thought;
Eagle, high look; wolf, secret cruelty;
Monkey, sweet breath; the cow her fair eyes brought;
The ermine, whitest skin, spotted with nought;[n]
　The sheep, mild-seeming face; climbing, the bear;　　　90
　The stag did give the harm-eschewing fear.

62 *blaying*: bleating.
66 *pewing*: plaintive crying.
68 *seech*: seek.
74 *swink*: labour, responsibility.
80 *ounce*: lynx.

The hare her sleights; the cat, his melancholy;
Ant, industry; the coney, skill to build;
Cranes, order; storks, to be appearing holy;
Chameleon, ease to change; duck, ease to yield;   95
Crocodile, tears, which might be falsely spilled;
    Ape great thing gave, though he did mowing stand:
    The instrument of instruments, the hand.

Each other beast likewise his present brings:
And, but they drad their prince they oft should want,   100
They all consented were to give him wings.
And aye more awe towards him for to plant,
To their own work this privilege they grant:
    That from thenceforth to all eternity
    No beast should freely speak, but only he.   105

Thus man was made; thus man their lord became;
Who at the first, wanting or hiding pride,
He did to beasts best use his cunning frame,
With water drink, herbs meat, and naked hide,[n]
And fellow-like let his dominion slide;   110
    Not in his sayings saying 'I', but 'we',
    As if he meant his lordship common be.

But when his seat so rooted he had found,
That they now skilled not how from him to wend;
Then gan in guiltless earth full many a wound   115
Iron to seek, which 'gainst itself should bend;
To tear the bowels, that good corn should send.
    But yet the common dam none did bemoan,
    Because, though hurt, they never heard her groan.

Then gan he factions in the beasts to breed,   120
Where helping weaker sort, the nobler beasts,
As tigers, leopards, bears, and lions' seed,
Disdained with this, in deserts sought their rests,
Where famine ravine taught their hungry chests,
    What craftily he forced them to do ill,   125
    Which being done, he afterwards would kill.

93 *coney*: rabbit.
97 *mowing*: making faces.
123 *Disdained*: angered, filled with disdain.

For murder done, which never erst was seen,
By those great beasts, as for the weaker's good,
He chose themselves his guarders for to been,
'Gainst those of might, of whom in fear they stood,   130
As horse and dog, not great, but gentle blood:
   Blithe were the commons, cattle of the field,
   Tho when they saw their foen of greatness killed.

But they, or spent, or made of slender might,
Then quickly did the meaner cattle find;   135
The great beams gone, the house on shoulders light;
For by and by, the horse fair bits did bind;
The dog was in a collar taught his kind;
   As for the gentle birds, like case might rue,
   When falcon they, and goshawk saw in mew.   140

Worst fell to smallest birds and meanest herd,
Who now his own, full like his own he used;
Yet first but wool or feathers off he teared,
And when they were well used to be abused,
For hungry throat their flesh with teeth he bruised;   145
   At length for glutton taste he did them kill;
   At last, for sport their silly lives did spill.

But yet, O man, rage not beyond thy need;
Deem it no glory to swell in tyranny.
Thou art of blood, joy not to make things bleed;   150
Thou fearest death, think they are loath to die;
A plaint of guiltless hurt doth pierce the sky.[n]
   And you, poor beasts, in patience bide your hell,
   Or know your strengths, and then you shall do well.

Thus did I sing and pipe eight sullen hours   155
To sheep, whom love, not knowledge, made to hear,
Now fancy's fits, now fortune's baleful stowers.
But then I homeward called my lambkins dear,
For to my dimmed eyes began to appear
   The night grown old, her black head waxen grey,   160
   Sure shepherd's sign that morn would soon fetch day.

133 *Tho*: then.
140 *mew*: cage.
157 *stowers*: tumults.

According to the nature of divers ears, divers judgements straight followed: some praising his voice; others the words, fit to frame a pastoral style; others the strangeness of the tale, and scanning what he should mean by it. But old Geron (who had borne him a grudge ever since, in one of their eclogues, he had taken him up over-bitterly) took hold of this occasion to make his revenge, and said he never saw thing worse proportioned than to bring in a tale of he knew not what beasts at such a banquet, when rather some song of love, or matter for joyful melody, was to be brought forth. 'But', said he, 'this is the right conceit of young men who think then they speak wiseliest, when they cannot understand themselves.' Then invited he Histor to answer him in eclogue-wise; who, indeed, having been long in love with the fair bride Kala, and now prevented, was grown into a detestation of marriage. But thus it was:

xxxi. A debate on marriage[n] [67]

Geron:
In faith, good Histor, long is your delay
   From holy marriage, sweet and surest mean
   Our foolish lusts in honest rules to stay.
I pray thee, do to Lalus' 'sample lean:
   Thou seest how frisk and jolly now he is,   5
   That last day seemed he could not chew a bean.
Believe me, man, there is no greater bliss
   Than is the quiet joy of loving wife;
   Which who so wants, half of himself doth miss.
Friend without change, playfellow without strife,   10
   Food without fullness, counsel without pride,
   Is this sweet doubling of our single life.

Histor:
No doubt, to whom so good chance did betide
   As for to find a pasture strowed with gold,
   He were a fool, if there he did not bide.   15
Who would not have a phoenix if he could?
   The humming wasp, if it had not a sting,
   Before all flies the wasp accept I would.

4 *'sample*: example.

But this bad world few golden fields doth bring;
　　Phoenix but one, of crows we millions have; 20
　　The wasp seems gay, but is a cumbrous thing.
If many Kalas our Arcadia gave,
　　Lalus' example I would soon ensue
　　And think I did myself from sorrow save.
But of such wives we find a slender crew; 25
　　Shrewdness so stirs, pride so puffs up their heart,
　　They seldom ponder what to them is due;
With meagre looks, as if they still did smart,
　　Puling and whimpering, or else scolding flat,
　　Make home more pain than following of the cart. 30
Either dull silence, or eternal chat,
　　Still contrary to what her husband says;
　　If he do praise the dog, she likes the cat.
Austere she is, when he would honest plays,
　　And gamesome then, when he thinks on his sheep; 35
　　She bids him go, and yet from journey stays.
She war doth ever with his kinsfolk keep,
　　And makes them fremd, who friends by nature are,
　　Envying shallow toys with malice deep.
And if forsooth there come some new-found ware, 40
　　The little coin his sweating brows have got
　　Must go for that, if for her lours he care,
Or else: 'Nay, faith, mine is the luckless'st lot
　　That ever fell to honest woman yet;
　　No wife but I hath such a man, God wot.' 45
Such is their speech, who be of sober wit;
　　But who do let their tongues show well their rage,
　　Lord, what by-words they speak, what spite they spit!
The house is made a very loathsome cage
　　Wherein the bird doth never sing, but cry; 50
　　With such a will that nothing can assuage.
Dearly the servants do their wages buy,
　　Reviled for each small fault, sometimes for none;
　　They better live, that in a gaol do lie.
Let other, fouler, spots away be blown; 55
　　For I seek not their shame; but still, methinks,
　　A better life it is to lie alone.

21 *cumbrous*: tiresome, troublesome.
38 *fremd*: hostile, unfriendly.
48 *by-words*: words of scorn.

Geron:
Who for each fickle fear from virtue shrinks
   Shall in this life embrace no worthy thing;
   No mortal man the cup of surety drinks.   60
The heavens do not good haps in handfuls bring;
   But let us pick our good from out much bad,
   That still our little world may know his king.
But certainly, so long we may be glad,
   While that we do what nature doth require;   65
   And for the event we never ought be sad.
Man oft is plagued with air, is burnt with fire,
   In water drowned, in earth his burial is;
   And shall we not therefore their use desire?
Nature above all things requireth this,   70
   That we our kind do labour to maintain,
   Which drawn-out line doth hold all human bliss.
Thy father justly may of thee complain,
   If thou do not repay his deeds for thee,
   In granting unto him a grandsire's name.[n]   75
Thy commonwealth may rightly grieved be,
   Which must by this immortal be preserved,
   If thus thou murder thy posterity.
His very being he hath not deserved
   Who for a self-conceit will that forbear,   80
   Whereby that being aye must be conserved.
And God forbid, women such cattle were
   As you paint them! But well in you I find,
   No man doth speak aright, who speaks in fear.
Who only sees the ill, is worse than blind.   85
   These fifty winters have I married been,
   And yet find no such faults in womankind.
I have a wife worthy to be a queen,
   So well she can command, and yet obey;
   In ruling of a house so well she's seen;   90
And yet in all this time, betwixt us tway,
   We bear our double yoke with such consent
   There never passed foul word, I dare well say.

66 *event*: outcome.
82 *cattle*: creatures.
90 *seen*: experienced, accomplished.
91 *tway*: two.

But these be your love-toys, which still are spent
   In lawless games, and love not as you should,   95
   But with much study learn late to repent.
How well last day before our prince you could
   Blind Cupid's works with wonder testify![n]
   Yet now the root of him abase you would.
Go to, go to, and Cupid now apply   100
   To that where thou thy Cupid may'st avow,
   And thou shalt find in women virtues lie:
Sweet supple minds, which soon to wisdom bow
   Where they by wisdom's rules directed are,
   And are not forced fond thraldom to allow.   105
As we to get are framed, so they to spare;
   We made for pain, our pains they made to cherish;
   We care abroad, and they of home have care.
O Histor, seek within thyself to flourish!
   Thy house by thee must live, or else be gone;   110
   And then who shall the name of Histor nourish?
Riches of children pass a prince's throne,
   Which touch the father's heart with secret joy
   When without shame he saith, 'These be mine own.'
Marry therefore; for marriage will destroy   115
   Those passions which to youthful head do climb,
   Mothers and nurses of all vain annoy.

Histor:
Perchance I will; but now, methinks it time
   We go unto the bride, and use this day
   To speak with her, while freely speak we may.[n]   120

He spake these last words with such affection as a curious eye
might easily have perceived he liked Lalus's fortune better than he
loved his person. But then, indeed, did all arise, and went to the
women; where spending all the day and good part of the night in
dancing, carolling, and wassailing, lastly they left Lalus where he
long desired to be left, and with many unfeigned thanks returned
every man to his home.

END OF THE THIRD ECLOGUES

106 *get*: earn a living.
107 *pain*: work, effort.

xxxii. A double sestina[n]   [71]

Strephon:

Ye goat-herd gods, that love the grassy mountains;
Ye nymphs, which haunt the springs in pleasant valleys;
Ye satyrs, joyed with free and quiet forests;
Vouchsafe your silent ears to plaining music,
Which to my woes gives still an early morning,   5
And draws the dolour on till weary evening.

Klaius:

O Mercury, foregoer to the evening;
O heavenly huntress of the savage mountains;
O lovely star, entitled of the morning;
While that my voice doth fill these woeful valleys,   10
Vouchsafe your silent ears to plaining music,
Which oft hath Echo tired in secret forests.

Strephon:

I, that was once free-burgess of the forests,
Where shade from sun, and sport I sought in evening;
I, that was once esteemed for pleasant music,   15
Am banished now among the monstrous mountains
Of huge despair, and foul affliction's valleys;
Am grown a scrich-owl to myself each morning.

Klaius:

I, that was once delighted every morning,
Hunting the wild inhabiters of forests;   20
I, that was once the music of these valleys.
So darkened am, that all my day is evening;
Heart-broken so, that molehills seem high mountains,
And fill the vales with cries instead of music.

1 *goat-herd gods*: Such as Faunus, or the fauns.
4 *plaining*: plaintive, complaining.
8 *heavenly huntress*: Diana.
9 *lovely star*: Venus.
18 *scrich-owl*: screech-owl.

Strephon:
Long since, alas, my deadly swannish music   25
Hath made itself a crier of the morning,
And hath with wailing strength climbed highest mountains;
Long since my thoughts more desert be than forests;
Long since I see my joys come to their evening,
And state thrown down to over-trodden valleys.   30

Klaius:
Long since the happy dwellers of these vallies
Have prayed me leave my strange exclaiming music,
Which troubles their day's work, and joys of evening;
Long since I hate the night, more hate the morning;
Long since my thoughts chase me like beasts in forests,   35
And make me wish myself laid under mountains.

Strephon:
Me seems I see the high and stately mountains
Transform themselves to low dejected valleys;
Me seems I hear, in these ill-changed forests,
The nightingales do learn of owls their music;   40
Me seems I feel the comfort of the morning
Turned to the mortal serene of an evening.

Klaius:
Me seems I see a filthy cloudy evening
As soon as sun begins to climb the mountains;
Me seems I feel a noisome scent, the morning,   45
When I do smell the flowers of these valleys;
Me seems I hear, when I do hear sweet music,
The dreadful cries of murdered men in forests.

Strephon:
I wish to fire the trees of all these forests;
I give the sun a last farewell each evening;   50
I curse the fiddling finders out of music;
With envy I do hate the lofty mountains,
And with despite despise the humble valleys;
I do detest night, evening, day and morning.

25 *swannish*: because it is like a song before death.
42 *mortal serene*: evening dew, believed to be death-bringing.

Klaius:
Curse to myself my prayer is, the morning;   55
My fire is more than can be made with forests;
My state more base, than are the basest valleys;
I wish no evening more to see, each evening;
Shamed I hate myself in sight of mountains,
And stop mine ears, lest I grow mad with music.   60

Strephon:
For she, whose parts maintained a perfect music,
Whose beauties shined more than the blushing morning;
Who much did pass in state the stately mountains,
In straightness passed the cedars of the forests,
Hath cast me, wretch, into eternal evening,   65
By taking her two suns from these dark valleys.

Klaius:
For she, with whom compared the Alps are valleys;
She, whose least word brings from the spheres their music;
At whose approach the sun rase in the evening;
Who, where she went, bare in her forehead morning,   70
Is gone, is gone, from these our spoiled forests,
Turning to deserts our best pastured mountains.

Strephon:
These mountains witness shall, so shall these valleys;

Klaius:
These forests eke, made wretched by our music;
Our morning hymn is this,[n] and song at evening.

61 *she*: Urania.

xxxiii. A double complaint[n]   [72]

Strephon:
I joy in grief, and do detest all joys;
Despise delight, am tired with thought of ease;
I turn my mind to all forms of annoys,
And with the change of them my fancy please;
I study that which most may me displease,   5
And in despite of that displeasure's might
Embrace that most, that most my soul destroys;
Blinded with beams, fell darkness is my sight;
Dwell in my ruins, feed with sucking smart;
I think from me, not from my woes, to part.   10

Klaius:
I think from me, not from my woes, to part,
And loathe this time called 'life'; nay, think that life
Nature to me for torment did impart;
Think, my hard haps have blunted death's sharp knife,
Not sparing me, in whom his works be rife;   15
And thinking this, think nature, life and death
Place sorrow's triumph on my conquered heart,
Whereto I yield, and seek no other breath
But from the scent of some infectious grave;
Nor of my fortune aught but mischief crave.   20

Strephon:
Nor of my fortune aught but mischief crave,
And seek to nourish that which now contains
All what I am; if I myself will save,
Then I must save what in me chiefly reigns,
Which is the hateful web of sorrow's pains.   25
Sorrow, then cherish me, for I am sorrow;
No being now but sorrow I can have;
Then deck me as thine own; thy help I borrow,
Since thou my riches art, and that thou hast
Enough to make a fertile mind lie waste.   30

Klaius:
Enough to make a fertile mind lie waste
Is that huge storm, which pours itself on me;
Hailstones of tears, of sighs a monstrous blast,
Thunders of cries; lightnings my wild looks be;
The darkened heaven, my soul, which nought can see;   35
The flying sprites which trees by roots up tear
Be those despairs, which have my hopes quite waste.
The difference is: all folks those storms forbear,
But I cannot, who then my self should fly,
So close unto my self my wracks do lie.   40

Strephon:
So close unto my self my wracks do lie,
Both cause, effect, beginning and the end
Are all in me; what help then can I try?
My ship, my self, whose course to love doth bend,
Sore beaten, doth her mast of comfort spend;   45
Her cable, reason, breaks from anchor, hope;
Fancy, her tackling, torn away doth fly;
Ruin, the wind, hath blown her from my scope;
Bruisèd with waves of care, but broken is
On rock, despair, the burial of my bliss.   50

Klaius:
On rock, despair, the burial of my bliss,
I long do plough with plough of deep desire;
The seed fast-meaning is, no truth to miss;
I harrow it with thoughts, which all conspire
Favour to make my chief and only hire.   55
But woe is me, the year is gone about,
And now I fain would reap, I reap but this:
Hate fully grown, absence new sprongen out,
So that I see, although my sight impair,
Vain is their pain, who labour in despair.   60

37 *waste*: wasted.
40 *wracks*: sufferings, ruins.
45 *spend*: break, destroy.
53 *fast-meaning*: sincerity, steadfast purpose.
58 *sprongen*: sprung.

Strephon:
Vain is their pain, who labour in despair:
For so did I, when with my angle, will,
I sought to catch the fish torpedo fair.[n]
Even then despair did hope already kill;
Yet fancy would perforce employ his skill,   65
And this hath got: the catcher now is caught,
Lamed with the angle which itself did bear,
And unto death, quite drowned in dolours, brought:
To death, as then disguised in her fair face.
Thus, thus, alas, I had my loss in chase.   70

Klaius:
Thus, thus, alas, I had my loss in chase,
When first that crowned basilisk I knew,
Whose footsteps I with kisses oft did trace,
Till by such hap as I must ever rue
Mine eyes did light upon her shining hue,   75
And hers on me, astonished with that sight.
Since then my heart did lose his wonted place,
Infected so with her sweet poison's might
That, leaving me for dead, to her it went:
But ah, her flight hath my dead relics spent.   80

Strephon:
But ah, her flight hath my dead relics spent;
Her flight from me, from me, though dead to me,
Yet living still in her, while her beams lent
Such vital spark that her mine eyes might see.
But now those living lights absented be,   85
Full dead before, I now to dust should fall,
But that eternal pains my soul have hent,
And keep it still within this body thrall,
That thus I must, while in this death I dwell,
In earthly fetters feel a lasting hell.   90

62 *angle*: fishing rod.
63 *torpedo*: an electric fish which kills the fisherman.
72 *basilisk*: a snake which kills with its gaze.
80 *spent*: destroyed.
87 *hent*: seized.

Klaius:

In earthly fetters feel a lasting hell,
Alas, I do; from which to find release
I would the earth, I would the heavens sell.
But vain it is to think those pains should cease,
Where life is death, and death can not breed peace.   95
O fair, O only fair, from thee, alas,
These foul, most foul disasters to me fell;
Since thou from me (O me!) O sun, didst pass:
Therefore, esteeming all good blessings toys,
I joy in grief, and do detest all joys.   100

Strephon:

I joy in grief, and do detest all joys.
But now an end, O Klaius, now an end,
For even the herbs our hateful music 'stroys,
And from our burning breath the trees do bend.

xxxiv. Philisides's vision[n]   [73]

Now was our heavenly vault deprived of the light,
With sun's depart; and now the darkness of the night
Did light those beamy stars, which greater light did dark;
Now each thing which enjoyed that fiery quickening spark,
Which 'life' is called, were moved their spirits to repose,   5
And wanting use of eyes, their eyes began to close.
A silence sweet each where with one consent embraced,
A music sweet to one in careful musing placed;
And mother earth, now clad in mourning weeds, did breathe
A dull desire to kiss the image of our death;   10
When I, disgraced wretch, not wretched then, did give
My senses such release, as they which quiet live,
Whose brains boil not in woes, nor breasts with beatings ache,
With nature's praise are wont in safest home to take.
Far from my thoughts was aught whereto their minds aspire   15
Who under courtly pomps do hatch a base desire;

103 *'stroys*: destroys.

Free all my powers were from those captiving snares,
Which heavenly purest gifts defile in muddy cares.
Ne could my soul accuse itself of such a fault
As tender conscience might with furious pangs assault:
But like the feeble flower, whose stalk cannot sustain   20
His weighty top, his top doth downward drooping lean;
Or as the silly bird in well acquainted nest
Doth hide his head with cares but only how to rest;
So I, in simple course, and unentangled mind,   25
Did suffer drowsy lids mine eyes, then clear, to blind,
And laying down my head, did nature's rule observe,
Which senses up doth shut the senses to preserve.
They first their use forgot; then fancies lost their force,
Till deadly sleep at length possessed my living corse.   30
A living corse I lay; but ah, my wakeful mind,
Which, made of heavenly stuff, no mortal change doth bind,
Flew up with freer wings of fleshly bondage free;
And having placed my thoughts, my thoughts thus placed
    me:
Me thought—nay, sure I was, I was in fairest wood   35
Of Samothea land;ⁿ a land which whilom stood
An honour to the world, while honour was their end,
And while their line of years they did in virtue spend.
But there I was, and there my calmy thoughts I fed
On nature's sweet repast, as healthful senses led.   40
Her gifts my study was, her beauties were my sport;
My work her works to know, her dwelling my resort.
Those lamps of heavenly fire to fixed motion bound,
The ever-turning spheres, the never-moving ground;
What essence dest'ny hath; if fortune be, or no;   45
Whence our immortal souls to mortal earth do flow;
What life it is, and how that all these lives do gather
With outward maker's force, or like an inward father;
Such thoughts, me thought, I thought, and strained my single
    mind,
Then void of nearer cares, the depth of things to find: 50
When lo, with hugest noise—such noise a tower makes,
When it blown up with mine a fall of ruin takes—
Or such a noise it was, as highest thunders send,
Or cannons, thunder-like, all shot together, lend:

30 *corse*: corpse.

The moon asunder rent (O gods, O pardon me,   55
That forced with grief reveals what grieved eyes did see!)
The moon asunder rent; whereat, with sudden fall,
More swift than falcon's stoop to feeding falconer's call,
There came a chariot fair by doves and sparrows guided,
Whose storm-like course stayed not, till hard by me it bided.   60
I, wretch, astonished was, and thought the deathful doom
Of heaven, of earth, of hell, of time and place was come.
But straight there issued forth two ladies (ladies, sure,
They seemed to me) on whom did wait a virgin pure.
Strange were the ladies' weeds; yet more unfit than strange.   65
The first with clothes tucked up, as nymphs in woods do range,
Tucked up, even with the knees, with bow and arrows prest;
Her right arm naked was; discovered was her breast;
But heavy was her pace, and such a meagre cheer,
As little hunting mind, God knows, did there appear.   70
The other had with art, more than our women know,
As stuff meant for the sale, set out to glaring show,
A wanton woman's face; and with curled knots had twined
Her hair, which by the help of painter's cunning shined.
When I such guests did see come out of such a house,   75
The mountains great with child I thought brought forth a mouse.
But walking forth, the first thus to the second said:
'Venus, come on'; said she, 'Dian, you are obeyed.'
These names abashed me much, when those great names I heard;
Although their fame, me seemed, from truth had greatly jarred.   80
As I thus musing stood, Diana called to her
Her waiting nymph; a nymph that did excel as far
All things that erst I saw, as orient pearls exceed
That which their mother hight, or else their silly seed;
Indeed a perfect hue; indeed a sweet consent   85
Of all those graces' gifts the heavens have ever lent.
And so she was attired, as one that did not prize
Too much her peerless parts, nor yet could them despise.
But called, she came apace; a pace wherein did move
The band of beauties all, the little world of love;   90
And bending humbled eyes (O eyes, the sun of sight!),
She waited mistress' will, who thus disclosed her sprite:
'Sweet Mira mine', quoth she, 'the pleasure of my mind,
In whom of all my rules the perfect proof I find,

67 *prest*: prompt, ready.
69 *meagre cheer*: melancholy expression.

To only thee, thou seest, we grant this special grace   95
Us to attend in this most private time and place.
Be silent therefore now, and so be silent still;
Of what thou seest close up in secret knot thy will.'
She answered was with look, and well-performed behest:
And Mira I admired: her shape sank in my breast.   100
But thus with ireful eyes, and face that shook with spite,
Diana did begin: 'What moved me to invite
Your presence, sister dear, first to my moony sphere,
And hither now, vouchsafe to take with willing ear.
I know full well you know what discord long hath reigned   105
Betwixt us two; how much that discord foul hath stained
Both our estates, while each the other did deprave;
Proof speaks too much to us, that feeling trial have.
Our names are quite forgot, our temples are defaced,
Our offerings spoiled, our priests from priesthood are displaced.   110
Is this thy fruit, O strife? Those thousand churches high,
Those thousand altars fair, now in the dust to lie?
In mortal minds our minds but planets' names preserve,
No knee once bowed, forsooth, for them they say we serve.
Are we their servants grown? No doubt, a noble stay;   115
Celestial powers to worms, Jove's children serve to clay.
But such, they say, we be: this praise our discord bred,
While we for mutual spite a striving passion fed.
But let us wiser be, and what foul discord brake,
So much more strong again let fastest concord make.   120
Our years do it require; you see we both do feel
The weakening work of time's for-ever-whirling wheel.
Although we be divine, our grandsire Saturn is
With age's force decayed; yet once the heaven was his.
And now, before we seek, by wise Apollo's skill,   125
Our young years to renew (for so he saith he will),
Let us a perfect peace betwixt us two resolve:
Which, lest the ruinous want of government dissolve,
Let one the princess be, to her the other yield;
For vain equality is but contention's field.   130
And let her have the gifts that should in both remain,
In her let beauty both, and chasteness, fully reign:
So as, if I prevail, you give your gifts to me,
If you, on you I lay what in my office be.
Now resteth only this: which of us two is she   135
To whom precedence shall of both accorded be?

For that, so that you like, hereby doth lie a youth',
She beckoned unto me: 'as yet of spotless truth,
Who may this doubt discern; for better wit than lot
Becometh us; in us fortune determines not.   140
This crown of amber fair', (an amber crown she held)[n]
'To worthiest let him give, when both he hath beheld,
And be it as he saith.' Venus was glad to hear
Such proffer made, which she well showed with smiling cheer,
As though she were the same, as when, by Paris' doom,   145
She had chief goddesses in beauty overcome,
And smirkly thus gan say: 'I never sought debate,
Diana dear; my mind to love, and not to hate,
Was ever apt; but you my pastimes did despise.
I never spited you, but thought you over-wise.   150
Now kindness proffered is, none kinder is than I;
And so most ready am this mean of peace to try.
And let him be our judge: the lad doth please me well.'
Thus both did come to me, and both began to tell—
For both together spake, each loath to be behind—   155
That they by solemn oath their deities would bind
To stand unto my will; their will they made me know.
I, that was first aghast, when first I saw their show,
Now bolder waxed, waxed proud, that I such sway might bear;
For near acquaintance doth diminish reverent fear.   160
And having bound them fast by Styx they should obey
To all what I decreed, did thus my verdict say:
'How ill both you can rule, well hath your discord taught;
Ne yet for what I see, your beauties merit ought.
To yonder nymph therefore'—to Mira I did point—   165
'The crown above you both for ever I appoint.'
I would have spoken out; but out they both did cry:
'Fie, fie, what have we done? Ungodly rebel, fie!
But now we needs must yield to what our oaths require.'
'Yet thou shalt not go free,' quoth Venus; 'such a fire   170
Her beauty kindle shall within thy foolish mind
That thou full oft shalt wish thy judging eyes were blind.'
'Nay, then,' Diana said, 'the chasteness I will give,
In ashes of despair, though burnt, shall make thee live.'

137 *so that*: provided that.
145 *doom*: judgement.
147 *smirkly*: smirkingly.

'Nay, thou,' said both, 'shalt see such beams shine in her face,   175
That thou shalt never dare seek help of wretched case.'
And with that cursed curse away to heaven they fled,
First having all their gifts upon fair Mira spread.
The rest I cannot tell; for therewithal, I waked,
And found with deadly fear that all my sinews shaked.   180
Was it a dream? O dream, how hast thou wrought in me,
That I things erst unseen should first in dreaming see?
And thou, O traitor sleep, made for to be our rest,
How hast thou framed the pain wherewith I am oppressed?
O coward Cupid, thus dost thou thy honour keep,   185
Unarmed, alas, unwarned, to take a man asleep?

xxxv. A pastoral elegy[n]   [75]

Since that to death is gone the shepherd high,
   Who most the silly shepherd's pipe did prize,
   Your doleful tunes, sweet muses, now apply.

And you, O trees, if any life there lies
   In trees, now through your porous barks receive   5
   The strange resound of these, my causeful cries,
And let my breath upon your branches cleave;
   My breath, distinguished into words of woe,
   That so I may signs of my sorrow leave.
But if among yourselves some one tree grow   10
   That aptest is to figure misery,
   Let it embassage bear your griefs to show.
The weeping myrrh, I think, will not deny
   Her help to this, this justest cause of plaint:
   Your doleful tunes, sweet muses, now apply.   15

And thou, poor earth, whom fortune doth attaint
   In nature's name to suffer such a harm
   As for to lose thy gem, our earthly saint,
Upon thy face let coaly ravens swarm;

13 *weeping myrrh*: exuding sap like tears.
16 *attaint*: condemn.

Let all the sea thy tears accounted be;   20
  Thy bowels with all killing metals arm.
Let gold now rust, let diamonds waste in thee;
  Let pearls be wan with woe their dam doth bear;
  Thyself henceforth the light do never see.
And you, O flowers, which sometimes princes were,   25
  Till these strange alterings you did hap to try,
  Of prince's loss yourselves for tokens rear.
Lily, in mourning black your whiteness die;
  O hyacinth, let 'AI' be on thee still.[n]
  Your doleful tunes, sweet muses, now apply.   30

O echo, all these woods with roaring fill,
  And do not only mark the accents last,
  But all, for all reach not my wailful will:
One echo to another echo cast
  Sound of my griefs, and let it never end,   35
  Till that it hath all woods and waters passed;
Nay, to the heavens your just complainings send,
  And stay the stars' inconstant constant race,
  Till that they do unto our dolours bend,
And ask the reason of that special grace,   40
  That they, which have no lives, should live so long,
  And virtuous souls so soon should lose their place?
Ask, if in great men, good men so do throng,
  That he for want of elbow room must die?
  Or if that they be scant, if this be wrong?   45
Did wisdom this our wretched time espy,
  In one true chest to rob all virtue's treasure?
  Your doleful tunes, sweet muses, now apply.

And if that any counsel you to measure
  Your doleful tunes, to them, still plaining, say: 50
  'To well-felt grief, plaint is the only pleasure.'
O light of sun, which is entitled day,
  O well thou dost, that thou no longer bidest,
  For mourning night her black weeds may display;
O Phoebus, with good cause thy face thou hidest,   55
  Rather than have thy all-beholding eye
  Fouled with this sight, while thou thy chariot guidest:

And well, methinks, becomes this vaulty sky
  A stately tomb to cover him deceased.
  Your doleful tunes, sweet muses, now apply.   60

O Philomela, with thy breast oppressed
  By shame and grief, help, help me to lament
  Such cursed harms as cannot be redressed;
Or if thy mourning notes be fully spent,
  Then give a quiet ear unto my plaining;   65
  For I to teach the world complaint am bent.
Ye dimmy clouds, which well employ your staining
  This cheerful air with your obscured cheer,
  Witness your woeful tears with daily raining;
And if, O sun, thou ever didst appear   70
  In shape which by man's eye might be perceived,
  Virtue is dead, now set thy triumph here.
Now set thy triumph in this world, bereaved
  Of what was good, where now no good doth lie;
  And by thy pomp our loss will be conceived.   75
O notes of mine, yourselves together tie:
  With too much grief, methinks, you are dissolved.
  Your doleful tunes, sweet muses, now apply.

Time ever old and young, is still revolved
  Within itself, and never taketh end;   80
  But mankind is for aye to nought resolved.
The filthy snake her aged coat can mend,
  And getting youth again, in youth doth flourish;
  But unto man, age ever death doth send.
The very trees with grafting we can cherish,   85
  So that we can long time produce their time;
  But man, which helpeth them, helpless must perish.
Thus, thus, the minds which over all do climb,
  When they by years' experience get best graces,
  Must finish them by death's detested crime.   90
We last short while, and build long-lasting places.
  Ah, let us all against foul nature cry:
  We nature's works do help, she us defaces.
For how can nature unto this reply,
  That she her child, I say, her best child killeth?   95
  Your doleful tunes, sweet muses, now apply.

61 *Philomela*: the nightingale, metamorphosed after her rape by Tereus.
86 *produce*: draw out, extend.

Alas, methinks, my weakened voice but spilleth
  The vehement course of this just lamentation;
  Methinks, my sound no place with sorrow filleth.
I know not I, but once in detestation   100
  I have myself, and all what life containeth,
  Since death on virtue's fort hath made invasion.
One word of woe another after traineth;
  Ne do I care how rude be my invention,
  So it be seen what sorrow in me reigneth.   105
O elements, by whose—they say—contention
  Our bodies be in living powers maintained,
  Was this man's death the fruit of your dissension?
O physic's power, which, some say, hath refrained
  Approach of death, alas, thou helpest meagrely,   110
  When once one is for Atropos distrained.
Great be physicians' brags; but aid is beggarly;
  When rooted moisture fails, or groweth dry,
  They leave off all, and say: 'Death comes too eagerly.'
They are but words, therefore, which men do buy   115
  Of any since god Aesculapius ceased.
  Your doleful tunes, sweet muses, now apply.

Justice, justice is now, alas, oppressed;
  Bountifulness hath made his last conclusion;
  Goodness for best attire in dust is dressed.   120
Shepherds, bewail your uttermost confusion,
  And see, by this picture to you presented,
  Death is our home, life is but a delusion.
For see, alas, who is from you absented:
  Absented? Nay, I say for ever banished   125
  From such as were to die for him contented.
Out of our sight, in turn of hand, is vanished
  Shepherd of shepherds, whose well-settled order,
  Private with wealth, public with quiet garnished.
While he did live, far, far, was all disorder;   130
  Example more prevailing than direction,
  Far was home strife, and far was foe from border.

97 *spilleth*: spoils, destroys.
111 *Atropos*: the third of the Fates, who cannot be avoided: death.
111 *distrained*: seized as payment for debt (legal term).
116 *Aesculapius*: the god of medicine, slain by Zeus for fear that he would outwit
  death.
127 *In turn of hand*: in the twinkling of an eye.

His life a law, his look a full correction:
   As in his health we healthful were preserved,
   So in his sickness grew our sure infection;   135
His death our death. But ah, my muse hath swerved
   From such deep plaint as should such woes descry,
   Which he of us for ever hath deserved.
The style of heavy heart can never fly
   So high, as should make such a pain notorious: 140
   Cease, muse, therefore; thy dart, O death, apply:
And farewell prince, whom goodness hath made glorious.

xxxvi. An elegiac sestina[n]   [76]

   Farewell, O sun, Arcadia's clearest light;
   Farewell, O pearl, the poor man's plenteous pleasure;
   Farewell, O golden staff, the weak man's might;
   Farewell, O joy, the woeful's only pleasure.
   Wisdom, farewell, the skill-less man's direction;   5
   Farewell with thee, farewell all our affection.

   For what place now is left for our affection,
   Now that of purest lamp is queint the light,
   Which to our darkened minds was best direction;
   Now that the mine is lost of all our treasure;   10
   Now death hath swallowed up our worldly pleasure,
   We orphans left, void of all public might?

   Orphans indeed, deprived of father's might:
   For he our father was in all affection,
   In our well-doing placing all his pleasure,   15
   Still studying how to us to be a light.
   As well he was in peace a safest treasure;
   In war his wit and word was our direction.

   Whence, whence, alas, shall we seek our direction?
   When that we fear our hateful neighbours' might,   20
   Who long have gaped to get Arcadians' treasure,

8 *queint*: quenched.

Shall we now find a guide of such affection,
Who for our sakes will think all travail light,
And make his pain to keep us safe, his pleasure?

No, no; for ever gone is all our pleasure;   25
For ever wandering from all good direction;
For ever blinded of our clearest light;
For ever lamed of our surest might;
For ever banished from well-placed affection;
For ever robbed of our royal treasure.   30

Let tears for him, therefore, be all our treasure,
And in our wailful naming him, our pleasure;
Let hating of ourselves be our affection,
And unto death bend still our thoughts' direction;
Let us against ourselves employ our might,   35
And putting out our eyes, seek we our light.

Farewell our light, farewell our spoiled treasure;
Farewell our might, farewell our daunted pleasure;
Farewell direction, farewell all affection.

xxxvii. Against the fear of death[n]   [77]

Since nature's works be good, and death doth serve
As nature's work, why should we fear to die?
Since fear is vain, but when it may preserve,
Why should we fear that which we cannot fly?
Fear is more pain than is the pain it fears,   5
Disarming human minds of native might,
While each conceit an ugly figure bears,
Which were not ill, well viewed in reason's light.
Our owly eyes, which dimmed with passions be,
And scarce discern the dawn of coming day,   10
Let them be cleared: and now begin to see,
Our life is but a step in dusty way.
    Then let us hold the bliss of peaceful mind;
    Since this we feel, great loss we cannot find.

Poems from Certain Sonnets

i. The surrender to love[n]　　　　　　　　　　　　　　[1]

Since, shunning pain, I ease can never find;
Since bashful dread seeks where he knows me harmed;
Since will is won, and stopped ears are charmed;
Since force doth faint, and sight doth make me blind;
Since loosing long, the faster still I bind;　　　　　　　　5
Since naked sense can conquer reason armed;
Since heart in chilling fear with ice is warmed;
In fine, since strife of thought but mars the mind:
I yield, O love, unto thy loathed yoke,
Yet craving law of arms, whose rule doth teach　　　　　10
That hardly used, whoever prison broke,
In justice quit, of honour made no breach:
　　Whereas, if I a grateful guardian have,
　　Thou art my lord, and I thy vowed slave.

ii. Love's torments　　　　　　　　　　　　　　　　[2]

When love, puffed up with rage of high disdain,
Resolved to make me pattern of his might,
Like foe, whose wits inclined to deadly spite,
Would often kill, to breed more feeling pain;
He would not, armed with beauty, only reign　　　　　　5
On those affects which easily yield to sight,
But virtue sets so high, that reason's light,
For all his strife, can only bondage gain:
So that I live to pay a mortal fee,
Dead-palsy-sick of all my chiefest parts;　　　　　　　10
Like those whom dreams make ugly monsters see,
And can cry 'Help!' with nought but groans and starts.
　　Longing to have, having no wit to wish,
　　To starving minds such is god Cupid's dish.

[2]　10 *Dead-palsy-sick*: paralysed

iii. To the tune of   [3]

Non credo gia che piu infelice amante[n]

> The fire to see my wrongs for anger burneth;
> The air in rain for my affliction weepeth;
> The sea to ebb for grief his flowing turneth;
> The earth with pity dull the centre keepeth;
>   Fame is with wonder blazed;   5
>   Time runs away for sorrow;
>   Place standeth still amazed,
>   To see my night of evils, which hath no morrow.
>   Alas, all only she no pity taketh
>   To know my miseries, but, chaste and cruel,   10
>   My fall her glory maketh:
>   Yet still her eyes give to my flames their fuel.
>
> Fire, burn me quite, till sense of burning leave me;
> Air, let me draw no more thy breath in anguish;
> Sea, drowned in thee, of tedious life bereave me;   15
> Earth, take this earth, wherein my spirits languish.
>   Fame, say I was not born;
>   Time, haste my dying hour;
>   Place, see my grave uptorn;
>   Fire, air, sea, earth, fame, time, place, show your power. 20
>   Alas, from all their helps I am exiled;
>   For hers am I, and death fears her displeasure.
>   Fie, death, thou art beguiled;
>   Though I be hers, she makes of me no treasure.

iv. To the same tune   [4]

> The nightingale, as soon as April bringeth
> Unto her rested sense a perfect waking,
> While late bare earth, proud of new clothing, springeth,
> Sings out her woes, a thorn her song-book making,

And mournfully bewailing   5
Her throat in tunes expresseth,
What grief her breast oppresseth
For Tereus' force on her chaste will prevailing.
  O Philomela fair, O take some gladness,
  That here is juster cause of plaintful sadness: 10
  Thine earth now springs, mine fadeth;
  Thy thorn without, my thorn my heart invadeth.

Alas, she hath no other cause of anguish
But Tereus' love, on her by strong hand wroken;
Wherein she, suffering all her spirits' languish,   15
Full woman-like, complains her will was broken.
  But I, who daily craving
  Cannot have to content me,
  Have more cause to lament me,
Since wanting is more woe than too much having.   20
  O Philomela fair, O take some gladness,
  That here is juster cause of plaintful sadness;
  Thine earth now springs, mine fadeth;
  Thy thorn without, my thorn my heart invadeth.

v. Rhymed sapphics[n]   [5]

$$- \cup - - - \cup \cup - \cup - -$$
$$- \cup \cup - -$$

O my thoughts' sweet food, my my only owner,
O my heaven's foretaste by thy heavenly pleasure,
O the fair nymph born to do women honour,
          Lady my treasure:

Where be now those joys that I lately tasted?   5
Where be now those eyes, ever inly piercers?
Where be now those words never idly wasted,
          Wounds to rehearsers?

[4]   14 *wroken*: wreaked, accomplished.

Where is, ah, that face, that a sun defaces?
Where be those welcomes, by no worth deserved?   10
Where be those movings, the delights, the graces?
    How be we swerved?

O hideous absence, by thee am I thralled:
O my vain word gone, ruin of my glory!
O due allegiance, by thee am I called   15
    Still to be sorry.

But no more words, though such a word be spoken,
Nor no more wording, with a word to spill me:
Peace, due allegiance; duty must be broken
    If duty kill me.   20

Then come, O come; then do I come, receive me,
Slay me not, for stay; do not hide thy blisses,
But between those arms; never else do leave me;
    Give me my kisses.

O my thoughts' sweet food, my my only owner,   25
O my heaven's foretaste by thy heavenly pleasure,
O the fair nymph born to do women honour,
    Lady my treasure.

vi. To the tune of Basciami vita mia[n]   [6]

Sleep, baby mine, desire; nurse beauty singeth;
Thy cries, O baby, set mine head on aching:
The babe cries: 'Way, thy love doth keep me waking.'

[5] 18 *spill*: destroy.
  23 *But*: except.

[6] 3 *Way*: alas, or mimetic word for baby's cry.

Lully, lully, my babe; hope cradle bringeth,
Unto my children alway good rest taking: 5
The babe cries: 'Way, thy love doth keep me waking.'

Since, baby mine, from me thy watching springeth;
Sleep then a little, pap content is making:
The babe cries: 'Nay, for that abide I waking.'

vii. To the tune of the Spanish song   [7]

Se tu señora no dueles di me[n]

O fair, O sweet, when I do look on thee,
In whom all joys so well agree,
Heart and soul do sing in me.
  This you hear is not my tongue,
  Which once said what I conceived,   5
  For it was of use bereaved,
  With a cruel answer stung.
    No, though tongue to roof be cleaved[n]
    Fearing lest he chastised be,
    Heart and soul do sing in me.   10

O fair, O sweet, when I do look on thee,
In whom all joys so well agree,
Heart and soul do sing in me.
  Just accord all music makes;
  In thee just accord excelleth,   15
  Where each part in such peace dwelleth,
  One of other beauty takes.
    Since then truth to all minds telleth
    That in thee lives harmony,
    Heart and soul do sing in me.   20

O fair, O sweet, when I do look on thee,
In whom all joys so well agree,
Heart and soul do sing in me.

[6]   9 *that*: satisfaction of desire.

They that heaven have known, do say
That who so that grace obtaineth   25
To see what fair sight there reigneth,
Forced are to sing alway:
 So then, since that heaven remaineth
 In thy face I plainly see,
 Heart and soul do sing in me.   30

O fair, O sweet, when I do look on thee,
In whom all joys so well agree,
Heart and soul do sing in me.
 Sweet, think not I am at ease
 For because my chief part singeth: 35
 This song from death's sorrow springeth,
 As to swan in last disease;
  For no dumbness nor death bringeth
  Stay to true love's melody:
  Heart and soul do sing in me.   40

viii. Translated out of Horace, which begins [12]

Rectius vives[n]

You better sure shall live, not evermore
 Trying high seas, nor while sea rage you flee,
 Pressing too much upon ill-harboured shore.

The golden mean who loves, lives safely free
 From filth of foreworn house, and quiet lives,   5
 Released from court, where envy needs must be.

The wind most oft the hugest pine-tree grieves;
 The stately towers come down with greater fall;
 The highest hills the bolt of thunder cleaves;

Ill haps do fill with hope, good hopes appal   10
 With fear of change the courage well prepared;
 Foul winters, as they come, away they shall.

Though present times and past with evils be snared,
    They shall not last; with cithern silent muse
    Apollo wakes, and bow hath sometime spared.   15

In hard estate with stout show valour use,
    The same man still in whom wisdom prevails;
    In too full wind draw in thy swelling sails.

ix. A lover's apology   [17]

My mistress lours, and saith I do not love;
I do protest, and seek with service due
In humble mind a constant faith to prove;
But for all this I cannot her remove
From deep vain thought that I may not be true.   5

If oaths might serve, even by the Stygian lake
Which poets say the gods themselves do fear,
I never did my vowed word forsake:
For why should I, whom free choice slave doth make,
Else what in face, than in my fancy bear?   10

My muse therefore—for only thou canst tell—
Tell me the cause of this my causeless woe,
Tell how ill thought disgraced my doing well,
Tell how my joys and hopes thus foully fell
To so low ebb, that wonted were to flow.   15

O this it is: the knotted straw is found
In tender hearts;[n] small things engender hate;
A horse's worth laid waste the Trojan ground;
A three-foot stool in Greece made trumpets sound;
And ass's shade ere now hath bred debate.   20

[12]   14 *cithern*: a kind of guitar.

If Greeks themselves were moved with so small cause
To twist those broils, which hardly would untwine,
Should ladies fair be tied to such hard laws
As in their moods to take a lingering pause?
I would it not, their metal is too fine.   25

My hand doth not bear witness with my heart,
She saith, because I make no woeful lays
To paint my living death and endless smart;
And so for one that felt god Cupid's dart
She thinks I lead and live too merry days.   30

Are poets then the only lovers true,
Whose hearts are set on measuring a verse,
Who think themselves well bless'd, if they renew
Some good old dump that Chaucer's mistress knew,
And use but you for matters to rehearse?   35

Then, good Apollo, do away thy bow;
Take harp, and sing, in this our versing time;
And in my brain some sacred humour flow,
That all the earth my woes, sighs, tears may know:
And see you not that I fall now to rhyme?   40

As for my mirth: how could I but be glad,
Whilst that, methought, I justly made my boast
That only I the only mistress had?
But now, if e'er my face with joy be clad,
Think Hannibal did laugh when Carthage lost.[n]   45

Sweet lady, as for those whose sullen cheer,
Compared to me, made me in lightness found;
Who stoic-like in cloudy hue appear;
Who silence force, to make their words more dear;
Whose eyes seem chaste, because they look on ground; 50
    Believe them not, for physic true doth find
    Choler adust is joyed in womankind.

24 *moods*: rages.
34 *dump*: melancholy song, complaint.
45 *Think*: consider, reflect upon the fact.
46 *cheer*: demeanour, expression.
52 *Choler adust*: black or dry melancholy.
52 *joyed*: made cheerful, rejoices.

x. A lover's landscape[n] [18]

In wonted walks, since wonted fancies change,
Some cause there is, which of strange cause doth rise:
For in each thing, whereto mine eye doth range,
Part of my pain, me seems, engraved lies.
The rocks, which were of constant mind the mark,   5
In climbing steep now hard refusal show;
The shading woods seem now my sun to dark,
And stately hills disdain to look so low.
The restful caves now restless visions give;
In dales I see each way a hard ascent;   10
Like late mown meads, late cut from joy I live;
Alas, sweet brooks do in my tears augment:
   Rocks, woods, hills, caves, dales, meads, brooks, answer me:
   Infected minds infect each thing they see.

xi. A farewell[n] [20]

Oft have I mused, but now at length I find
Why those that die, men say they do depart;
'Depart', a word so gentle to my mind,
Weakly did seem to paint death's ugly dart.
But now the stars with their strange course do bind   5
Me one to leave, with whom I leave my heart,
I hear a cry of spirits faint and blind,
That, parting thus, my chiefest part I part.
Part of my life, the loathed part to me,
Lives to impart my weary clay some breath;   10
But that good part, wherein all comforts be,
Now dead, doth show departure is a death,
   Yea, worse than death; death parts both woe and joy;
   From joy I part, still living in annoy.

[18]   7 *dark*: darken.

xii. The Seven Wonders of England[n]   [22]

Near Wilton sweet, huge heaps of stone are found;
But so confused, that neither any eye
Can count them just, nor reason reason try
What force brought them to so unlikely ground.[n]

To stranger weights my mind's waste soil is bound,   5
Of passion's hills, reaching to reason's sky,
From fancy's earth passing all number's bound,
Passing all guess whence into me should fly
   So mazed a mass; or if in me it grows,
   A simple soul should breed so mixed woes.   10

The Breretons have a lake, which when the sun
Approaching warms—not else—dead logs up sends,
From hidd'nest depth, which tribute when it ends,
Sore sign it is the lord's last thread is spun.[n]

My lake is sense, whose still streams never run,   15
But when my sun her shining twins there bends;
Then from his depth with force in her begun,
Long drowned hopes to watery eyes it lends;
   But when that fails my dead hopes up to take,
   Their master is fair warned his will to make.   20

We have a fish, by strangers much admired,
Which, caught, to cruel search yields his chief part,
With gall cut out, closed up again by art;
Yet lives until his life be new required.[n]

A stranger fish myself, not yet expired,   25
Though rapt with beauty's hook, I did impart
Myself unto th'anatomy desired,
Instead of gall, leaving to her my heart;
   Yet live with thoughts closed up, till that she will
   By conquest's right, instead of searching, kill.   30

1 *huge heaps of stone*: Stonehenge.
3 *just*: accurately.
21 *a fish*: the pike.
27 *anatomy*: dissection.

Peak hath a cave whose narrow entries find
Large rooms within, where drops distil amain,
Till knit with cold, though there unknown, remain,
Deck that poor place with alabaster lined.[n]

Mine eyes the strait, the roomy cave my mind,
Whose cloudy thoughts let fall an inward rain
Of sorrow's drops, till colder reason bind
Their running fall into a constant vein
    Of truth, far more than alabaster pure;
      Which, though despised, yet still doth truth endure.   40

A field there is, where, if a stake be pressed
Deep in the earth, what hath in earth receipt
Is changed to stone, in hardness, cold, and weight;
The wood above doth soon consuming rest.[n]

The earth, her ears; the stake is my request;   45
Of which, how much may pierce to that sweet seat,
To honour turned, doth dwell in honour's nest,
Keeping that form, though void of wonted heat;
    But all the rest, which fear durst not apply,
      Failing themselves, with withered conscience die.   50

Of ships by shipwreck cast on Albion coast,
Which rotting on the rocks their death do die,
From wooden bones, and blood of pitch, doth fly
A bird which gets more life than ship had lost.[n]

My ship, desire, with wind of lust long tossed,   55
Brake on fair cleeves of constant chastity;
Where, plagued for rash attempt, gives up his ghost,
So deep in seas of virtue beauties lie.
    But of his death flies up a purest love,
      Which, seeming less, yet nobler life doth move.   60

31 *a cave*: possibly Poole's Cave, near Buxton; see note.
41 *A field*: near Bath; see note.
54 *A bird*: the barnacle goose; see note.
56 *cleeves*: cliffs.

These wonders England breeds; the last remains,
A lady, in despite of nature chaste,
On whom all love, in whom no love is placed,
Where fairness yields to wisdom's shortest reins.

An humble pride, a scorn that favour stains;   65
A woman's mould, but like an angel graced;
An angel's mind, but in a woman cast;
A heaven on earth, or earth that heaven contains;
   Now thus this wonder to myself I frame:
   She is the cause that all the rest I am.   70

xiii. To the tune of   [23]

Wilhelmus van Nassouwe, & c.[n]

Who hath his fancy pleased
With fruits of happy sight,
Let here his eyes be raised
On nature's sweetest light:
A light which doth dissever   5
And yet unite the eyes,
A light which, dying never,
Is cause the looker dies.

She never dies, but lasteth
In life of lover's heart;   10
He ever dies, that wasteth
In love his chiefest part.
Thus is her life still guarded
In never dying faith;
Thus is his death rewarded,   15
Since she lives in his death.

Look then, and die; the pleasure
Doth answer well the pain;
Small loss of mortal treasure,
Who may immortal gain.   20

Immortal be her graces,
Immortal is her mind;
They fit for heavenly places,
This heaven in it doth bind.

But eyes those beauties see not,   25
Nor sense that grace descries;
Yet eyes deprived be not
From sight of her fair eyes:
Which, as of inward glory
They are the outward seal,   30
So may they live still sorry
Which die not in that weal.

But who hath fancies pleased
With fruits of happy sight
Let here his eyes be raised   35
On nature's sweetest light.

xiv. To the tune of [24]

The Smokes of Melancholy[n]

Who hath ever felt the change of love
And known those pangs that the losers prove
  May paint my face without seeing me,
  And write the state how my fancies be
  The loathsome buds grown on sorrow's tree: 5
But who by hearsay speaks, and hath not fully felt
What kind of fires they be in which those spirits melt
  Shall guess, and fail, what doth displease;
  Feeling my pulse, miss my disease.

O no, O no; trial only shows   10
The bitter juice of forsaken woes,
  Where former bliss present ills do stain—
  Nay, former bliss adds to present pain,
  While remembrance doth both states contain.

Come, learners, then, to me, the model of mishap,   15
Engulfed in despair, slid down from fortune's lap;
  And as you like my double lot,
   Tread in my steps, or follow not.

For me, alas, I am full resolved
Those bands, alas, shall not be dissolved,   20
  Nor break my word, though reward come late,
   Nor fail my faith in my failing fate,
    Nor change in change, though change change my state:
But always one myself with eagle-eyed truth to fly
Up to the sun, although the sun my wings do fry: 25
  For if those flames burn my desire,
   Yet shall I die in Phoenix' fire.

xv. Aristophanics[n]   [25]

−∪∪−∪−−

  When to my deadly pleasure,
  When to my lively torment,
  Lady, mine eyes remained,
  Joined, alas, to your beams,
  With violence of heavenly   5
  Beauty tied to virtue,
  Reason abashed retired,
  Gladly my senses yielded.
  Gladly my senses yielding
  Thus to betray my heart's fort   10
  Left me devoid of all life.
  They to the beamy suns went,
  Where, by the death of all deaths,
  Find to what harm they hastened;
  Like to the silly sylvan   15
  Burned by the light he best liked,
  When with a fire he first met.

[24] 27 *in Phoenix' fire*: in the expectation of rising again, like the Phoenix from his ashes.

[25] 15 *the silly sylvan*: the satyr who on first seeing fire kissed it.

Yet, yet, a life to their death,
Lady, you have reserved;
Lady, the life of all love;   20
For though my sense be from me,
And I be dead, who want sense;
Yet do we both live in you;
Turned anew by your means
Unto the flower that aye turns,   25
As you, alas, my sun bends.
Thus do I fall, to rise thus;
Thus do I die, to live thus;
Changed to a change, I change not.
Thus may I not be from you;   30
Thus be my senses on you;
Thus what I think is of you;
Thus what I seek is in you;
All what I am, it is you.

xvi. To the tune of a Neapolitan song[n]   [26]

No, no, no, no, I cannot hate my foe;
  Although with cruel fire
  First thrown on my desire
  She sacks my rendered sprite:
    For so fair a flame embraces   5
      All the places
    Where that heat of all heats springeth
      That it bringeth
    To my dying heart some pleasure,
      Since his treasure   10
    Burneth bright in fairest light: no, no, no, no.

No, no, no, no, I cannot hate my foe;
  Although with cruel fire
  First thrown on my desire
  She sacks my rendered sprite: 15

[25]   25 *the flower*: the heliotrope, which turns towards the sun.

Since our lives be not immortal,
  But to mortal
Fetters tied, do wait the hour
  Of death's power,
They have no cause to be sorry   20
  Who with glory
End the way where all men stay: no, no, no, no.

No, no, no, no, I cannot hate my foe;
  Although with cruel fire
First thrown on my desire   25
She sacks my rendered sprite:
  No man doubts, whom beauty killeth,
    Fair death feeleth;
  And in whom fair death proceedeth,
    Glory breedeth;   30
  So that I, in her beams dying,
    Glory trying,
Though in pain, cannot complain: no, no, no, no.

xvii. To the tune of a Neapolitan villanelle[n]   [27]

All my sense thy sweetness gained,
Thy fair hair my heart enchained,
My poor reason thy words moved,
So that thee like heaven I loved:
  Fa la la leridan, dan dan dan deridan,   5
  Dan dan dan deridan deridan dei:
    While to my mind the outside stood
    For messenger of inward good.

[26] 27 *whom*: that he whom.
      32 *trying*: experiencing.

Now thy sweetness sour is deemed,
Thy hair not a hair esteemed;   10
Reason hath thy words removed,
Finding that but words they proved:
   Fa la la leridan, dan dan dan deridan,
   Dan dan dan deridan deridan dei:
     For no fair sign can credit win   15
     If that the substance fail within.

No more in thy sweetness glory;
For thy knitting hair be sorry;
Use thy words but to bewail thee,
That no more thy beams avail thee: 20
   Fa la la leridan, dan dan dan deridan,
   Dan dan dan deridan deridan dei:
     Lay not thy colours more to view
     Without the picture be found true.

Woe to me, alas, she weepeth: 25
Fool in me, what folly creepeth?
Was I to blaspheme enraged
Where my soul I have engaged?
   Fa la la leridan, dan dan dan deridan,
   Dan dan dan deridan deridan dei: 30
     And wretched I must yield to this;
     The fault I blame her chasteness is.

Sweetness, sweetly pardon folly;
Tie me, hair, your captive wholly;
Words, O words, of heavenly knowledge,   35
Know my words their faults acknowledge:
   Fa la la leridan, dan dan dan deridan,
   Dan dan dan deridan deridan dei:
     And all my life I will confess,
     The less I love, I live the less.   40

[28]

xviii. Translated out of the Diana of Montemayor[n]

in Spanish, where Sireno, a shepherd, pulling out a little of his
mistress Diana's hair, wrapped about with green silk, who now had
utterly forsaken him: to the hair he thus bewailed himself:

> What changes here, O hair,
> I see since I saw you:
> How ill fits you this green to wear,
> For hope the colour due.[n]
> Indeed, I well did hope,   5
> Though hope were mixed with fear,
> No other shepherd should have scope
> Once to approach this hair.
>
> Ah hair, how many days,
> My Dian made me show,   10
> With thousand pretty childish plays
> If I ware you, or no:
> Alas, how oft with tears,
> O tears of guileful breast,
> She seemed full of jealous fears,   15
> Whereat I did but jest.
>
> Tell me, O hair of gold,
> If I then faulty be
> That trust those killing eyes I would,
> Since they did warrant me.   20
> Have you not seen her mood,
> What streams of tears she spent,
> Till that I sware my faith so stood
> As her words had it bent?
>
> Who hath such beauty seen   25
> In one that changeth so?
> Or where one's love so constant been,
> Who ever saw such woe?

21 _mood_: anger.
27 _so constant been_: has been so constant.

Ah hair, are you not grieved,
To come from whence you be,   30
Seeing how once, you saw, I lived,
To see me as you see?

On sandy bank of late
I saw this woman sit,
Where, 'Sooner die than change my state',[n]   35
She with her finger writ:
Thus my belief was stayed—
Behold love's mighty hand!—
On things were by a woman said
And written in the sand.[n]   40

xix. The same Sireno in Montemayor[n]   [29]

**holding his mistress's glass before her, looking upon her while she
viewed herself, thus sang:**

Of this high grace, with bliss conjoined,
    No further debt on me is laid,
Since that in self-same metal coined,
    Sweet lady, you remain well paid.
        For if my place give me great pleasure,   5
        Having before me nature's treasure,
        In face and eyes unmatched being,
        You have the same in my hands, seeing
        What in your face mine eyes do measure.

Nor think the match unev'nly made,   10
    That of those beams in you do tarry
The glass to you but gives a shade,
    To me mine eyes the true shape carry;
        For such a thought, most highly prized,
        Which ever hath love's yoke despised,   15
        Better than one captived perceiveth:
        Though he the lively form receiveth,
        The other sees it but disguised.

13 *To me*: whereas to me.
15 *Which*: she who, i.e. Diana.

xx. Love's funeral[n]   [30]

Ring out your bells, let mourning shows be spread,
  For love is dead:
    All love is dead, infected
    With plague of deep disdain,
    Worth as naught worth rejected,   5
    And faith fair scorn doth gain.
      From so ungrateful fancy,
      From such a female franzy,
      From them that use men thus:
      Good lord, deliver us.   10

Weep, neighbours, weep: do you not hear it said
  That love is dead?
    His death-bed peacock's folly,
    His winding-sheet is shame,
    His will false-seeming holy,   15
    His sole executor blame.
      From so ungrateful fancy,
      From such a female franzy,
      From them that use men thus:
      Good lord, deliver us.   20

Let dirge be sung, and trentals rightly read,
  For love is dead.
    Sir wrong his tomb ordaineth,
    My mistress' marble heart,
    Which epitaph containeth: 25
    'Her eyes were once his dart.'
      From so ungrateful fancy,
      From such a female franzy,
      From them that use men thus:
      Good lord, deliver us.   30

8 *franzy*: frenzy.
21 *trentals*: sets of thirty requiem masses.

Alas, I lie: rage hath this error bred;
  Love is not dead.
    Love is not dead, but sleepeth
    In her unmatched mind,
    Where she his counsel keepeth   35
    Till due desert she find.
      Therefore from so vile fancy,
      To call such wit a franzy
      Who love can temper thus:
      Good lord, deliver us.   40

xxi. The curse on desire   [31]

Thou blind man's mark, thou fool's self-chosen snare,
Fond fancy's scum, and dregs of scattered thought,
Band of all evils, cradle of causeless care,
Thou web of will, whose end is never wrought;
Desire, desire, I have too dearly bought,   5
With price of mangled mind, thy worthless ware;
Too long, too long, asleep thou hast me brought,
Who should my mind to higher things prepare.
  But yet in vain thou hast my ruin sought:
  In vain thou madest me to vain things aspire,   10
  In vain thou kindlest all thy smoky fire;
  For virtue hath this better lesson taught,
  Within myself to seek my only hire,
  Desiring naught but how to kill desire.

1 *mark*: target.
3 *Band*: perhaps swaddling band.
4 *web*: piece of (endless) woven cloth.

xxii. The farewell to desire   [32]

Leave me, O love which reachest but to dust,
And thou, my mind, aspire to higher things;
Grow rich in that which never taketh rust;
What ever fades, but fading pleasure brings.
Draw in thy beams, and humble all thy might   5
To that sweet yoke[n] where lasting freedoms be,
Which breaks the clouds, and opens forth the light
That doth both shine, and give us sight to see.
O take fast hold, let that light be thy guide
In this small course which birth draws out to death,   10
And think how ill becometh him to slide,
Who seeketh heaven, and comes of heavenly breath:
      Then farewell, world; thy uttermost I see;
      Eternal love, maintain thy life in me.

Splendidis longum valedico nugis[n]

Astrophil and Stella

Astrophil and Stella

1[n]

Loving in truth, and fain in verse my love to show,
That she (dear she)[n] might take some pleasure of my pain;
Pleasure might cause her read, reading might make her know;
Knowledge might pity win, and pity grace obtain;
    I sought fit words to paint the blackest face of woe,   5
Studying inventions fine, her wits to entertain;
Oft turning others' leaves, to see if thence would flow
Some fresh and fruitful showers upon my sunburnt brain.
    But words came halting forth, wanting invention's stay;
Invention, nature's child, fled step-dame study's blows;   10
And others' feet still seemed but strangers in my way.
Thus great with child to speak, and helpless in my throes,
    Biting my truant pen, beating myself for spite,
    'Fool,' said my muse to me; 'look in thy heart, and write.'[n]

2[n]

Not at first sight, nor with a dribbed shot,
    Love gave the wound which while I breathe will bleed:
    But known worth did in mine of time proceed,
Till by degrees it had full conquest got.
I saw, and liked; I liked, but loved not;   5
    I loved, but straight did not what love decreed:
    At length to love's decrees I, forced, agreed,
Yet with repining at so partial lot.
    Now even that footstep of lost liberty
Is gone, and now like slave-born Muscovite[n]   10
I call it praise to suffer tyranny;
And now employ the remnant of my wit
    To make myself believe that all is well,
    While with a feeling skill I paint my hell.

2 1 *dribbed*: ineffectual, random.

3

Let dainty wits cry on the sisters nine,
That bravely masked, their fancies may be told:
Or Pindar's apes, flaunt they in phrases fine,
Enam'lling with pied flowers their thoughts of gold:
    Or else let them in statelier glory shine,   5
Ennobling new-found tropes with problems old:
Or with strange similes enrich each line,
Of herbs or beasts, which Ind or Afric hold.[n]
    For me, in sooth, no muse but one I know;
    Phrases and problems from my reach do grow,   10
And strange things cost too dear for my poor sprites.
    How then? Even thus: in Stella's face I read
    What love and beauty be; then all my deed
But copying is, what in her nature writes.

4

Virtue, alas, now let me take some rest:
Thou sett'st a bate between my will and wit.
If vain love have my simple soul oppressed,
Leave what thou lik'st not, deal not thou with it.
    Thy sceptre use in some old Cato's breast;   5
Churches or schools are for thy seat more fit.
I do confess—pardon a fault confessed—
My mouth too tender is for thy hard bit.
    But if that needs thou wilt usurping be
    The little reason that is left in me,   10
And still the effect of thy persuasions prove:
    I swear, my heart such one shall show to thee
    That shrines in flesh so true a deity,
That, virtue, thou thy self shalt be in love.

---

3 1 *sisters nine*: the nine Muses.
    2 *masked*: in masquing costume.
    3 *Pindar's apes*: imitators of the Greek lyric poet Pindar, such as the poets of
      the French Pléiade.
    6 *problems*: questions in logical syllogisms.
    13 *deed*: activity, occupation.

4 2 *bate*: quarrel, debate.
    5 *Cato*: Cato the Censor, a Roman disciplinarian.

5

It is most true, that eyes are formed to serve
The inward light; and that the heavenly part
Ought to be king, from whose rules who do swerve,
Rebels to Nature, strive for their own smart.
   It is most true, what we call Cupid's dart,   5
An image is, which for ourselves we carve;
And, fools, adore in temple of our heart,
Till that good god make Church and churchmen starve.
   True, that true beauty virtue is indeed,
Whereof this beauty can be but a shade,   10
Which elements with mortal mixture breed;[n]
True, that on earth we are but pilgrims made,
   And should in soul up to our country move;
True; and yet true, that I must Stella love.

6[n]

Some lovers speak, when they their muses entertain,
Of hopes begot by fear, of wot not what desires,
Of force of heavenly beams, infusing hellish pain,
Of living deaths, dear wounds, fair storms and freezing fires.[n]
   Some one his song in Jove, and Jove's strange tales, attires,   5
Broidered with bulls and swans, powdered with golden rain.[n]
Another, humbler, wit to shepherd's pipe retires,
Yet hiding royal blood full oft in rural vein.
   To some a sweetest plaint a sweetest style affords,
   While tears pour out his ink, and sighs breathe out his words,   10
His paper, pale despair, and pain his pen doth move.[n]
   I can speak what I feel,[n] and feel as much as they,
   But think that all the map of my state I display,
When trembling voice brings forth, that I do Stella love.

5 13 *our country*: Heaven.

6 6 *Broidered*: embroidered, decorated.
   6 *powdered*: spotted, spangled.

7^n

When nature made her chief work, Stella's eyes,
In colour black why wrapped she beams so bright?
Would she in beamy black, like painter wise,
Frame daintiest lustre, mixed of shades and light?
     Or did she else that sober hue devise   5
In object best to knit and strength our sight,
Lest, if no veil those brave gleams did disguise,
They, sun-like, should more dazzle than delight?
     Or would she her miraculous power show,
That, whereas black seems beauty's contrary,   10
She even in black doth make all beauties flow?
Both so, and thus: she minding love should be
     Placed ever there, gave him this mourning weed
     To honour all their deaths, who for her bleed.

8

Love, born in Greece, of late fled from his native place,
     Forced by a tedious proof, that Turkish hardened heart^n
     Is no fit mark to pierce with his fine pointed dart;
And pleased with our soft peace, stayed here his flying race.
But finding these North climes too^n coldly him embrace,   5
     Not used to frozen clips, he strave to find some part
     Where with most ease and warmth he might employ his art.
At length he perched himself in Stella's joyful face,
     Whose fair skin, beamy eyes, like morning sun on snow,
Deceived the quaking boy, who thought from so pure light   10
Effects of lively heat must needs in nature grow.
But she, most fair, most cold, made him thence take his flight
     To my close heart, where, while some firebrands he did lay,
     He burnt unwares his wings, and cannot fly away.

7   6 *strength*: strengthen.

8   6 *clips*: embraces.

9

Queen Virtue's court, which some call Stella's face,
  Prepared by Nature's chiefest furniture,
  Hath his front built of alablaster pure;
Gold is the covering of that stately place.
The door, by which sometimes comes forth her grace,   5
  Red porphyr is, which lock of pearl makes sure;
  Whose porches rich (which name of 'cheeks' endure)
Marble, mixed red and white, do interlace.
  The windows now through which this heavenly guest
Looks o'er the world, and can find nothing such   10
Which dare claim from those lights the name of 'best',
Of touch they are that without touch doth touch,
  Which Cupid's self from Beauty's mine did draw:
  Of touch they are, and poor I am their straw.[n]

10

Reason, in faith thou art well served, that still
Would'st brabbling be with sense and love in me.
I rather wished thee climb the muses' hill,
Or reach the fruit of nature's choicest tree,
  Or seek heaven's course, or heaven's inside, to see.   5
Why should'st thou toil our thorny soil to till?
Leave sense, and those which sense's objects be:
Deal thou with powers of thoughts, leave love to will.
  But thou would'st needs fight both with love and sense,
With sword of wit giving wounds of dispraise,   10
Till downright blows did foil thy cunning fence:
For soon as they strake thee with Stella's rays,
  Reason, thou kneeled'st, and offered'st straight to prove
  By reason good, good reason her to love.

9 12 *touch*: touchstone, or a kind of black quartz used for testing the quality
    of gold; suggests also jet which attracts straws.

10 2 *brabbling*: quarrelling
    11 *fence*: defensive strategy in swordsmanship.

11

In truth, O Love, with what a boyish kind
   Thou dost proceed in thy most serious ways:
   That when the heaven to thee his best displays
Yet of that best thou leav'st the best behind.
For like a child, that some fair book doth find,   5
   With gilded leaves or coloured vellum plays,
   Or at the most, on some fine picture stays,
But never heeds the fruit of writer's mind:
   So when thou saw'st, in nature's cabinet,
Stella, thou straight look'st babies in her eyes,   10
In her cheek's pit thou did'st thy pit-fold set,
And in her breast bo-peep or couching lies,
   Playing and shining in each outward part:
   But, fool, seek'st not to get into her heart.

12

Cupid, because thou shin'st in Stella's eyes,
   That from her locks, thy day-nets, none 'scapes free,
   That those lips swell, so full of thee they be,
That her sweet breath makes oft thy flames to rise,
That in her breast thy pap well sugared lies,   5
   That her grace gracious makes thy wrongs, that she,
   What words so e'er she speaks, persuades for thee,
That her clear voice lifts thy fame to the skies;
   Thou countest Stella thine, like those whose powers,
Having got up a breach by fighting well,   10
Cry, 'Victory, this fair day all is ours!'
O no, her heart is such a citadel,
   So fortified with wit, stored with disdain,
   That to win it, is all the skill and pain.

11   11 *pit-fold*: pitfall.

12   2 *day-nets*: traps for birds made of nets and small mirrors.
    10 *got up a breach*: made a gap in the enemy's ranks.

13

Phoebus was judge between Jove, Mars, and Love,
   Of those three gods, whose arms the fairest were.
   Jove's golden shield did eagle sables bear,
Whose talents held young Ganymede above:
But in vert field Mars bare a golden spear   5
   Which through a bleeding heart his point did shove.[n]
   Each had his crest: Mars carried Venus' glove,
Jove on his helm the thunderbolt did rear.
Cupid then smiles, for on his crest there lies
   Stella's fair hair, her face he makes his shield,   10
   Where roses gules are borne in silver field.[n]
Phoebus drew wide the curtains of the skies
   To blaze[n] these last, and sware devoutly then,
   The first, thus matched, were scarcely gentlemen.

14[n]

Alas, have I not pain enough, my friend,
   Upon whose breast a fiercer gripe doth tire
   Than did on him who first stale down the fire,
While Love on me doth all his quiver spend,
But with your rhubarb words you must contend   5
   To grieve me worse, in saying that desire
   Doth plunge my well-formed soul even in the mire
Of sinful thoughts, which do in ruin end?
   If that be sin, which doth the manners frame,
Well stayed with truth in word, and faith of deed,   10
Ready of wit, and fearing nought but shame:
If that be sin, which in fixed hearts doth breed
   A loathing of all loose unchastity:
   Then love is sin, and let me sinful be.

---

13 3 *sables*: sable, black.
    5 *vert*: green (heraldic).
   11 *gules*: red (heraldic).
   13 *blaze*: describe the arms of.
   14 *gentlemen*: entitled to coats of arms.

14 2 *gripe*: clutching grip, as of vulture.
    2 *tire*: tear, prey.
    3 *him*: Prometheus, whose liver was torn perpetually by a vulture for bring-
      ing fire to mankind.
    5 *rhubarb*: a bitter purgative.

15[n]

You that do search for every purling spring
   Which from the ribs of old Parnassus flows;
   And every flower, not sweet perhaps, which grows
Near thereabouts, into your poesy wring;[n]
You that do dictionary's method bring   5
   Into your rhymes, running in rattling rows;[n]
   You that poor Petrarch's long-deceased woes
With new-born sighs and denizened wit do sing:[n]
   You take wrong ways, those far-fet helps be such
   As do bewray a want of inward touch: 10
And sure at length stol'n goods do come to light.
   But if (both for your love and skill) your name
   You seek to nurse at fullest breasts of fame,
Stella behold, and then begin to endite.

16

In nature apt to like, when I did see,
   Beauties, which were of many carats fine,
   My boiling sprites did thither soon incline,
And, love, I thought that I was full of thee.
But finding not those restless flames in me   5
   Which others said did make their souls to pine,
   I thought those babes of some pin's hurt did whine,
By my love judging what love's pain might be.
   But while I thus with this young lion played,[n]
Mine eyes (shall I say cursed or blessed?) beheld   10
Stella: now she is named, need more be said?
In her sight I a lesson new have spelled;
   I now have learned love right, and learned even so
   As who by being poisoned doth poison know.

15 1 *purling*: bubbling, flowing.
    8 *denizened*: naturalized (as foreigner or colonizer).
    9 *far-fet*: far-fetched.

17

His mother dear Cupid offended late,
　Because that Mars, grown slacker in her love,
　With pricking shot he did not throughly move,
To keep the pace of their first loving state.
The boy refused, for fear of Mars's hate,　　　　　　5
　Who threatened stripes if he his wrath did prove.
　But she in chafe him from her lap did shove,
Brake bow, brake shafts, while Cupid weeping sate:
　Till that his grandame, Nature, pitying it,
Of Stella's brows made him two better bows,　　　　10
And in her eyes of arrows infinite.
O how for joy he leaps, O how he crows,
　And straight therewith, like wags new got to play,
　Falls to shrewd turns; and I was in his way.

18

With what sharp checks I in myself am shent
　When into reason's audit I do go,
　And by just counts myself a bankrupt know
Of all those goods, which heaven to me hath lent,
Unable quite to pay even nature's rent,　　　　　　5
　Which unto it by birthright I do owe:
　And which is worse, no good excuse can show,
But that my wealth I have most idly spent.
　My youth doth waste, my knowledge brings forth toys,
My wit doth strive those passions to defend　　　　10
Which for reward spoil it with vain annoys.
I see my course to lose myself doth bend:
　I see, and yet no greater sorrow take
　Than that I lose no more for Stella's sake.[n]

17　1 *his mother dear*: Venus, the grammatical object.
　　1 *Cupid*: the subject.

18　1 *checks*: rebukes.
　　1 *shent*: shamed.

19

On Cupid's bow how are my heart-strings bent,
   That see my wrack, and yet embrace the same!
   When most I glory, then I feel most shame:
I willing run, yet while I run, repent.
My best wits still their own disgrace invent;   5
   My very ink turns straight to Stella's name;
   And yet my words, as them my pen doth frame,
Avise themselves that they are vainly spent.
   For though she pass all things, yet what is all
That unto me, who fare like him that both   10
Looks to the skies, and in a ditch doth fall?^{n}
O let me prop my mind, yet in his growth,
   And not in nature for best fruits unfit.
   'Scholar,' saith Love, 'bend hitherward your wit.'

20

Fly, fly, my friends, I have my death wound, fly;
See there that boy, that murth'ring boy I say,
Who like a thief hid in dark bush doth lie,
Till bloody bullet get him wrongful prey.
   So tyrant he no fitter place could spy,   5
Nor so fair level in so secret stay
As that sweet black which veils the heavn'ly eye;
There himself with his shot he close doth lay.
   Poor passenger, pass now thereby I did,
And stayed, pleased with the prospect of the place,   10
While that black hue from me the bad guest hid:
But straight I saw motions of lightning grace,
   And then descried the glist'ring of his dart:
   But ere I could fly thence, it pierced my heart.

19 2 *wrack*: wreck, ruin.
     8 *Avise*: inform.

20 6 *level*: position for aiming from.
     9 *passenger*: passer-by.

21

Your words, my friend, right healthful caustics, blame
  My young mind marred, whom love doth windlass so
  That mine own writings like bad servants show,
My wits, quick in vain thoughts, in virtue lame;
That Plato I read for nought, but if he tame   5
  Such coltish gyres;[n] that to my birth I owe
  Nobler desires, lest else that friendly foe,
Great expectation, wear a train of shame.
  For since mad March great promise made of me,[n]
If now the May of my years much decline,   10
What can be hoped my harvest time will be?
Sure you say well; your wisdom's golden mine
  Dig deep with learning's spade; now tell me this,
  Hath this world aught so fair as Stella is?

22

In highest way of heaven the sun did ride,
  Progressing then from fair twins' golden place,
  Having no scarf of clouds before his face,
But shining forth of heat in his chief pride,
When some fair ladies, by hard promise tied,   5
  On horseback met him in his furious race;
  Yet each prepared, with fan's well-shielding grace,
From that foe's wounds their tender skins to hide.
Stella alone with face unarmed marched,
  Either to do like him, which open shone,   10
  Or careless of the wealth because her own.
Yet were the hid and meaner beauties parched,
  Her daintiest bare went free. The cause was this:
  The sun, which others burned, did her but kiss.

21 2 *windlass*: decoy, ensnare.

22 2 *twins*: Gemini, the sign from which the sun emerges in June.

23

The curious wits, seeing dull pensiveness
   Bewray itself in my long settled eyes,
   Whence these same fumes of melancholy rise
With idle pains, and missing aim, do guess.
Some, that know how my spring I did address,   5
   Deem that my muse some fruit of knowledge plies;
   Others, because the prince my service tries,
Think that I think state errors to redress.
   But harder judges judge ambition's rage,
Scourge of itself, still climbing slippery place,   10
Holds my young brain captived in golden cage.
O fools, or over-wise: alas, the race
   Of all my thoughts hath neither stop nor start
   But only Stella's eyes and Stella's heart.

24[n]

Rich fools there be, whose base and filthy heart
Lies hatching still the goods wherein they flow;
And damning their own selves to Tantal's smart,
Wealth breeding want, more blessed, more wretched grow.
   Yet to those fools heaven such wit doth impart   5
As what their hands do hold, their heads do know,
And knowing, love, and loving, lay apart,
As sacred things, far from all danger's show.
   But that rich fool, who by blind fortune's lot
The richest gem of love and life enjoys,   10
And can with foul abuse such beauties blot,
Let him, deprived of sweet but unfelt joys,
   Exiled for aye from those high treasures which
   He knows not, grow in only folly rich.

23   7 *the prince*: the Queen.

24   3 *Tantal's smart*: the torment of the miser Tantalus, condemned to
perpetual thirst amid water.

25

The wisest scholar of the wight most wise,[n]
By Phoebus' doom, with sugared sentence says,
That virtue, if it once met with our eyes,
Strange flames of love it in our souls would raise;
    But for that man with pain this truth descries,   5
While he each thing in sense's balance weighs,
And so nor will, nor can, behold those skies
Which inward sun to heroic mind displays:
    Virtue of late, with virtuous care to stir
Love of herself, takes Stella's shape, that she   10
To mortal eyes might sweetly shine in her.
It is most true, for since I her did see,
    Virtue's great beauty in that face I prove,
    And find the effect, for I do burn in love.

26

Though dusty wits dare scorn astrology,
And fools can think those lamps of purest light,
Whose numbers, ways, greatness, eternity,
Promising wonders, wonder to invite,
    To have for no cause birthright in the sky,   5
But for to spangle the black weeds of night;
Or for some brawl, which in that chamber high
They should still dance, to please a gazer's sight:
    For me, I do Nature unidle know,
And know great causes great effects procure,   10
And know those bodies high reign on the low.[n]
And if these rules did fail, proof makes me sure,
    Who oft fore-judge my after-following race
    By only those two eyes in Stella's face.

25 1 *The wisest scholar*: Plato, pupil of Socrates.
     2 *By Phoebus' doom*: adjudged most wise by the oracle of Apollo at Delphi.

26 1 *dusty*: earth-bound.
     7 *brawl*: a country dance.
    12 *proof*: experience.

27

Because I oft, in dark abstracted guise,
　Seem most alone in greatest company,
　With dearth of words, or answers quite awry,
To them that would make speech of speech arise,
They deem, and of that doom the rumour flies,   5
　That poison foul of bubbling pride doth lie
　So in my swelling breast, that only I
Fawn on myself, and others do despise.
　Yet pride, I think, doth not my soul possess,
Which looks too oft in his unflatt'ring glass;   10
But one worse fault, ambition, I confess,
That makes me oft my best friends overpass,
　Unseen, unheard, while thought to highest place
　Bends all his powers, even unto Stella's grace.

28

You that with allegory's curious frame
　Of others' children changelings use to make,
　With me those pains, for God's sake, do not take;
I list not dig so deep for brazen fame.
When I say 'Stella', I do mean the same   5
　Princess of beauty, for whose only sake
　The reins of love I love, though never slake,
And joy therein, though nations count it shame.
　I beg no subject to use eloquence,
Nor in hid ways to guide philosophy.   10
Look at my hands for no such quintessence,
But know that I, in pure simplicity,
　Breathe out the flames which burn within my heart,
　Love only reading unto me this art.

28 7 *slake*: slacken, loosen.

29[n]

Like some weak lords, neighboured by mighty kings,
  To keep themselves and their chief cities free,
  Do easily yield, that all their coasts may be
Ready to store their camps of needful things:
So Stella's heart, finding what power love brings,   5
  To keep itself in life and liberty,
  Doth willing grant, that in the frontiers he
Use all to help his other conquerings.
And thus her heart escapes; but thus her eyes
  Serve him with shot, her lips his heralds are,   10
  Her breasts his tents, legs his triumphal car,
Her flesh his food, her skin his armour brave;
And I, but for because my prospect lies
Upon that coast, am giv'n up for a slave.

30[n]

Whether the Turkish new moon minded be
  To fill his horns this year on Christian coast;[n]
  How Pole's right king means, without leave of host,
To warm with ill-made fire cold Muscovy;[n]
If French can yet three parts in one agree;[n]   5
  What now the Dutch in their full diets boast;[n]
  How Holland hearts, now so good towns be lost,
Trust in the pleasing shade of Orange tree;[n]
  How Ulster likes of that same golden bit
Wherewith my father once made it half tame;[n]   10
If in the Scottish court be welt'ring yet;[n]
These questions busy wits to me do frame.
  I, cumbered with good manners, answer do,
  But know not how, for still I think of you.

29 13 *but for because*: only because.

30 6 *diets*: councils.
    11 *welt'ring*: turbulence, confusion.

31

With how sad steps, O moon, thou climb'st the skies;
   How silently, and with how wan a face.
   What, may it be that even in heav'nly place
That busy archer his sharp arrows tries?
Sure, if that long-with-love-acquainted eyes
   Can judge of love, thou feel'st a lover's case;
   I read it in thy looks; thy languished grace
To me, that feel the like, thy state descries.
   Then even of fellowship, O moon, tell me,
Is constant love deemed there but want of wit?   10
Are beauties there as proud as here they be?
Do they above love to be loved, and yet
   Those lovers scorn whom that love doth possess?
   Do they call virtue there ungratefulness?[n]

32

Morpheus, the lively son of deadly sleep,
   Witness of life to them that living die;[n]
   A prophet oft, and oft an history,
A poet eke, as humours fly or creep;
Since thou in me so sure a power dost keep   5
   That never I with closed-up sense do lie
   But by thy work my Stella I descry
Teaching blind eyes both how to smile and weep,
   Vouchsafe of all acquaintance this to tell:
Whence hast thou ivory, rubies, pearl and gold   10
To show her skin, lips, teeth and head so well?
'Fool,' answers he; 'no Ind's such treasures hold,
   But from thy heart, while my sire charmeth thee,
   Sweet Stella's image I do steal to me.'

32 1 *Morpheus*: dream-bringing son of Somnus; see note.
    12 *Ind's*: Indies.

33[n]

I might (unhappy word), O me, I might,
And then would not, or could not, see my bliss:
Till now, wrapped in a most infernal night,
I find how heavenly day, wretch, I did miss.[n]
   Heart, rend thyself, thou dost thyself but right;   5
No lovely Paris made thy Helen his;
No force, no fraud, robbed thee of thy delight;
Nor Fortune of thy fortune author is;
   But to myself myself did give the blow,
While too much wit (forsooth) so troubled me   10
That I respects for both our sakes must show:
And yet could not by rising morn foresee
   How fair a day was near. O punished eyes,
   That I had been more foolish, or more wise!

34

Come, let me write. 'And to what end?' To ease
   A burdened heart. 'How can words ease, which are
   The glasses of thy daily vexing care?'
Oft cruel fights well pictured forth do please.[n]
'Art not ashamed to publish thy disease?'   5
   Nay, that may breed my fame, it is so rare.
   'But will not wise men think thy words fond ware?'
Then be they close, and so none shall displease.
   'What idler thing, than speak and not be heard?'
What harder thing than smart, and not to speak?   10
Peace, foolish wit; with wit my wit is marred.
Thus write I while I doubt to write, and wreak
   My harms on ink's poor loss; perhaps some find
   Stella's great powers, that so confuse my mind.

34 7 *fond ware*: useless trifles.
    8 *close*: private, secret.

35

What may words say, or what may words not say,
Where truth itself must speak like flattery?
Within what bounds can one his liking stay,
Where nature doth with infinite agree?
    What Nestor's counsels can my flames allay,   5
Since reason's self doth blow the coal in me?
And ah, what hope that hope should once see day,
Where Cupid is sworn page to chastity?
Honour is honoured, that thou dost possess
    Him as thy slave; and now long needy fame   10
    Doth even grow rich, naming my Stella's name.
Wit learns in thee perfection to express;
    Not thou by praise, but praise in thee is raised;
    It is a praise to praise, when thou art praised.

36

Stella, whence doth this new assault arise,
A conquered, yelden, ransacked heart to win?
Whereto long since, through my long battered eyes,
Whole armies of thy beauties entered in;
    And there, long since, love, thy lieutenant lies   5
My forces razed, thy banners raised within,
Of conquest do not these effects suffice,
But wilt new war upon thine own begin?
    With so sweet voice, and by sweet nature so,
In sweetest strength, so sweetly skilled withal,   10
In all sweet stratagems sweet art can show,
That not my soul, which at thy foot did fall,
    Long since forced by thy beams, but stone nor tree,
    By sense's privilege, can 'scape from thee.[n]

---

35 5 *Nestor's counsels* : Nestor, the old Greek leader in the *Iliad*, was a by-
     word for sage advice.
    11 *my Stella's name*: Penelope Devereux, Lady Rich.
    14 *It is a praise to praise, when thou art praised*: praise itself is praiseworthy
    when Stella is its object.

36 2 *yelden*: yielded.

37[n]

My mouth doth water, and my breast doth swell,
  My tongue doth itch, my thoughts in labour be;
  Listen then, lordings, with good ear to me,
For of my life a riddle I must tell.
Towards Aurora's court a nymph doth dwell,   5
  Rich in all beauties which man's eye can see;
  Beauties so far from reach of words, that we
Abase her praise, saying she doth excel;
  Rich in the treasure of deserved renown;
Rich in the riches of a royal heart;   10
Rich in those gifts that give the eternal crown;
Who though most rich in these, and every part
  Which make the patents of true worldly bliss,
  Hath no misfortune, but that Rich she is.

38

This night, while sleep begins with heavy wings
  To hatch mine eyes, and that unbitted thought
  Doth fall to stray, and my chief powers are brought
To leave the sceptre of all subject things,
The first that straight my fancy's error brings   5
  Unto my mind, is Stella's image, wrought
  By love's own self; but with so curious draught
That she, methinks, not only shines, but sings.
  I start, look, heark; but what in closed-up sense
Was held, in opened sense it flies away,   10
Leaving me nought but wailing eloquence.
I, seeing better sights in sight's decay,
  Called it anew, and wooed sleep again:
  But him, her host, that unkind guest had slain.

37 5 *Towards Aurora's court*: in the East; see note.
    13 *make the patents*: constitute the grants, endowments.

38 2 *hatch*: close.
    2 *unbitted*: uncontrolled.
    7 *curious draught*: elaborate draftsmanship, clever representation.

39

Come sleep, O sleep, the certain knot of peace,
The baiting place of wit, the balm of woe,
The poor man's wealth, the prisoner's release,
The indifferent judge between the high and low;
    With shield of proof shield me from out the prease   5
Of those fierce darts despair at me doth throw:
O make in me those civil wars to cease;
I will good tribute pay, if thou do so.
    Take thou of me sweet pillows, sweetest bed,
A chamber deaf to noise, and blind to light;   10
A rosy garland, and a weary head;
And if these things, as being thine by right,
    Move not thy heavy grace, thou shalt in me,
    Livelier than elsewhere, Stella's image see.[n]

40

As good to write, as for to lie and groan.
    O Stella dear, how much thy power hath wrought,
    That hast my mind, none of the basest, brought
My still kept course, while others sleep, to moan.
Alas, if from the height of virtue's throne   5
    Thou canst vouchsafe the influence of a thought
    Upon a wretch, that long thy grace hath sought;
Weigh then how I by thee am overthrown:
    And then, think thus: although thy beauty be
    Made manifest by such a victory,   10
Yet noblest conquerors do wrecks avoid.
    Since then thou hast so far subdued me,
    That in my heart I offer still to thee,
    O, do not let thy temple be destroyed.

39 2 *baiting place*: resting place.
    5 *prease*: press, onslaught.

41

Having this day my horse, my hand, my lance,
  Guided so well, that I obtained the prize,
  Both by the judgement of the English eyes
And of some sent from that sweet enemy, France;[n]
Horsemen my skill in horsemanship advance;   5
  Town-folks my strength; a daintier judge applies
  His praise to sleight, which from good use doth rise;
Some lucky wits impute it but to chance;
  Others, because of both sides I do take
My blood from them, who did excel in this,   10
Think nature me a man of arms did make.[n]
How far they shoot awry! The true cause is,
  Stella looked on, and from her heavenly face
  Sent forth the beams, which made so fair my race.

42

O eyes, which do the spheres of beauty move,
Whose beams be joys, whose joys all virtues be,
Who, while they make love conquer, conquer love;
The schools where Venus hath learned chastity;
  O eyes, where humble looks most glorious prove,   5
Only loved tyrants, just in cruelty;
Do not, O do not, from poor me remove;
Keep still my zenith, ever shine on me.
  For though I never see them, but straight ways
My life forgets to nourish languished sprites;   10
Yet still on me, O eyes, dart down your rays;
And if from majesty of sacred lights,
  Oppressing mortal sense, my death proceed,
  Wracks triumphs be, which love (high set) doth breed.[n]

41 7 *sleight*: dexterity, achieved by practice.

42 14 *wracks*: wrecks, overthrows.

43

Fair eyes, sweet lips, dear heart, that foolish I
Could hope by Cupid's help on you to prey;
Since to himself he doth your gifts apply,
And his main force, choice sport, and easeful stay.
    For when he will see who dare him gainsay,   5
Then with those eyes he looks; lo, by and by
Each soul doth at love's feet his weapons lay,
Glad if for her he give them leave to die.
    When he will play, then in her lips he is,
Where, blushing red, that love's self doth them love,   10
With either lip he doth the other kiss
But when he will for quiet's sake remove
    From all the world, her heart is then his room,
    Where well he knows, no man to him can come.

44

My words, I know, do well set forth my mind;
    My mind bemoans his sense of inward smart;
    Such smart may pity claim of any heart;
Her heart (sweet heart) is of no tiger's kind:
And yet she hears, yet I no pity find,   5
    But more I cry, less grace she doth impart.[n]
    Alas, what cause is there so overthwart,
That nobleness itself makes thus unkind?
    I much do guess, yet find no truth save this:
That when the breath of my complaints doth touch   10
Those dainty doors unto the court of bliss,
The heavenly nature of that place is such
    That once come there, the sobs of mine annoys
    Are metamorphosed straight to tunes of joys.

45

Stella oft sees the very face of woe
   Painted in my beclouded stormy face;
   But cannot skill to pity my disgrace,
Not though thereof the cause herself she know;
Yet hearing late a fable, which did show   5
   Of lovers never known a grievous case,
   Pity thereof gat in her breast such place
That, from that sea derived, tears' springs did flow.
   Alas, if fancy drawn by imaged things,
Though false, yet with free scope more grace doth breed   10
Than servant's wrack, where new doubts honour brings;
Then think, my dear, that you in me do read
   Of lover's ruin some sad tragedy:
   I am not I, pity the tale of me.[n]

46

I cursed thee oft; I pity now thy case,
   Blind-hitting boy, since she that thee and me
   Rules with a beck, so tyrannizeth thee,
That thou must want or food, or dwelling-place.
For she protests to banish thee her face—   5
   Her face? O love, a rogue thou then shouldst be,
   If love learn not alone to love and see,
Without desire to feed of further grace.
   Alas poor wag, that now a scholar art
To such a school-mistress, whose lessons new   10
Thou needs must miss, and so thou needs must smart.
Yet dear, let me this pardon get of you,
   So long (though he from book mich to desire)
   Till without fuel you can make hot fire.[n]

45 3 *cannot skill*: is unable.
    11 *wrack*: destruction.

46 4 *or . . . or*: both . . . and.
    11 *miss*: mistake, perform amiss.
    13 *mich*: play truant.

47

What, have I thus betrayed my liberty?
  Can those black beams such burning marks engrave
  In my free side? or am I born a slave,
Whose neck becomes such yoke of tyranny?
Or want I sense to feel my misery?   5
  Or sprite, disdain of such disdain to have,
  Who for long faith, though daily help I crave,
May get no alms, but scorn of beggary?
  Virtue, awake: beauty but beauty is;
I may, I must, I can, I will, I do,   10
Leave following that, which it is gain to miss.
Let her go. Soft, but here she comes. Go to,
  Unkind, I love you not—: O me, that eye
  Doth make my heart give to my tongue the lie.

48

Soul's joy, bend not those morning stars from me,
  Where virtue is made strong by beauty's might,
  Where love is chasteness, pain doth learn delight,
And humbleness grows one with majesty.
Whatever may ensue, O let me be   5
  Co-partner of the riches of that sight;
  Let not mine eyes be hell-driven from that light;
O look, O shine, O let me die, and see.
  For though I oft my self of them bemoan,
  That through my heart their beamy darts be gone,   10
Whose cureless wounds even now most freshly bleed;
  Yet since my death-wound is already got,
  Dear killer, spare not thy sweet cruel shot:
A kind of grace it is to slay with speed.

49

I on my horse, and love on me, doth try
   Our horsemanships, while by strange work I prove
   A horseman to my horse, a horse to love;
And now man's wrongs in me, poor beast, descry.
The reins wherewith my rider doth me tie   5
   Are humbled thoughts, which bit of reverence move,
   Curbed in with fear, but with gilt boss above
Of hope, which makes it seem fair to the eye.
   The wand is will; thou, fancy, saddle art,
Girt fast by memory; and while I spur   10
My horse, he spurs with sharp desire my heart;
He sits me fast, however I do stir;
   And now hath made me to his hand so right
   That in the manage myself takes delight.

50[n]

Stella, the fullness of my thoughts of thee
Cannot be stayed within my panting breast,
But they do swell and struggle forth of me,
Till that in words thy figure be expressed.
   And yet, as soon as they so formed be,   5
According to my lord love's own behest,
With sad eyes I their weak proportion see,
To portrait that which in this world is best;
   So that I cannot choose but write my mind,
And cannot choose but put out what I write,   10
While those poor babes their death in birth do find:
And now my pen these lines had dashed quite,
   But that they stopped his fury from the same,
   Because their forefront bare sweet Stella's name.

---

49 7 *boss*: metal knob, horse brass.
    9 *wand*: crop.
    14 *manage*: process of training a horse (himself).

50 8 *portrait*: portray, depict.

51[n]

Pardon, mine ears, both I and they do pray,
  So may your tongue still fluently proceed,
  To them that do such entertainment need,
So may you still have somewhat new to say.
On silly me do not the burden lay   •   5
  Of all the grave conceits your brain doth breed;
  But find some Hercules to bear, in steed
Of Atlas tired, your wisdom's heavenly sway.
  For me, while you discourse of courtly tides,
Of cunning'st fishers in most troubled streams,   10
Of straying ways, when valiant error guides;
Meanwhile my heart confers with Stella's beams,
  And is even irked that so sweet comedy
  By such unsuited speech should hindered be.

52

A strife is grown between virtue and love,
  While each pretends that Stella must be his.
  Her eyes, her lips, her all, saith love, do this,
Since they do wear his badge, most firmly prove.
But virtue thus that title doth disprove: 5
  That Stella (O dear name) that Stella is
  That virtuous soul, sure heir of heavenly bliss,
Not this fair outside, which our hearts doth move;
  And therefore, though her beauty and her grace
Be love's indeed, in Stella's self he may   10
By no pretence claim any manner place.
Well, love, since this demur our suit doth stay,
  Let virtue have that Stella's self; yet thus,
  That virtue but that body grant to us.

51   7 *in steed*: instead, in place of.
     8 *Atlas*: the god who held up the heavens.

52   12 *demur*: legal scruple, objection.

53[n]

In martial sports I had my cunning tried,
  And yet to break more staves did me address,
  While with the people's shouts, I must confess,
Youth, luck and praise even filled my veins with pride;
When Cupid, having me, his slave, descried   5
  In Mars's livery, prancing in the press:
  'What now, sir fool,' said he; 'I would no less,
Look here, I say.' I looked, and Stella spied,
  Who hard by made a window send forth light.
My heart then quaked, then dazzled were mine eyes,   10
One hand forgot to rule, th'other to fight;
Nor trumpet's sound I heard, nor friendly cries;
  My foe came on, and beat the air for me,
  Till that her blush taught me my shame to see.

54

Because I breathe not love to every one,
  Nor do not use set colours for to wear,
  Nor nourish special locks of vowed hair,
Nor give each speech a full point of a groan,
The courtly nymphs, acquainted with the moan   5
  Of them, who in their lips love's standard bear:
  'What, he?' say they of me, 'now I dare swear,
He cannot love; no, no, let him alone.'
  And think so still, so Stella know my mind.
Profess indeed I do not Cupid's art;   10
But you fair maids, at length this true shall find,
That his right badge is but worn in the heart;
  Dumb swans, not chattering pies, do lovers prove;[n]
  They love indeed, who quake to say they love.

53 2 *staves*: tilting staffs.
    7 *I would no less*: I desire no less honour than Mars.
    11 *rule*: control the horse.
    12 *trumpet*: signal for combat to begin.

54 13 *pies*: magpies.

55

Muses, I oft invoked your holy aid,
  With choicest flowers my speech to engarland so
  That it, despised in true but naked show,
Might win some grace in your sweet skill arrayed;
And oft whole troops of saddest words I stayed,   5
  Striving abroad a-foraging to go,
  Until by your inspiring I might know
How their black banner might be best displayed.[n]
  But now I mean no more your help to try,
Nor other sugaring of my speech to prove,   10
But on her name incessantly to cry:
For let me but name her, whom I do love,
  So sweet sounds straight mine ear and heart do hit
  That I well find no eloquence like it.

56

Fie, school of patience, fie; your lesson is
  Far, far too long to learn it without book:
  What, a whole week without one piece of look,
And think I should not your large precepts miss?
When I might read those letters fair of bliss,   5
  Which in her face teach virtue, I could brook
  Somewhat thy leaden counsels, which I took
As of a friend that meant not much amiss:
  But now that I, alas, do want her sight,
What, dost thou think that I can ever take   10
In thy cold stuff a phlegmatique delight?
No, patience; if thou wilt my good, then make
  Her come, and hear with patience my desire,
  And then with patience bid me bear my fire.

56 4 *miss*: mistake, disobey.
    11 *phlegmatique*: phlegmatic (old spelling for metrical reasons).

57

Woe, having made with many fights his own
    Each sense of mine, each gift, each power of mind,
    Grown now his slaves, he forced them out to find
The thorough'st words, fit for woe's self to groan,
Hoping that when they might find Stella alone,   5
    Before she could prepare to be unkind,
    Her soul, armed but with such a dainty rind,
Should soon be pierced with sharpness of the moan.
    She heard my plaints, and did not only hear,
But them (so sweet she is) most sweetly sing,[n]   10
With that fair breast making woe's darkness clear.
A pretty case! I hoped her to bring
    To feel my griefs, and she with face and voice
    So sweets my pains, that my pains me rejoice.

58

Doubt there hath been, when with his golden chain
    The orator so far men's hearts doth bind
    That no pace else their guided steps can find
But as he them more short or slack doth rein
Whether with words this sovereignty he gain,   5
    Clothed with fine tropes, with strongest reasons lined,
    Or else pronouncing grace, wherewith his mind
Prints his own lively form in rudest brain.[n]
    Now judge by this: in piercing phrases late
    The anatomy of all my woes I wrate,   10
Stella's sweet breath the same to me did read.
    O voice, O face, maugre my speech's might,
    Which wooed woe, most ravishing delight
Even those sad words even in sad me did breed.

58 12 *maugre*: in spite of.

59

Dear, why make you more of a dog than me?
  If he do love, I burn, I burn in love;
  If he wait well, I never thence would move;
If he be fair, yet but a dog can be.
Little he is, so little worth is he;   5
  He barks, my songs thy own voice oft doth prove;
  Bidden, perhaps he fetcheth thee a glove;
But I unbid fetch even my soul to thee.
  Yet while I languish, him that bosom clips,
That lap doth lap, nay lets, in spite of spite,   10
This sour-breathed mate taste of those sugared lips.
Alas, if you grant only such delight
  To witless things, then love, I hope (since wit
  Becomes a clog) will soon ease me of it.

60

When my good angel guides me to the place[n]
  Where all my good I do in Stella see,
  That heaven of joys throws only down on me
Thundered disdains, and lightnings of disgrace;
But when the rugged'st step of fortune's race   5
  Makes me fall from her sight, then sweetly she
  With words, wherein the muses' treasures be,
Shows love and pity to my absent case.
  Now I, wit-beaten long by hardest fate,
So dull am, that I cannot look into   10
The ground of this fierce love and lovely hate,
Then some good body tell me how I do,
  Whose presence absence, absence presence is;
  Blessed in my curse, and cursed in my bliss.

61

Oft with true sighs, oft with uncalled tears,
Now with slow words, now with dumb eloquence,
I Stella's eyes assail, invade her ears;
But this at last is her sweet-breathed defence:
   That who indeed infelt affection bears,   5
So captives to his saint both soul and sense
That wholly hers, all selfness he forbears;
Thence his desires he learns, his life's course thence.
   Now since her chaste mind hates this love in me,
   With chastened mind I straight must show that she 10
Shall quickly me from what she hates remove.
   O doctor Cupid, thou for me reply;
   Driven else to grant, by angel's sophistry,
That I love not, without I leave to love.

62

Late tired with woe, even ready for to pine
With rage of love, I called my love unkind;
She in whose eyes love, though unfelt, doth shine,
Sweet said that I true love in her should find.
   I joyed, but straight thus watered was my wine,   5
That love she did, but loved a love not blind,[n]
Which would not let me, whom she loved, decline
From nobler course, fit for my birth and mind:
   And therefore, by her love's authority,
   Willed me these tempests of vain love to fly,   10
And anchor fast myself on virtue's shore.
   Alas, if this the only metal be
   Of love, new-coined to help my beggary,
Dear, love me not, that you may love me more.

61 12 *doctor*: teacher, instructor.

63

O grammar rules, O now your virtues show:
   So children still read you with awful eyes,
   As my young dove may in your precepts wise,
Her grant to me, by her own virtue, know.
For late, with heart most high, with eyes most low,   5
   I craved the thing, which ever she denies:
   She, lightning love, displaying Venus' skies,
Lest once should not be heard, twice said, 'No, no.'
   Sing then, my muse, now Io Paean sing;
   Heavens, envy not at my high triumphing,   10
But grammar's force with sweet success confirm.
   For grammar says (O this, dear Stella, weigh),
   For grammar says (to grammar who says nay?)
That in one speech two negatives affirm.[n]

First song

Doubt you to whom my muse these songs intendeth,
Which now my breast, o'ercharged, to music lendeth?
To you, to you, all song of praise is due;
Only in you my song begins and endeth.[n]

Who hath the eyes which marry state with pleasure,   5
Who keeps the key of nature's chiefest treasure?
To you, to you, all song of praise is due;
Only for you the heaven forgat all measure.

Who hath the lips, where wit in fairness reigneth,
Who womankind at once both decks and staineth?   10
To you, to you, all song of praise is due;
Only by you Cupid his crown maintaineth.

Who hath the feet, whose step all sweetness planteth,
Who else for whom fame worthy trumpets wanteth?
To you, to you, all song of praise is due;   15
Only to you her sceptre Venus granteth.

Who hath the breast, whose milk doth passions nourish,
Whose grace is such, that when it chides doth cherish?
To you, to you, all song of praise is due;
Only through you the tree of life doth flourish.   20

Who hath the hand which without stroke subdueth,
Who long-dead beauty with increase reneweth?
To you, to you, all song of praise is due;
Only at you all envy hopeless rueth.

Who hath the hair which loosest, fastest, tieth?   25
Who makes a man live then glad, when he dieth?
To you, to you, all song of praise is due;
Only of you the flatterer never lieth.

Who hath the voice which soul from senses sunders?
Whose force but yours the bolt of beauty thunders?   30
To you, to you, all song of praise is due;
Only with you not miracles are wonders.

Doubt you to whom my muse these notes intendeth,
Which now my breast, o'ercharged, to music lendeth?
To you, to you, all song of praise is due;   35
Only in you my song begins and endeth.

64[n]

No more, my dear, no more these counsels try;
   O give my passions leave to run their race.
   Let fortune lay on me her worst disgrace,
Let folk o'ercharged with brain against me cry,
Let clouds bedim my face, break in mine eye,   5
   Let me no steps but of lost labour trace,
   Let all the earth with scorn recount my case,
But do not will me from my love to fly.
   I do not envy Aristotle's wit,
Nor do aspire to Caesar's bleeding fame,   10
Nor aught do care, though some above me sit,
Nor hope, nor wish, another course to frame,
   But that which once may win thy cruel heart.
   Thou art my wit, and thou my virtue art.

32 *not miracles are wonders*: wonders are not miracles; i.e. they are part of the
  natural order of things.

64 10 *bleeding fame*: the fame Caesar gained by being murdered.

65

Love, by sure proof I may call thee unkind,
That giv'st no better ear to my just cries;
Thou whom to me such my good turns should bind,
As I may well recount, but none can prize.
    For when, nak'd boy, thou could'st no harbour find   5
In this old world, grown now so too too wise,
I lodged thee in my heart; and being blind
By nature born, I gave to thee mine eyes.
    Mine eyes, my light, my heart, my life, alas,
If so great services may scorned be,   10
Yet let this thought thy tigerish courage pass,
That I, perhaps, am somewhat kin to thee:
    Since in thine arms, if learn'd fame truth hath spread,
    Thou bear'st the arrow, I the arrow head.[n]

66

And do I see some cause a hope to feed,
Or doth the tedious burden of long woe
In weakened minds, quick apprehending breed,
Of every image, which may comfort show?
    I cannot brag of word, much less of deed;   5
Fortune wheels still with me in one sort slow;
My wealth no more, and no whit less my need;
Desire still on the stilts of fear doth go.
    And yet amid all fears, a hope there is
Stol'n to my heart, since last fair night, nay day: 10
Stella's eyes sent to me the beams of bliss,
Looking on me, while I looked other way;
    But when mine eyes back to their heaven did move,
    They fled with blush, which guilty seemed of love.

67

Hope, art thou true, or dost thou flatter me?
  Doth Stella now begin with piteous eye
  The ruins of her conquest to espy;
Will she take time, before all wracked be?
Her eyes' speech is translated thus by thee: 5
  But fail'st thou not, in phrase so heavenly-high?
  Look on again, the fair text better try;
What blushing notes dost thou in margin see?ⁿ
  What sighs stol'n out, or killed before full born?
Hast thou found such, and such-like arguments?   10
Or art thou else to comfort me forsworn?
Well, how so thou interpret the contents,
  I am resolved thy error to maintain,
  Rather than by more truth to get more pain.

68

Stella, the only planet of my light,
  Light of my life, and life of my desire,
  Chief good whereto my hope doth only aspire,
World of my wealth, and heaven of my delight;
Why dost thou spend the treasures of thy sprite   5
  With voice more fit to wed Amphion's lyre,
  Seeking to quench in me the noble fire
Fed by thy worth, and kindled by thy sight?
  And all in vain, for while thy breath most sweet
With choicest words, thy words with reasons rare,   10
Thy reasons firmly set on virtue's feet,
Labour to kill in me this killing care:
  O think I then, what paradise of joy
  It is, so fair a virtue to enjoy.

67   4 *wracked*: destroyed, ruined.
     5 *eyes' speech*: cf. preceding sonnet.

68   6 *Amphion*: the Greek poet whose music moved stones and built Thebes.

69

O joy too high for my low style to show;
  O bliss, fit for a nobler state than me;
  Envy, put out thine eyes, lest thou do see
What oceans of delight in me do flow.
My friend, that oft saw through all masks of woe,   5
  Come, come, and let me pour myself on thee;
  Gone is the winter of my misery,
My spring appears; O see what here doth grow!
  For Stella hath, with words where faith doth shine,
Of her high heart giv'n me the monarchy;   10
I, I, O I may say, that she is mine.
And though she give but thus conditionally
  This realm of bliss, while virtuous course I take,
  No kings be crowned, but they some covenants make.[n]

70

My muse may well grudge at my heavenly joy,
If still I force her in sad rhymes to creep;
She oft hath drunk my tears, now hopes to enjoy
Nectar of mirth, since I Jove's cup do keep.[n]
  Sonnets be not bound prentice to annoy;   5
Trebles sing high, as well as basses deep;
Grief but love's winter livery is; the boy
Hath cheeks to smile, as well as eyes to weep.
  Come then my muse, show thou height of delight
In well raised notes; my pen the best it may   10
Shall paint out joy, though but in black and white.
Cease, eager muse; peace pen, for my sake stay;
  I give you here my hand for truth of this:
  Wise silence is best music unto bliss.

70 5 *annoy*: grief, sadness.

71

Who will in fairest book of nature know
  How virtue may best lodged in beauty be,
  Let him but learn of love to read in thee,
Stella, those fair lines which true goodness show.
There shall he find all vices' overthrow,   5
  Not by rude force, but sweetest sovereignty
  Of reason, from whose light those night-birds fly,
That inward sun in thine eyes shineth so.
  And not content to be perfection's heir
Thy self, dost strive all minds that way to move,   10
Who mark in thee what is in thee most fair;
So while thy beauty draws the heart to love,
  As fast thy virtue bends that love to good.
  But ah, desire still cries: 'Give me some food.'

72

Desire, though thou my old companion art,
  And oft so clings to my pure love, that I
  One from the other scarcely can descry,
While each doth blow the fire of my heart;
Now from thy fellowship I needs must part;   5
  Venus is taught with Dian's wings to fly;
  I must no more in thy sweet passions lie;
Virtue's gold now must head my Cupid's dart.[n]
  Service and honour, wonder with delight,
Fear to offend, will worthy to appear,   10
Care shining in mine eyes, faith in my sprite;
These things are left me by my only dear.
  But thou, desire, because thou would'st have all,
  Now banished art—but yet, alas, how shall?

72 6 *Venus is taught* . . .: the goddess of love is taught chastity.

Second song

Have I caught my heavenly jewel
Teaching sleep most fair to be?
Now will I teach her that she,
When she wakes, is too too cruel.

Since sweet sleep her eyes hath charmed,   5
The two only darts of love:
Now will I with that boy prove
Some play, while he is disarmed.

Her tongue waking still refuseth,
Giving frankly niggard 'no';   10
Now will I attempt to know
What 'no' her tongue sleeping useth.

See, the hand which, waking, guardeth,
Sleeping, grants a free resort;
Now will I invade the fort;   15
Cowards love with loss rewardeth.

But, O fool, think of the danger
Of her just and high disdain;
Now will I, alas, refrain;
Love fears nothing else but anger.   20

Yet those lips so sweetly swelling
Do invite a stealing kiss:
Now will I but venture this;
Who will read, must first learn spelling.

O sweet kiss—but ah, she is waking,   25
Louring beauty chastens me;
Now will I away hence flee;
Fool, more fool, for no more taking.[n]

73

Love still a boy, and oft a wanton is,
Schooled only by his mother's tender eye;
What wonder then if he his lesson miss,
When for so soft a rod dear play he try?
　And yet my Star, because a sugared kiss   5
In sport I sucked, while she asleep did lie,
Doth lour, nay chide; nay, threat, for only this.
Sweet, it was saucy love, not humble I.
　　But no 'scuse serves, she makes her wrath appear
　　In beauty's throne; see now, who dares come near   10
Those scarlet judges, threatening bloody pain?
　　O heavenly fool, thy most kiss-worthy face
　　Anger invests with such a lovely grace
That anger's self I needs must kiss again.

74

I never drank of Aganippe well,
Nor ever did in shade of Tempe sit;
And muses scorn with vulgar brains to dwell;
Poor layman I, for sacred rites unfit.
　Some do I hear of poet's fury tell,[n]   5
But (God wot) wot not what they mean by it;
And this I swear, by blackest brook of hell,
I am no pick-purse of another's wit.
　　How falls it then, that with so smooth an ease
　　My thoughts I speak, and what I speak doth flow   10
In verse, and that my verse best wits doth please?
Guess we the cause: 'What, is it thus?' Fie, no;
　　'Or so?' Much less. 'How then?' Sure, thus it is:
　　My lips are sweet, inspired with Stella's kiss.

73 11 *judges*: lips.

74 1 *Aganippe*: spring in Greece dedicated to the muses.
　　2 *Tempe*: valley in Thessaly where Apollo pursued Daphne.

75

Of all the kings that ever here did reign,
Edward, named fourth, as first in praise I name;
Not for his fair outside, nor well lined brain,
Although less gifts imp feathers oft on fame;
    Nor that he could, young-wise, wise-valiant, frame   5
His sire's revenge, joined with a kingdom's gain;
And gained by Mars, could yet mad Mars so tame,[n]
That balance weighed what sword did late obtain;
    Nor that he made the flower-de-luce so 'fraid,
Though strongly hedged of bloody lion's paws,   10
That witty Lewis to him a tribute paid;[n]
Nor this, nor that, nor any such small cause;
    But only for this worthy knight durst prove
    To lose his crown, rather than fail his love.[n]

76[n]

She comes, and straight therewith her shining twins do move
    Their rays to me, who in her tedious absence lay
    Benighted in cold woe; but now appears my day,
The only light of joy, the only warmth of love.
She comes, with light and warmth, which like Aurora prove   5
    Of gentle force, so that mine eyes dare gladly play
    With such a rosy morn, whose beams most freshly gay
Scorch not, but only do dark chilling sprites remove.
    But lo, while I do speak, it groweth noon with me;
Her flamy glistering lights increase with time and place;   10
My heart cries, 'Ah, it burns;' mine eyes now dazzled be;
No wind, no shade, can cool; what help then in my case,
    But with short breath, long looks, staid feet and walking
       head,
    Pray that my sun go down with meeker beams to bed.

75   4 *imp*: engraft.
       8 *balance*: justice, equity.
       9 *flower-de-luce*: France.
       10 *bloody lion*: Scotland.

76   5 *Aurora*: the dawn.
       13 *walking*: agitated, in motion.

77[n]

Those looks, whose beams be joy, whose motion is delight;
That face, whose lecture shows what perfect beauty is;
That presence, which doth give dark hearts a living light;
That grace, which Venus weeps that she herself doth miss;
  That hand, which without touch holds more than Atlas'
    might;   5
Those lips, which make death's pay a mean price for a kiss;
That skin, whose pass-praise hue scorns this poor term of
    'white';
Those words, which do sublime the quintessence of bliss;
  That voice, which makes the soul plant himself in the ears;
That conversation sweet, where such high comforts be,   10
As construed in true speech, the name of heaven it bears,
Makes me in my best thoughts and quiet'st judgement see
  That in no more but these I might be fully blessed:
  Yet ah, my maiden muse doth blush to tell the rest.

78[n]

O how the pleasant airs of true love be
  Infected by those vapours which arise
  From out that noisome gulf, which gaping lies
Between the jaws of hellish jealousy:
A monster, others' harm, self-misery,   5
  Beauty's plague, virtue's scourge, succour of lies;
  Who his own joy to his own hurt applies,
And only cherish doth with injury;
  Who, since he hath, by nature's special grace,
  So piercing paws, as spoil when they embrace;   10
So nimble feet, as stir still, though on thorns;
  So many eyes, ay seeking their own woe;
  So ample ears, as never good news know:
Is it not ill that such a devil wants horns?

77 2 *whose lecture*: the reading of which.
    4 *miss*: lack.
    8 *sublime*: extract, make pure (as in alchemy).
    8 *quintessence*: the purest part, the essence obtained by refining.

79

Sweet kiss, thy sweets I fain would sweetly endite,
   Which even of sweetness sweetest sweetener art:
   Pleasing'st consort, where each sense holds a part;
Which, coupling doves, guides Venus' chariot right;
Best charge, and bravest retreat in Cupid's fight;   5
   A double key, which opens to the heart,
   Most rich, when most his riches it impart;
Nest of young joys, schoolmaster of delight,
   Teaching the mean at once to take and give;
The friendly fray, where blows both wound and heal;   10
The pretty death, while each in other live;
Poor hope's first wealth, hostage of promised weal,
   Breakfast of love—but lo, lo, where she is:
   Cease we to praise, now pray we for a kiss.[n]

80

Sweet swelling lip, well may'st thou swell in pride,
   Since best wits think it wit thee to admire;
   Nature's praise, virtue's stall, Cupid's cold fire,
Whence words, not words, but heavenly graces slide;
The new Parnassus, where the muses bide;   5
   Sweetener of music, wisdom's beautifier;
   Breather of life, and fastener of desire,
Where beauty's blush in honour's grain is dyed.
   Thus much my heart compelled my mouth to say:
   But now, spite of my heart, my mouth will stay,   10
Loathing all lies, doubting this flattery is,
   And no spur can his resty race renew,
   Without how far this praise is short of you,
Sweet lip, you teach my mouth with one sweet kiss.

79   3 *consort*: group of instruments of the same family.

80   3 *stall*: seat.
     8 *grain*: texture, fibre; = dyed fast. Cf. gloss on sonnet 102 l. 6.
     12 *resty*: restive.

81

O kiss, which dost those ruddy gems impart,
Or gems, or fruits of new-found paradise,
Breathing all bliss, and sweetening to the heart,
Teaching dumb lips a nobler exercise;
   O kiss, which souls, even souls together ties   5
By links of love, and only nature's art;
How fain would I paint thee to all men's eyes,
Or of thy gifts at least shade out some part.
   But she forbids; with blushing words, she says
   She builds her fame on higher seated praise;   10
But my heart burns, I cannot silent be.
   Then since (dear life) you fain would have me peace,
   And I, mad with delight, want wit to cease,
Stop you my mouth with still still kissing me.

82

Nymph of the garden where all beauties be;
   Beauties, which do in excellency pass
· His who till death looked in a watery glass,
Or hers whom naked the Trojan boy did see:
Sweet garden nymph, which keeps the cherry tree,   5
   Whose fruit doth far th'Hesperian taste surpass;
   Most sweet-fair, most fair-sweet, do not, alas,
From coming near those cherries banish me.
   For though, full of desire, empty of wit,
Admitted late by your best-graced grace,   10
I caught at one of them a hungry bit;
Pardon that fault, once more grant me the place,
   And I do swear, even by the same delight,
   I will but kiss, I never more will bite.

81 2 *gems*: pun on *gemmae* = buds.
    4 *nobler*: nobler than speech.

82 3 *His*: Narcissus.
    4 *hers*: Venus, seen by Paris.
    6 *th'Hesperian taste*: the golden apples of the Hesperides, given as a
    wedding present to Juno by the Earth.

83

Good brother Philip,[n] I have borne you long;
   I was content you should in favour creep,
   While craftily you seemed your cut to keep,
As though that fair soft hand did you great wrong.
I bare (with envy) yet I bare your song,   5
   When in her neck you did love-ditties peep;
   Nay, more fool I, oft suffered you to sleep
In lilies' nest, where love's self lies along.
   What, doth high place ambitious thoughts augment?
Is sauciness reward of courtesy?   10
Cannot such grace your silly self content,
But you must needs with those lips billing be,
   And through those lips drink nectar from that tongue?
   Leave that, sir Phip, lest off your neck be wrung.

Third song

If Orpheus' voice had force to breathe such music's love
Through pores of senseless trees, as it could make them move;
If stones good measure danced, the Theban walls to build,
To cadence of the tunes, which Amphion's lyre did yield;
More cause a like effect at leastwise bringeth: 5
O stones, O trees, learn hearing: Stella singeth.

If love might sweeten so a boy of shepherd brood,
To make a lizard dull to taste love's dainty food;
If eagle fierce could so in Grecian maid delight,
As his light was her eyes, her death his endless night;[n]   10
Earth gave that love, Heaven I trow love refineth:
O birds, O beasts, look, love: lo, Stella shineth.

---

83   3 *cut to keep*: know your place, act with propriety.

4 *Amphion's lyre*: see gloss on sonnet 68 l. 6.

The birds, beasts, stones, and trees feel this, and feeling, love;
And if the trees, nor stones, stir not, the same to prove,
Nor beasts nor birds do come unto this blessed gaze,   15
Know, that small love is quick, and great love doth amaze:
They are amazed, but you with reason armed:
O eyes, O ears of men, how are you charmed!

84

Highway, since you my chief Parnassus be,
   And that my muse, to some ears not unsweet,[n]
   Tempers her words to trampling horse's feet
More oft than to a chamber melody;
Now blessed you, bear onward blessed me   5
   To her, where I my heart safeliest shall meet.
   My muse and I must you of duty greet,
With thanks and wishes, wishing thankfully.
   Be you still fair, honoured by public heed,
By no encroachment wronged, nor time forgot;   10
Nor blamed for blood, nor shamed for sinful deed.
   And that you know, I envy you no lot
   Of highest wish, I wish you so much bliss,
   Hundreds of years you Stella's feet may kiss.

85

I see the house; my heart, thy self contain;
   Beware full sails drown not thy tottering barge,
   Lest joy, by nature apt sprites to enlarge,
Thee to thy wrack beyond thy limits strain;
Nor do like lords, whose weak confused brain,   5
   Not pointing to fit folks each undercharge,
   While every office themselves will discharge,
With doing all, leave nothing done but pain.[n]
   But give apt servants their due place; let eyes
See beauty's total sum summed in her face;   10
Let ears hear speech, which wit to wonder ties;
Let breath suck up those sweets; let arms embrace
   The globe of weal; lips love's indentures make;
   Thou but of all the kingly tribute take.

85   6 *Not pointing* . . . : not delegating duties to suitable people.
   13 *indentures*: agreements, contracts.

Fourth song

Only joy, now here you are,
Fit to hear and ease my care;
Let my whispering voice obtain
Sweet reward for sharpest pain:
Take me to thee and thee to me.   5
'No, no, no, no, my dear, let be.'

Night hath closed all in her cloak,
Twinkling stars love-thoughts provoke;
Danger hence good care doth keep;
Jealousy itself doth sleep: 10
Take me to thee and thee to me.
'No, no, no, no, my dear, let be.'

Better place can no man find
Cupid's yoke to loose or bind;
These sweet flowers on fine bed too   15
Us in their best language woo:
Take me to thee and thee to me.
'No, no, no, no, my dear, let be.'

This small light the moon bestows
Serves thy beams but to disclose,   20
So to raise my hap more high;
Fear not else, none can us spy:
Take me to thee and thee to me.
'No, no, no, no, my dear, let be.'

That you heard was but a mouse;   25
Dumb sleep holdeth all the house;
Yet asleep, methinks, they say,
Young folks, take time while you may:
Take me to thee and thee to me.
'No, no, no, no, my dear, let be.'   30

15 *sweet flowers*: presumably embroidered on a coverlet, since the scene is
happening indoors.

Niggard time threats, if we miss
This large offer of our bliss
Long stay ere he grant the same;
Sweet then, while each thing doth frame:
Take me to thee and thee to me.   35
'No, no, no, no, my dear, let be.'

Your fair mother is abed,
Candles out, and curtains spread;
She thinks you do letters write;
Write, but first let me endite: 40
Take me to thee and thee to me.
'No, no, no, no, my dear, let be.'

Sweet, alas, why strive you thus?
Concord better fitteth us.
Leave to Mars the force of hands,   45
Your power in your beauty stands:
Take me to thee and thee to me.
'No, no, no, no, my dear, let be.'

Woe to me, and do you swear
Me to hate, but I forbear?   50
Cursed be my destinies all,
That brought me so high, to fall;
Soon with my death I will please thee.
'No, no, no, no, my dear, let be.'

86

Alas, whence came this change of looks? If I
    Have changed desert, let mine own conscience be
    A still felt plague, to self condemning me:
Let woe gripe on my heart, shame load mine eye.
But if all faith, like spotless ermine,[n] lie   5
    Safe in my soul, which only doth to thee
    (As his sole object of felicity)
With wings of love in air of wonder fly,

50 *but*: unless.

86 4 *gripe*: grip, tear.

O ease your hand, treat not so hard your slave;
In justice pains come not till faults do call;   10
Or if I needs, sweet judge, must torments have,
Use something else to chasten me withal
 Than those blessed eyes, where all my hopes do dwell.
 No doom should make one's heaven become his hell.

Fifth song[n]

While favour fed my hope, delight with hope was brought;
Thought waited on delight, and speech did follow thought;
Then grew my tongue and pen records unto thy glory;
I thought all words were lost, that were not spent of thee;
I thought each place was dark but where thy lights would be,   5
And all ears worse than deaf, that heard not out thy story.

I said thou wert most fair, and so indeed thou art;
I said thou wert most sweet, sweet poison to my heart;
I said my soul was thine—O that I then had lied!
I said thine eyes were stars, thy breasts the milken way,   10
Thy fingers Cupid's shafts, thy voice the angels' lay,
And all I said so well, as no man it denied.

But now that hope is lost, unkindness kills delight,
Yet thought and speech do live, though metamorphosed quite;
For rage now rules the reins, which guided were by pleasure.   15
I think now of thy faults, who late thought of thy praise;
That speech falls now to blame, which did thy honour raise;
The same key open can, which did lock up a treasure.

Thou then, whom partial heavens conspired in one to frame,
The proof of beauty's worth, th'inheritrix of fame,   20
The mansion seat of bliss, and just excuse of lovers;
See now those feathers plucked, wherewith thou flew'st most
 high;
See what clouds of reproach shall dark thy honour's sky;
Whose own fault casts him down, hardly high seat recovers.

86 14 *doom*: judgement.

And O my muse, though oft you lulled her in your lap,   25
And then, a heavenly child, gave her ambrosian pap,
And to that brain of hers your hidd'nest gifts infused;
Since she, disdaining me, doth you in me disdain,
Suffer her not to laugh, while we both suffer pain;
Princes in subjects wronged, must deem themselves abused.   30

Your client poor my self, shall Stella handle so?
Revenge, revenge, my muse; defiance' trumpet blow;
Threaten what may be done, yet do more than you threaten.
Ah, my suit granted is; I feel my breast to swell;
Now child, a lesson new you shall begin to spell: 35
Sweet babes must babies have, but shrewd girls must be beaten.

Think now no more to hear of warm fine-odoured snow,
Nor blushing lilies, nor pearls' ruby-hidden row,
Nor of that golden sea, whose waves in curls are broken:
But of thy soul, so fraught with such ungratefulness,   40
As where thou soon might'st help, most faith doth most oppress;
Ungrateful who is called, the worst of evils is spoken.[n]

Yet worse than worst, I say thou art a thief. A thief?
No God forbid. A thief, and of worst thieves the chief;
Thieves steal for need, and steal but goods, which pain recovers, 45
But thou, rich in all joys, dost rob my joys from me,
Which cannot be restored by time nor industry.
Of foes the spoil is evil, far worse of constant lovers.

Yet gentle English thieves do rob, but will not slay;
Thou, English murdering thief, wilt have hearts for thy prey;   50
The name of 'murderer' now on thy fair forehead sitteth;
And even while I do speak, my death wounds bleeding be,
Which, I protest, proceed from only cruel thee.
Who may, and will not, save, murder in truth committeth.

But murder, private fault, seems but a toy to thee;   55
I lay then to thy charge, unjustest tyranny,
If rule by force without all claim a tyrant showeth.
For thou dost lord my heart, who am not born thy slave;
And which is worse, makes me, most guiltless, torments have;
A rightful prince by unright deeds a tyrant groweth.   60

36 *babies*: dolls.
36 *shrewd*: shrewish, naughty.

Lo, you grow proud with this, for tyrants make folk bow.
Of foul rebellion then I do appeach thee now;
Rebel by nature's law, rebel by law of reason.
Thou, sweetest subject, wert born in the realm of love,
And yet against thy prince thy force dost daily prove;   65
No virtue merits praise, once touched with blot of treason.

But valiant rebels oft in fools' mouths purchase fame;
I now then stain thy white with vagabonding shame,
Both rebel to the son, and vagrant from the mother:
For wearing Venus' badge in every part of thee   70
Unto Diana's train thou, runaway, did'st flee:
Who faileth one, is false, though trusty to another.

What, is not this enough? Nay, far worse cometh here:
A witch I say thou art, though thou so fair appear;
For I protest, my sight never thy face enjoyeth,   75
But I in me am changed; I am alive and dead;
My feet are turned to roots; my heart becometh lead.
No witchcraft is so evil, as which man's mind destroyeth.

Yet witches may repent; thou art far worse than they;
Alas, that I am forced such evil of thee to say!   80
I say thou art a devil, though clothed in angel's shining;
For thy face tempts my soul to leave the heaven for thee,
And thy words of refuse do pour even hell on me.
Who tempt, and tempted plague, are devils in true defining.

You then, ungrateful thief; you murdering tyrant, you;   85
You rebel runaway, to lord and lady untrue;
You witch, you devil, alas—you still of me beloved;
You see what I can say; mend yet your froward mind,
And such skill in my muse you, reconciled, shall find,
That all these cruel words your praises shall be proved.   90

62 *appeach*: impeach, accuse.
83 *refuse*: refusal.

Sixth song

O you that hear this voice,
O you that see this face,
Say whether of the choice
Deserves the former place:
Fear not to judge this bate,   5
For it is void of hate.

This side doth beauty take;
For that, doth music speak;
Fit orators to make
The strongest judgements weak: 10
The bar to plead their right
Is only true delight.

Thus doth the voice and face,
These gentle lawyers, wage,
Like loving brothers' case   15
For father's heritage,
That each, while each contends,
Itself to other lends.

For beauty beautifies
With heavenly hue and grace   20
The heavenly harmonies;
And in this faultless face
The perfect beauties be
A perfect harmony.

Music more lofty swells   25
In speeches nobly placed;
Beauty as far excels
In action aptly graced;
A friend each party draws
To countenance his cause.   30

3 *whether*: which.
4 *former*: first.
5 *bate*: debate, dispute.

Love more affected seems
To beauty's lovely light,
And wonder more esteems
Of music's wondrous might;
But both to both so bent   35
As both in both are spent.

Music doth witness call
The ear, his truth to try;
Beauty brings to the hall
The judgement of the eye: 40
Both in their objects such,
As no exceptions touch.

The common sense, which might
Be arbiter of this,
To be, forsooth, upright,   45
To both sides partial is:
He lays on this chief praise,
Chief praise on that he lays.

Then reason, princess high,
Whose throne is in the mind,   50
Which music can in sky
And hidden beauties find:
Say whether thou wilt crown
With limitless renown.

Seventh song[n]

Whose senses in so ill consort their stepdame nature lays,
That ravishing delight in them most sweet tunes do not raise;
Or if they do delight therein, yet are so cloyed with wit,
As with sententious lips to set a title vain on it;
O let them hear these sacred tunes, and learn in wonder's schools   5
To be, in things past bounds of wit, fools, if they be not fools.

42 *exceptions*: legal objections.
53 *whether*: which of the two.

1 *ill consort*: disharmony.

Who have so leaden eyes, as not to see sweet beauty's show;
Or seeing, have so wooden wits, as not that worth to know;
Or knowing, have so muddy minds, as not to be in love;
Or loving, have so frothy thoughts as eas'ly thence to move: 10
O, let them see these heavenly beams, and in fair letters read
A lesson fit, both sight and skill, love and firm love to breed.

Hear then, but then with wonder hear; see, but adoring see;
No mortal gifts, no earthly fruits, now here descended be;
See; do you see this face? A face? Nay, image of the skies,   15
Of which the two life-giving lights are figured in her eyes.
Hear you this soul-invading voice, and call it but a voice?
The very essence of their tunes, when angels do rejoice.

Eighth song[n]

In a grove most rich of shade,[n]
Where birds wanton music made,
May then young his pied weeds showing,
New perfumed with flowers fresh growing,

Astrophil with Stella sweet   5
Did for mutual comfort meet;
Both within themselves oppressed,
But each in the other blessed.

Him great harms had taught much care:
Her fair neck a foul yoke bare: 10
But her sight his cares did banish,
In his sight her yoke did vanish.

Wept they had, alas the while;
But now tears themselves did smile,
While their eyes, by love directed,   15
Interchangeably reflected.

Sigh they did; but now betwixt
Sighs of woes were glad sighs mixed,
With arms crossed, yet testifying
Restless rest, and living dying.   20

Their ears hungry of each word,
Which the dear tongue would afford,
But their tongues restrained from walking,
Till their hearts had ended talking.

But when their tongues could not speak   25
Love itself did silence break;
Love did set his lips asunder,
Thus to speak in love and wonder:

'Stella, sovereign of my joy,
Fair triumpher of annoy,   30
Stella, star of heavenly fire,
Stella, lodestar of desire;

Stella, in whose shining eyes
Are the lights of Cupid's skies;
Whose beams, where they once are darted,   35
Love therewith is straight imparted;

Stella, whose voice when it speaks
Senses all asunder breaks;
Stella, whose voice when it singeth
Angels to acquaintance bringeth;   40

Stella, in whose body is
Writ each character of bliss;
Whose face all, all beauty passeth,
Save thy mind, which yet surpasseth:

Grant, O grant—but speech, alas,   45
Fails me, fearing on to pass;
Grant—O me, what am I saying?
But no fault there is in praying:

19 *arms crossed*: gesture of melancholy, as in figure on tomb-stone.

Grant, O dear, on knees I pray'—
(Knees on ground he then did stay)   50
'That not I, but since I love you,
Time and place for me may move you.

Never season was more fit,
Never room more apt for it;
Smiling air allows my reason;   55
These birds sing, "Now use the season";

This small wind, which so sweet is,
See how it the leaves doth kiss,
Each tree in his best attiring
Sense of love to love inspiring.   60

Love makes earth the water drink,
Love to earth makes water sink;
And if dumb things be so witty,
Shall a heavenly grace want pity?'

There his hands in their speech fain   65
Would have made tongue's language plain:
But her hands, his hands repelling,
Gave repulse, all grace excelling.

Then she spake; her speech was such
As not ears, but heart did touch;   70
While such wise she love denied,
As yet love she signified.

'Astrophil,' said she, 'my love
Cease in these effects to prove:
Now be still; yet still believe me,   75
Thy grief more than death would grieve me.

If that any thought in me
Can taste comfort but of thee,
Let me, fed with hopeless anguish,
Joyless, hopeless, endless languish.   80

54 *room*: place.
71 *such wise*: in such a way.
74 *in these effects to prove*: to test by these manifestations.

If those eyes you praised be
Half so dear as you to me,
Let me home return, stark blinded
Of those eyes, and blinder minded.

If to secret of my heart   .   85
I do any wish impart
Where thou art not foremost placed,
Be both wish and I defaced.

If more may be said, I say:
All my bliss in thee I lay;   90
If thou love, my love content thee,
For all love, all faith is meant thee.

Trust me, while I thee deny,
In my self the smart I try;
Tyrant honour thus doth use thee;   95
Stella's self might not refuse thee.

Therefore, dear, this no more move,
Lest, though I leave not thy love,
Which too deep in me is framed,
I should blush when thou art named.'   100

Therewithal away she went,
Leaving him so passion-rent
With what she had done and spoken,
That therewith my song is broken.[n]

94 *try*: experience.

Ninth song

Go, my flock, go get you hence,
Seek a better place of feeding,
Where you may have some defence
From the storms in my breast breeding,
And showers from my eyes proceeding.   5

Leave a wretch, in whom all woe
Can abide to keep no measure;
Merry flock, such one forego,
Unto whom mirth is displeasure,
Only rich in mischief's treasure.   10

Yet, alas, before you go,
Hear your woeful master's story,
Which to stones I else would show:
Sorrow only then hath glory,
When 'tis excellently sorry.   15

Stella, fiercest shepherdess,
Fiercest, but yet fairest ever;
Stella, whom, O heavens, still bless,
Though against me she persevere,
Though I bliss inherit never;   20

Stella hath refused me,
Stella, who more love hath proved
In this caitiff heart to be
Than can in good ewes be moved
Toward lambkins best beloved.   25

Stella hath refused me;
Astrophil, that so well served,
In this pleasant spring must see,
While in pride flowers be preserved,
Himself only winter-starved.   30

Why, alas, doth she then swear
That she loveth me so dearly,
Seeing me so long to bear
Coals of love, that burn so clearly,
And yet leave me helpless merely?   35

Is that love? Forsooth, I trow,
If I saw my good dog grieved,
And a help for him did know,
My love should not be believed
But he were by me relieved.   40

No, she hates me, wellaway,
Faining love somewhat, to please me;
For she knows, if she display
All her hate, death soon would seize me,
And of hideous torments ease me.   45

Then adieu, dear flock, adieu:
But alas, if in your straying
Heavenly Stella meet with you,
Tell her, in your piteous blaying,
Her poor slave's unjust decaying.   50

87

When I was forced from Stella, ever dear,
Stella, food of my thoughts, heart of my heart,
Stella, whose eyes make all my tempests clear,
By iron laws of duty to depart;[n]
   Alas, I found that she with me did smart,   5
I saw that tears did in her eyes appear;
I saw that sighs her sweetest lips did part,
And her sad words my sadded sense did hear.
   For me, I wept, to see pearls scattered so;
   I sighed her sighs, and wailed for her woe;   10
Yet swam in joy, such love in her was seen.
   Thus while th'effect most bitter was to me,
   And nothing than the cause more sweet could be,
I had been vexed, if vexed I had not been.

49 *blaying*: bleating, baaing.

88

Out, traitor absence; darest thou counsel me
From my dear captainess to run away,
Because in brave array here marcheth she
That to win me, oft shows a present pay?
   Is faith so weak? Or is such force in thee?   5
When sun is hid, can stars such beams display?
Cannot heaven's food, once felt, keep stomachs free
From base desire on earthly cates to prey?
   Tush, absence; while thy mists eclipse that light,
   My orphan sense flies to the inward sight,   10
Where memory sets forth the beams of love;
   That where before heart loved and eyes did see,
   In heart both sight and love now coupled be;
United powers make each the stronger be.

89

Now that of absence the most irksome night
   With darkest shade doth overcome my day;
   Since Stella's eyes, wont to give me my day,
Leaving my hemisphere, leave me in night;
Each day seems long, and longs for long-stayed night;   5
   The night as tedious, woos the approach of day;
   Tired with the dusty toils of busy day,
Languished with horrors of the silent night,
Suffering the ills both of the day and night,
   While no night is more dark than is my day,   10
Nor no day hath less quiet than my night;
   With such bad mixture of my night and day,
That living thus in blackest winter night,
   I feel the flames of hottest summer day.[n]

90

Stella, think not that I by verse seek fame;
  Who seek, who hope, who love, who live, but thee:
  Thine eyes my pride, thy lips my history;
If thou praise not, all other praise is shame.
Nor so ambitious am I, as to frame   5
  A nest for my young praise in laurel tree;
  In truth I swear, I wish not there should be
Graved in mine epitaph a poet's name:
  Ne if I would, could I just title make,
That any laud to me thereof should grow,   10
Without my plumes from others' wings I take.
For nothing from my wit or will doth flow,
  Since all my words thy beauty doth endite,
  And love doth hold my hand, and makes me write.[n]

91

Stella, while now, by honour's cruel might,
  I am from you, light of my life, misled,
  And that fair you, my sun, thus overspread
With absence' veil, I live in sorrow's night;
If this dark place yet show, like candle light,   5
  Some beauty's piece, as amber-coloured head,
  Milk hands, rose cheeks, or lips more sweet, more red,
Or seeing jets, black, but in blackness bright:
  They please, I do confess, they please mine eyes.
But why? Because of you they models be,   10
Models such be wood-globes of glistering skies.[n]
Dear, therefore be not jealous over me;
  If you hear that they seem my heart to move,
  Not them, O no, but you in them I love.

90   9 *Ne*: nor.

92

Be your words made, good sir, of Indian ware,[n]
   That you allow me them by so small rate?
   Or do you cutted Spartans imitate?
Or do you mean my tender ears to spare,
That to my questions you so total are?   5
   When I demand of Phoenix Stella's state,
   You say, forsooth, you left her well of late.
O God, think you that satisfies my care?
   I would know whether she did sit or walk,
How clothed, how waited on? Sighed she or smiled?   10
Whereof, with whom, how often did she talk?
With what pastime, time's journey she beguiled?
   If her lips deigned to sweeten my poor name?
   Say all, and all well said, still say the same.

Tenth song

O dear life, when shall it be
   That mine eyes thine eyes may see,
   And in them my mind discover,
   Whether absence have had force
   Thy remembrance to divorce   5
   From the image of thy lover?

O if I myself find not
   After parting aught forgot,
   Nor debarred from beauty's treasure,
   Let no tongue aspire to tell   10
   In what high joys I shall dwell;
   Only thought aims at the pleasure.

92   3 *cutted*: concise, laconic.
     5 *total*: brief.

Thought, therefore, I will send thee
  To take up the place for me
  Long I will not after tarry.   15
  There unseen thou may'st be bold
  Those fair wonders to behold,
  Which in them my hopes do carry.

Thought, see thou no place forbear;
  Enter bravely everywhere,   20
  Seize on all to her belonging;
  But if thou would'st guarded be,
  Fearing her beams, take with thee
  Strength of liking, rage of longing.

Think of that most grateful time   25
  When my leaping heart will climb
  In my lips to have his biding,
  There those roses for to kiss
  Which do breathe a sugared bliss,
  Opening rubies, pearls dividing.   30

Think of my most princely power,
  When I, blessed, shall devour
  With my greedy lickerous senses,
  Beauty, music, sweetness, love,
  While she doth against me prove   35
  Her strong darts but weak defences.

Think, think, of those dallyings,
  When with dove-like murmurings,
  With glad moaning passed anguish,
  We change eyes, and heart for heart   40
  Each to other do impart,
  Joying, till joy make us languish.

O my thought, my thoughts, surcease;
  Thy delights my woes increase,
  My life melts with too much thinking.   45
  Think no more, but die in me,
  Till thou shalt revived be
  At her lips my nectar drinking.

33 *lickerous*: greedy, lecherous.

93[n]

O fate, O fault, O curse, child of my bliss;
  What sobs can give words grace my grief to show?
  What ink is black enough to paint my woe?
Through me, wretch me, even Stella vexed is.
Yet truth—if caitiff's breath might call thee—this   5
  Witness with me, that my foul stumbling so
  From carelessness did in no manner grow;
But wit, confused with too much care, did miss.
  And do I then myself this vain 'scuse give?
I have (live I, and know this?) harmed thee;   10
Though worlds quite me, shall I myself forgive?
Only with pains my pains thus eased be,
  That all my hurts in my heart's wrack I read;
  I cry thy sighs; my dear, thy tears I bleed.

94

Grief, find the words; for thou hast made my brain
  So dark with misty vapours, which arise
  From out thy heavy mould, that inbent eyes
Can scarce discern the shape of mine own pain.
Do thou then (for thou canst), do thou complain,   5
  For my poor soul, which now that sickness tries
  Which even to sense, sense of itself denies,
Thou harbingers of death lodge there his train.
  Or if thy love of plaint yet mine forbears,
As of a caitiff, worthy so to die;   10
Yet wail thyself, and wail with causeful tears,
That though in wretchedness thy life doth lie,
Yet grow'st more wretched than thy nature bears,
By being placed in such a wretch as I.

93 8 *miss*: go astray, do wrong.
   11 *quite*: acquit, or requite.

95

Yet sighs, dear sighs, indeed true friends you are,
   That do not leave your least friend at the worst;
   But as you with my breast I oft have nursed,
So grateful now you wait upon my care.
Faint coward joy no longer tarry dare,   5
   Seeing hope yield when this woe strake him first;
   Delight protests he is not for the accursed,
Though oft himself my mate-in-arms he sware.
   Nay, sorrow comes with such main rage, that he
Kills his own children, tears, finding that they   10
By love were made apt to consort with me.
Only true sighs, you do not go away:
   Thank may you have for such a thankful part,
   Thank-worthiest yet, when you shall break my heart.

96

Thought, with good cause thou lik'st so well the night,
   Since kind or chance gives both one livery:
   Both sadly black, both blackly darkened be,
Night barred from sun, thou from thy own sun's light.
Silence in both displays his sullen might;   5
   Slow heaviness in both holds one degree,
   That full of doubts, thou of perplexity;
Thy tears express night's native moisture right.
   In both a mazefull solitariness:
In night, of sprites the ghastly powers stir,   10
In thee, or sprites, or sprited ghastliness,
But, but, alas, night's side the odds hath, far,
   For that at length yet doth invite some rest,
   Thou, though still tired, yet still dost it detest.

96 2 *kind*: nature.
    8 *express*: squeeze out (literal meaning), as well as communicate.
    9 *mazefull*: confused, bewildered.
    12 *far*: spelt 'fur' in Sidney's holographs, and so rhyming with 'stir'.

97[n]

Dian, that fain would cheer her friend, the night,
　　Shows her oft at the full her fairest face,
　　Bringing with her those starry nymphs, whose chase
From heavenly standing hits each mortal wight.
But ah, poor night, in love with Phoebus' light,　　　　　5
　　And endlessly despairing of his grace,
　　Herself (to show no other joy hath place)
Silent and sad, in mourning weeds doth dight:
　　Even so, alas, a lady, Dian's peer,
With choice delights and rarest company　　　　　　　10
Would fain drive clouds from out my heavy cheer.
But woe is me, though joy itself were she,
　　She could not show my blind brain ways of joy,
　　While I despair my sun's sight to enjoy.

98

Ah bed, the field where joy's peace some do see,
　　The field where all my thoughts to war be trained,
　　How is thy grace by my strange fortune stained!
How thy lee shores by my sighs stormed be!
With sweet soft shades thou oft invitest me　　　　　5
　　To steal some rest; but, wretch, I am constrained
　　(Spurred with love's spur, though galled and shortly reined
With care's hard hand) to turn and toss in thee,
　　While the black horrors of the silent night
Paint woe's black face so lively to my sight　　　　　10
That tedious leisure marks each wrinkled line.
　　But when Aurora leads out Phoebus' dance,
　　Mine eyes then only wink, for spite, perchance,
That worms should have their sun, and I want mine.

97　4 *standing*: position (as in shooting).
　　8 *dight*: dress.

98　2 *trained*: drawn, attracted.
　　13 *wink*: close.

99

When far spent night persuades each mortal eye,
  To whom nor art nor nature granteth light,
  To lay his then mark-wanting shafts of sight,
Closed with their quivers, in sleep's armoury;
With windows ope then most my mind doth lie,   5
  Viewing the shape of darkness and delight,
  Takes in that sad hue, which with the inward night
Of his mazed powers keeps perfect harmony.
  But when birds charm, and that sweet air, which is
Morn's messenger, with rose-enamelled skies,   10
Calls each wight to salute the flower of bliss:
In tomb of lids then buried are mine eyes,
  Forced by their lord, who is ashamed to find
  Such light in sense, with such a darkened mind.

100

O tears, no tears, but rain from beauty's skies,[n]
  Making those lilies and those roses grow
  Which aye most fair, now more than most fair show,
While graceful pity beauty beautifies:
O honeyed sighs, which from that breast do rise   5
  Whose pants do make unspilling cream to flow,
  Winged with whose breath so pleasing zephyrs blow,
As can refresh the hell where my soul fries:
  O plaints, conserved in such a sugared phrase
  That eloquence itself envies your praise,   10
While sobbed-out words a perfect music give:
  Such tears, sighs, plaints, no sorrow is, but joy;
  Or if such heavenly signs must prove annoy,
All mirth farewell, let me in sorrow live.

99 3 *mark-wanting*: lacking a target.
    8 *mazed*: confused.
    9 *charm*: sing in chorus.
    14 *light in sense*: visible light, as distinct from inner light.

101

Stella is sick, and in that sick-bed lies
Sweetness, that breathes and pants as oft as she;
And grace, sick too, such fine conclusions tries
That sickness brags itself best graced to be.
   Beauty is sick, but sick in so fair guise   5
That in that paleness beauty's white we see;
And joy, which is inseparate from these eyes,
Stella now learns (strange case!) to weep in thee.
   Love moves thy pain, and like a faithful page,
As thy looks stir, runs up and down, to make   10
All folks prest at thy will thy pain to assuage;
Nature with care sweats for her darling's sake,
     Knowing worlds pass, ere she enough can find
     Of such heaven stuff, to clothe so heavenly mind.

102[n]

Where be the roses gone, which sweetened so our eyes?
   Where those red cheeks, which oft with fair increase did frame
   The height of honour in the kindly badge of shame?
Who hath the crimson weeds stolen from my morning skies?
How doth the colour vade of those vermilion dyes,   5
   Which nature's self did make, and self engrained the same!
   I would know by what right this paleness overcame
That hue, whose force my heart still unto thraldom ties?
   Galen's adoptive sons, who by a beaten way
   Their judgements hackney on, the fault on sickness lay;   10
But feeling proof makes me say they mistake it far:
   It is but love, which makes his paper perfect white
   To write therein more fresh the story of delight,
While beauty's reddest ink Venus for him doth stir.

---

101   7 *inseparate*: inseparable.
     11 *prest*: prompt, eager.

102   3 *kindly*: natural, appropriate.
     5 *vade*: disappear, fade.
     6 *engrained*: dyed in grain, i.e. fast.
     9 *Galen's adoptive sons*: doctors.
     11 *far*: cf. gloss on sonnet 96 l. 12.

103

O happy Thames, that didst my Stella bear!
I saw thyself, with many a smiling line[n]
Upon thy cheerful face, joy's livery wear,
While those fair planets on thy streams did shine.
    The boat for joy could not to dance forbear,   5
While wanton winds, with beauties so divine
Ravished, stayed not, till in her golden hair
They did themselves (O sweetest prison!) twine.
    And fain those Aeol's youths there would their stay
Have made; but forced by nature still to fly,   10
First did with puffing kiss those locks display.
She, so dishevelled, blushed; from window I
    With sight thereof cried out, 'O fair disgrace;
    Let honour's self to thee grant highest place.'

104

Envious wits, what hath been mine offence,
    That with such poisonous care my looks you mark,
    That to each word, nay, sigh, of mine you hark,
As grudging me my sorrow's eloquence?
Ah, is it not enough, that I am thence,   5
Thence, so far thence, that scarcely any spark
    Of comfort dare come to this dungeon dark,
Where rigorous exile locks up all my sense?
    But if I by a happy window pass;
If I but stars upon my armour bear;[n]   10
Sick, thirsty, glad, though but of empty glass;
Your moral notes straight my hid meaning tear
    From out my ribs, and puffing prove that I
    Do Stella love. Fools, who doth it deny?

103 4 *fair planets*: Stella's eyes.
     9 *Aeol's youths*: sons of Aeolus, breezes.

104 5 *thence*: away from where I want to be.

Eleventh song

'Who is it that this dark night
Underneath my window plaineth?'
It is one that from thy sight
Being, ah, exiled, disdaineth
Every other vulgar light.   5

'Why, alas, and are you he?
Be not yet those fancies changed?'
Dear, when you find change in me,
Though from me you be estranged,
Let my change to ruin be.   10

'Well, in absence this will die;
Leave to see, and leave to wonder.'
Absence sure will help, if I
Can learn, how myself to sunder
From what in my heart doth lie.   15

'But time will these thoughts remove;
Time doth work what no man knoweth.'
Time doth as the subject prove;
With time still the affection groweth
In the faithful turtle dove.   20

'What if you new beauties see,
Will they not stir new affection?'
I will think they pictures be,
Image-like of saint's perfection,
Poorly counterfeiting thee.   25

'But your reason's purest light
Bids you leave such minds to nourish.'
Dear, do reason no such spite;
Never doth thy beauty flourish
More than in my reason's sight.   30

'But the wrongs love bears, will make
Love at length leave undertaking.'
No, the more men do it shake
In a ground of so firm making
Deeper still they drive the stake.   35

'Peace, I think that some give ear;
Come no more, lest I get anger.'
Bliss, I will my bliss forbear,
Fearing, sweet, you to endanger,
But my soul shall harbour there.   40

'Well, be gone, be gone, I say,
Lest that Argus' eyes perceive you.'
O, unjust is^n fortune's sway,
Which can make me thus to leave you,
And from louts to run away.   45

105^n

Unhappy sight, and hath she vanished by,
   So near, in so good time, so free a place?
   Dead glass, dost thou thy object so embrace
As what my heart still sees, thou canst not spy?
I swear by her I love and lack, that I   5
   Was not in fault, who bent thy dazzling race
   Only unto the heaven of Stella's face,
Counting but dust what in the way did lie.
   But cease, mine eyes, your tears do witness well
That you, guiltless thereof, your nectar missed.   10
Cursed be the page from whom the bad torch fell,
Cursed be the night which did your strife resist,
   Cursed be the coachman, which did drive so fast,
   With no worse curse than absence makes me taste.

---

42 *Argus' eyes*: watchful jealousy; Argus was the dog set by Juno to watch over
Io.

106

O absent presence, Stella is not here;
  False flattering hope, that with so fair a face
  Bare me in hand, that in this orphan place
Stella, I say my Stella, should appear.
What say'st thou now? Where is that dainty cheer   5
  Thou told'st mine eyes should help their famished case?
  But thou art gone, now that self-felt disgrace
Doth make me most to wish thy comfort near.
  But here I do store of fair ladies meet,
  Who may with charm of conversation sweet   10
Make in my heavy mould new thoughts to grow:
  Sure they prevail as much with me, as he
  That bade his friend, but then new maimed, to be
Merry with him, and not think of his woe.

107

  Stella, since thou so right a princess art
    Of all the powers which life bestows on me,
    That ere by them aught undertaken be
  They first resort unto that sovereign part;
  Sweet, for a while give respite to my heart,   5
    Which pants as though it still should leap to thee;
    And on my thoughts give thy lieutenancy
  To this great cause, which needs both use and art;[n]
    And as a queen, who from her presence sends
  Whom she employs, dismiss from thee my wit,   10
  Till it have wrought what thy own will attends.
  On servants' shame oft master's blame doth sit;
    O, let not fools in me thy works reprove,
    And scorning say, 'See, what it is to love!'

106 3 *Bare me in hand*: deceived me, misled me.
    10 *charm*: harmony, musical murmur.

107 7 *lieutenancy*: delegated authority.

108[n]

When sorrow, using mine own fire's might,
  Melts down his lead into my boiling breast,
  Through that dark furnace to my heart oppressed
There shines a joy from thee, my only light;
But soon as thought of thee breeds my delight,   5
  And my young soul flutters to thee, his nest;
  Most rude despair, my daily unbidden guest,
Clips straight my wings, straight wraps me in his night,
  And makes me then bow down my head, and say:
'Ah, what doth Phoebus' gold that wretch avail   10
Whom iron doors do keep from use of day?'
So strangely, alas, thy works in me prevail,
  That in my woes for thee thou art my joy,
  And in my joys for thee my only annoy.

108 10 *Phoebus' gold*: sunlight.

Additional poem

Philisides absent from Mira: a canzone[n]   [OP 5]

The lad Philisides
Lay by a river's side,
In flowery field a gladder eye to please;
His pipe was at his foot,
His lambs were him beside;   5
A widow turtle near on bared root
Sate wailing without boot;
Each thing, both sweet and sad,
Did draw his boiling brain
To think, and think with pain,   10
Of Mira's beams, eclipsed by absence bad.
And thus, with eyes made dim
With tears, he said, or sorrow said for him:

'O earth, once answer give:
So may thy stately grace   15
By north or south still rich adorned live;
So Mira long may be
On thy then blessed face,
Whose foot doth set a heaven on cursed thee;
I ask—now answer me—   20
If th'author of thy bliss,
Phoebus, that shepherd high,
Do turn from thee his eye,
Doth not thyself, when he long absent is,
Like rogue all ragged go,   25
And pine away with daily wasting woe?

'Tell me, you wanton brook:
So may your sliding race
Shun loathed-loving banks with cunning crook;
So in you ever new   30
Mira may look her face,
And make you fair with shadow of her hue,
So when to pay your due
To mother sea you come,
She chide you not for stay,   35
Nor beat you for your play:

31 *look*: look at.

Tell me, if your diverted streams become
Absented quite from you,
Are you not dried? Can you yourself renew?

'Tell me, you flowers fair,   40
Cowslip and columbine:
So may your make, this wholesome spring-time air,
With you embraced lie,
And lately thence untwine,
But with dew-drops engender children high;[n]   45
So may you never die,
But pulled by Mira's hand
Dress bosom hers, or head,
Or scatter on her bed:
Tell me, if husband spring-time leave your land,   50
When he from you is sent,
Wither not you, languished with discontent?

'Tell me, my seely pipe:
So may thee still betide
A cleanly cloth thy moistness for to wipe;   55
So may the cherries red
Of Mira's lips divide
Their sugared selves to kiss thy happy head;
So may her ears be led,
Her ears, where music lives,   60
To hear, and not despise,
Thy liribliring cries:
Tell, if that breath which thee thy sounding gives
Be absent far from thee,
Absent alone canst thou then piping be?   65

'Tell me, my lamb of gold:
So may'st thou long abide
The day well fed, the night in faithful fold;
So grow thy wool of note
In time, that, richly dyed,   70
It may be part of Mira's petticoat;

42 *make*: mate, sweetheart.
53 *seely*: silly; pitiful, innocent.
62 *liribliring*: onomatopoeic word for warbling of pipe, coined by Sidney.

Tell me, if wolves the throat
Have caught of thy dear dam,
Or she from thee be stayed,
Or thou from her be strayed,　　　　　　　75
Canst thou, poor lamb, become another's lamb?
Or rather, till thou die,
Still for thy dam with bea-waymenting cry?

'Tell me, O turtle true:
So may no fortune breed　　　　　　　　80
To make thee, nor thy better-loved, rue;
So may thy blessings swarm
That Mira may thee feed
With hand and mouth; with lap and breast keep warm:
Tell me, if greedy arm　　　　　　　　85
Do fondly take away
With traitor lime the one,
The other left alone;
Tell me, poor wretch, parted from wretched prey,
Disdain not you the green,　　　　　　　90
Wailing till death; shun you not to be seen?

'Earth, brook, flowers, pipe, lamb, dove,
Say all, and I with them:
'Absence is death, or worse, to them that love.'
So I, unlucky lad,　　　　　　　　95
Whom hills from her do hem,
What fits me now but tears, and sighings sad?
O fortune too too bad:
I rather would my sheep
Th'had'st killed with a stroke,　　　　　100
Burnt cabin, lost my cloak,
Than want one hour those eyes which my joys keep.
O, what doth wailing win?
Speech without end were better not begin.

'My song, climb thou the wind　　　　　105
Which Holland sweet now gently sendeth in,
That on his wings the level thou may'st find

77 *Or rather*: Or will you rather.
78 *bea-waymenting*: lamenting with baas or bleats.
105 *the wind*: i.e. the East wind.
107 *the level*: aim, line of fire (archery term).

To hit, but kissing hit,
Her ears, the weights of wit.
If thou know not for whom thy master dies,   110
These marks shall make thee wise:
She is the herdess fair that shines in dark,
And gives her kids no food but willow's bark.'

This said, at length he ended
His oft sigh-broken ditty,   115
Then rase; but rase on legs with faintness bended,
With skin in sorrow dyed,
With face the plot of pity,
With thoughts, which thoughts their own
    tormentors tried,
He rase, and straight espied   120
His ram, who to recover
The ewe another loved
With him proud battle proved:
He envied such a death in sight of lover,
And always westward eyeing,   125
More envied Phoebus for his western flying.[n]

113 *willow's bark*: i.e. she forsakes her kids.
116 *rase*: rose.
118 *plot*: map.

The Psalms of David

Psalm 13: Usque quo domine

1. How long, O lord, shall I forgotten be?
   What, ever?
   How long wilt thou thy hidden face from me
   Dissever?
2. How long shall I consult with careful sprite   5
   In anguish?
   How long shall I with foes triumphant might
   Thus languish?

3. Behold me, lord; let to thy hearing creep
   My crying;   10
   Nay, give me eyes, and light, lest that I sleep
   In dying.
4. Lest my foe brag, that in my ruin he
   Prevailed,
   And at my fall they joy that, troublous, me   15
   Assailed.

5. No, no; I trust on thee, and joy in thy
   Great pity:
   Still therefore of thy graces shall be my
   Song's ditty.   20

Psalm 23: Dominus regit me

1. The lord, the lord, my shepherd is,
   And so can never I
   Taste misery.
2. He rests me in green pasture his;
   By waters still and sweet   5
   He guides my feet.

3. He me revives; leads me the way
  Which righteousness doth take,
   For his name's sake.
4. Yea, though I should through valleys stray 10
  Of death's dark shade, I will
   No whit fear ill.

For thou, dear lord, thou me besett'st;
  Thy rod and thy staff be
   To comfort me. 15
5. Before me thou a table sett'st,
  Even when foe's envious eye
   Doth it espy.

With oil thou dost anoint my head,
  And so my cup dost fill 20
   That it doth spill.
6. Thus, thus, shall all my days be fed;
  This mercy is so sure
   It shall endure;
And long, yea, long abide I shall 25
  There where the lord of all
   Doth hold his hall.

Psalm 29: Afferte domino

1. Ascribe unto the lord of light,
  Ye men of power, even by birth-right,
  Ascribe all glory and might.
2. Ascribe due glory to his name,
  And in his ever glorious frame 5
  Of sanctuary do the same.

3. His voice is on the waters found;
   His voice doth threatening thunders sound,
   Yea, through the waters doth resound.
4. The voice of that lord, ruling us,   10
   Is strong, though he be gracious,
   And ever, ever glorious.
5. By voice of great Jehovah we
   The highest cedars broken see,
   Even cedars which on Leban be;   15
6. Nay, like young calves in leaps are borne,
   And Leban self, with nature's scorn,
   And Sirion like young unicorn.[n]
7. His voice doth flashing flames divide;
   His voice have trembling deserts tried,   20
   Even deserts, where the Arabs bide.
8. His voice makes hinds their calves to cast;
   His voice makes bald the forest waste;
   But in his church his fame is placed.
9. His justice seat the world sustains;   25
   Of furious floods he holds the reins,
   And this his rule for aye remains.
10. God to his people strength shall give,
   That they in peace shall blessed live.

Psalm 38: Domine ne in furore

1. Lord, while that thy rage doth bide,
   Do not chide,
   Nor in anger chastise me;
2. For thy shafts have pierced me sore,
   And yet more: 5
   Still thy hands upon me be.

15 *Leban*: Mount Lebanon.

   3. No sound part (caused by thy wrath)
      My flesh hath,
   Nor my sins let my bones rest;
   4. For my faults are highly spread   10
      On my head,
   Whose foul weights have me oppressed.

   5. My wounds putrify and stink,
      In the sink
   6. Of my filthy folly laid;   15
   Earthly I do bow and crook,
      With a look
   Still in mourning cheer arrayed.

   7. In my reins hot torment reigns;
      There remains   20
   8. Nothing in my body sound;
   I am weak and broken sore,
      Yea, I roar,
   In my heart such grief is found.

   9. Lord, before thee I do lay   25
      What I pray;
   My sighs are not hid from thee;
  10. My heart pants; gone is my might;
      Even the light
   Of mine eyes abandons me.   30

  11. From my plague kin, neighbour, friend,
      Far off wend;
  12. But who for my life do wait,
   They lay snares; they nimble be,
      Who hunt me,   35
   Speaking evil, thinking deceit.

  13. But I like a man become
      Deaf and dumb,
   Little hearing, speaking less;
  14. I even as such kind of wight,   40
      Senseless quite,
   Word with word do not repress.

16 *Earthly*: earthwards.

15. For on thee, lord, without end
    I attend;
  My God, thou wilt hear my voice: 45
16. For I said, 'Hear, lest they be
    Glad on me,
  Whom my fall doth make rejoice.'

17. Sure, I do but halting go,
    And my woe   50
  Still my o'erthwart neighbour is.
18. Lo, I now to mourn begin
    For my sin,
  Telling mine iniquities.

19. But the while they live and grow   55
    In great show;
20. Many mighty wrongful foes
  Who do evil for good, to me
    Enemies be:
  Why? Because I virtue chose.   60

21. Do not, lord, then, me forsake;
    Do not take
22. Thy dear presence far from me;
  Haste, O lord, that I be stayed
    By thy aid;   65
  My salvation is in thee.

Notes

Poems from The Old Arcadia

i. This sonnet is sung by the prince Pyrocles (who is disguised as an Amazon to gain access to the Arcadian princess Philoclea) at the end of his argument with his friend Musidorus about love. Musidorus has asserted that 'as the love of heaven makes one heavenly, the love of virtue virtuous, so doth the love of the world make one become worldly, and this effeminate love of a woman doth so womanize a man that, if you yield to it, it will not only make you a famous Amazon, but a launderer, a distaff spinner, or whatsoever other vile occupations their idle heads can imagine and their weak hands perform' (a reference to the humiliations undergone by Hercules for love of Omphale). Pyrocles agrees that the love of a woman makes a man womanish, but asserts, as in this sonnet, that such a love is glorious. (*Old Arcadia*, pp. 28–9.) In the *New Arcadia* the sonnet is used in a more dramatic way; Musidorus comes upon a splendidly dressed Amazon whom he does not recognize as his friend Pyrocles, and hears her sing the song, which makes him suspect her identity (*Works*, i. 75–6).

ii. This poem belongs to the tradition of the *contreblason*, or catalogue of uglinesses rather than beauties, of which there are many examples from the fourteenth century onwards. Donne's *The Anagram* is a familiar later example (Gardner (ed.), *Elegies and Songs and Sonnets* (1965), p. 21); and Shakespeare's 'Dark Lady' sonnets bear some relation to the tradition. Mopsa, the daughter of the herdsman Dametas, is described in this poem, which is ascribed in the *Old Arcadia* to 'Alethes, an honest man of that time'; in the *New Arcadia* the hospitable Kalander quotes it, ascribing it to 'a pleasant fellow of my acquaintance' (*Old Arcadia*, pp. 30–1; *Works*, i. 21).

iii. This singing competition is the second item in the First Eclogues in the *Old Arcadia*; Lalus, an Arcadian shepherd 'accounted one of the best singers among them', challenges the seeming-shepherd Dorus—who is the prince Musidorus of Macedon in disguise—having observed his skill in dancing in the symbolic contest between happy and unhappy shepherds which went before. The singing contest occurred in classical eclogues (Theocritus, *Idylls*, 5–9, Virgil, Eclogue 5); but Sidney's immediate models were probably Sannazaro and Montemayor (Sannazaro, *Arcadia*, Ecloga 2; Montemayor, *Diana*, pp. 224–7). The method of the contest is for each singer to introduce fresh and more taxing verse-forms, which his opponent must continue. The forms used by Sidney are even more taxing than those of Sannazaro and Montemayor. Lalus opens in *terza rima* with trisyllabic rhymes, which he himself abandons, outdone by Dorus, for disyllabic rhymes in line 72.

iii. 7. Cf. note on *Astrophil and Stella*, 54. 13.

iii. 63. *To set a pearl in steel so meanly varnished*: Cf. Pamela's *impresa* in the *New Arcadia* of 'a very rich diamond set but in a black horn', with the motto '*yet still myself*', referring to her constant nobility even in the simple dress imposed on her by her father (*Works*, i. 90). Dorus's image also refers to Pamela, though he avoids naming her, since he is attempting to conceal his love for her from the company at large.

iii. 72. *Of fairer death how can I make election?*: an almost proverbial sentiment; cf. the last line of Petrarch's *Canzoniere*, cxl, translated by Surrey as 'Sweet is his death, that takes his end by love'; cf. also *Astrophil and Stella*, 42. 14.

iii. 87. At the end of Book I of the *Old Arcadia* Philoclea and Pamela are pursued by a lion and bear respectively: Pamela, 'whether it were she had heard that such was the best refuge against that beast, or that fear . . . brought forth the effects of wisdom . . . no sooner saw the bear coming towards her, but she fell down flat upon her face' (*Old Arcadia*, p. 51; *Works*, i. 122).

iii. 101.   A reference to the procedure, in either black or white magic, of making a charmed circle into which a spirit is summoned.

iii. 115.   Lalus abandons *terza rima*, having descended to masculine rhymes in line 100, for medial rhymes, which are used in several poems in Sannazaro's *Arcadia* (Ecloga 2, 20–39; 10, 79–163).

iii. 147.   Dorus having easily adopted Lalus's medial rhymes, Lalus introduces a complex stanza-form, which, however, Dorus complexifies still further by making each stanza open with the final line of its predecessor. Lalus, defeated by this, gives up the struggle in line 166, returning to the trisyllabic *terza rima* with which he opened; Dorus, however, outdoing him in courtesy as well as in poetic skill, echoes his acknowledgement of defeat (173), and concludes in the same form.

iii. 156–72.   Most of the MSS. contain an earlier version of these lines, in which the similes are 'a beast' and 'a vision', rather than 'a flower' and 'a shade' (see Ringler, p. 20).

iii. 166.   *O, he is marred, that is for others made*: quoted by Nashe in *Will Summer's Last Will and Testament* (*Works*, ed. McKerrow, iii. 238, line 145).

iv.   This description of Cupid is attributed in the *Old Arcadia* to Dicus, one of the Arcadian shepherds, in the First Eclogues; in the *New Arcadia* Miso quotes the poem, which she says a 'good wold woman' gave her. Dicus wears a picture of the monstrous Cupid in his bosom, and the 'good wold woman' shows Miso the picture of 'Love' (*Old Arcadia*, pp. 64–6; *Works*, i. 238–9). The poem, an attack on the sensual love of which the heroes of the *Arcadia* are victims, is a kind of *contre-blason* of Cupid (cf. OA iii). The notion of Cupid as a hangman may derive from the common association of marriage and hanging, as in the proverb 'Wedding and hanging is destiny' (Tilley, *Proverbs*, W2327). Cupid himself is associated with hanging in some of the emblem books (Achilles Bocchius, *Symbolicarum quaestionum libri quinque* (Bologna, 1555), xi and xii). Cf. also *Much Ado about Nothing*, III. ii. 11–12.

v.   This poem, from the First Eclogues, is closely modelled on Sannazaro's eighth eclogue (lines 62–5). In Sannazaro's poem old Eugenio offers advice against love to the melancholy Clonico; its form, however, is less complex than Sidney's, being *terza rima* throughout. In the First Eclogues the poem forms an interruption to Histor's narrative of Erona; as Histor is about to recite the dialogue-poem relating to her story (OA xv), Geron starts up and strikes on the shoulder the young shepherd Philisides, who 'had all this time lain upon the ground, at the foot of a cypress tree, leaning upon his elbow with so deep a melancholy that his senses carried to his mind no delight from any of their objects' (*Old Arcadia*, pp. 71–6). The poem does not appear in the *New Arcadia*, where the role of Philisides is much diminished.

v. 55.   This imagery of woman's fickleness derives originally from Ovid (*Heroides*, v, 115–16), and had become traditional; cf., for instance, Wyatt's 'Since in a net I seek to hold the wind' (translating Petrarch). Sidney's immediate source, however, is Sannazaro's Ecloga 8, lines 10–12, which are exactly translated here, except that 'hand' is substituted for 'heart'. This is the only direct translation which has been traced in Sidney's original poetry.

v. 63–5.   In the mouth of Histor, who interrupts the dialogue at this point (see opening note on this poem), Sidney pays tribute to his friend Sir Edward Dyer, whose best-known poem, 'A Fancy', contains the couplet: O fraile unconstant kynd, and safe in trust to noe man! Noe woomen angels be, and loe, my mystris is a woeman; (R. M. Sargent, *Life and Lyrics of Dyer* (1935), p. 186). These lines, in couplets rather than *terza rima*, seem to have been added by Sidney in revision.

v. 86.   *No man doth wish his horse should aged be*: Amphialus, in the *New Arcadia*, wins a contest with the showy Phalantus thanks to choosing 'a horse, whom (though he was near twenty years old) he preferred, for a piece of sure service, before a great number of younger' (*Works*, i. 414).

v. 123-34. This list of tasks which drive away thoughts of love derives from Ovid's *Remedia Amoris*, 315-16, 178-210, though there is also an analogous passage in Sannazaro's Ecloga 8, 121-32.

vi. Musidorus (Dorus) sings these elegiacs to Pamela as part of the First Eclogues, accompanying himself with a lute which he finds lying under her feet, and gazing at her as he sings (*Old Arcadia*, pp. 79-80). The poem is not used in the *New Arcadia*.

vii. Pyrocles (Cleophila) seizes the lute from Musidorus's hands (see preceding note), and sings these sapphics while gazing at Philoclea, though thinly disguising the object of his love by addressing himself to Hope, rather than directly to Philoclea (*Old Arcadia*, pp. 81-2; *Works*, i. 143-4). Metrically and poetically this is perhaps the most successful of Sidney's poems in quantitative verse.

viii. This dialogue in hexameters is the final item in the *Old Arcadia* First Eclogues (it does not appear in the *New Arcadia*). Musidorus and Pyrocles covertly discuss their respective situations in love, each disguised and as yet unaccepted by the princess he loves.

viii. 56. *of virtue you have left proofs to the whole world*: Pyrocles's heroic adventures are told in detail by Musidorus in the *New Arcadia* (*Works*, i. 189-215, 261-307); they are more briefly described in the *Old Arcadia* (*Old Arcadia*, p. 11 and *passim*).

viii. 71. Cf. Romeo's 'He jests at scars that never felt a wound' (*Romeo and Juliet*, ii. ii. 1).

viii. 92. *Come from the marble bowers, many times the gay arbour of anguish*: quoted late in her life by Lady Anne Clifford, whose first husband was Sidney's nephew, Philip Herbert: 'The marble pillars of Knole in Kent and Wilton in Wiltshire were to me oftentimes but the gay Harbours of anguish' (G. C. Williamson, *Lady Anne Clifford* 1922, p. 173).

viii. 115-43. The tree catalogue is a traditional poetic exercise deriving from the classical poets; e.g. Ovid, *Metamorphoses*, x, 90-104. Cf. Chaucer's *Parliament of Fowls*, line 178f.; *Knight's Tale*, line 2921f.; *The Faerie Queene*, i. i. 8-9. Sidney's catalogue is a little confused; the palm tree appears twice (lines 127-8, 137-8) for instance. Sidney appears to have planned to write a catalogue of trees in prose for the bathing scene in the *New Arcadia*, to judge by a hiatus in that passage (*Works*, i. 216).

viii. 138. Both the attributes of the palm tree employed by Sidney here—its rising under a burden and its joining of male to female—were used in *imprese* (i.e. emblems with a personal reference) known to him (Paolo Giovio, *Dialogo dell' Imprese* (Lyons, 1574), pp. 81, 221; Bodleian MS. Rawl. D. 345, fol. 23); Sidney used the loving nature of palm trees for the *impresa* of the loving husband Argalus in the *New Arcadia* (*Works*, i. 423). He is fond of playing on different meanings of the word 'sense'; cf. note on AS 36.

viii. 141-3. Pamela is consistently associated with stately trees; in Book 3 of the *Old Arcadia* Pamela and Musidorus cut verses in the bark of a pine tree (*Old Arcadia*, pp. 198-9).

ix. Sung by Pyrocles in a cave and overheard by Gynecia (*Works*, iv. 88-90). Cf. the repetitions of 'in vain' here with those in CS xxi, and also perhaps with Sidney's death-bed assertion that all things in his former life had been 'vain, vain, vain' (*Misc. Prose*, p. 169).

xi. 6. *My weeds, desire, cut out in endless folds*: This image is of a piece with the emblematic costumes worn by characters in the *Arcadia*; its specific source may be the opening of Montemayor's *Diana*, where the forsaken Sireno wears 'a long grey coat as rugged as his haps' (*Diana*, p. 11).

xii.   Out of context this sonnet has a riddling effect; in its context the meaning is clear. Pyrocles is loved by both of Philoclea's parents, Basilius, who has not penetrated his disguise, and Gynecia, who has; but not by Philoclea herself (*Old Arcadia*, pp. 113–14).

xiii. 15–16.   The image of writing in the sand, a traditional one for vain endeavour, occurs in one of the poems of Montemayor translated by Sidney, which is perhaps his immediate source here (CS xviii).

xiv.   This rustic singing competition, from the Second Eclogues in the *Old Arcadia*, succeeds a more courtly and dignified one, between Dicus and Musidorus, in which Dicus reproached Musidorus with being in love. The debate of Nico and Pas is in comic contrast, both in theme, language, and the comparative simplicity of its verse-forms; there are no feminine rhymes, and only the simplest variation in line length, from iambic hexameters to pentameters (line 51 to end); contrast OA vii. Cf. Sidney's comment on the pastoral poem in the *Defence of Poetry*, that it can 'sometimes show that contentions for trifles can get but a trifling victory' (*Misc. Prose*, p. 93).

xiv. 25.   *by my hat*: The duck uses this simple oath in Chaucer's *Parliament of Fowls*, line 589.

xiv. 85.   The white sparrow probably derives from Skelton's Philip Sparrow; cf. also AS 83.

xiv. 92.   Cf. the image of Cupid as a hangman in OA iv. The implication presumably is that Pas should hang himself.

xiv. 106.   *beauties from her fell*: Probably this means 'beauties from her skin (fell)', rather than 'beauties which fell from her'. Greville uses a similar conceit in *Caelica*, xxii:

> Was it for this that I might Mira see
> Washing the water with her beauties white?
>   (Greville, *Poems and Dramas*, ed. Bullough (1938), i. 85.)

xiv. 116.   This image is probably taken from the poem of Montemayor's which Sidney translated (CS xix), on *Sireno . . . holding his mistress's glass before her, looking upon her while she viewed herself.*

xiv. 141–6.   The answer to both these riddles might be 'a lover': one who moves and sees only with his mistress's eyes, her eyes and limbs being made his by love; and a hopeless lover who will find peace only in death. This interpretation would suit both the feeble-mindedness of Nico and Pas and their use of sub-Petrarchan imagery. The final riddles and award of the prize occur at the end of Virgil's Third Eclogue, on which this poem is freely based.

xv.   This poem belongs to the most elaborate sub-plot in the *Old Arcadia*, the story of Erona and Plangus, which the shepherd Histor begins to tell in the First Eclogues. Erona, daughter of the king of Lydia, out of contempt for love defaces and destroys all the images of Cupid in the realm; Cupid avenges this blasphemy by making her fall in love with the base-born Antiphilus, who despises her, while a neighbouring tyrant, King Otaves, makes war on Lydia for the sake of her love. Pyrocles and Musidorus rescue her from Otaves, but meanwhile Antiphilus, now her husband, allies with Artaxia, the queen of Persia, who puts Erona in prison and threatens to put her to death if Pyrocles and Musidorus do not rescue her within two years. A young man called Plangus falls in love with her while she is in prison, and wanders through Asia Minor in search of the princes. On his way through Arcadia he meets the sage shepherd Boulon, with whom he has this debate, reported by another shepherd, Histor, in the Second Eclogues. The story of Erona, and in particular the character of Plangus, is developed much further in the *New Arcadia*, where Plangus's interlocutor in the debate (rather inappropriately, since he is scarcely a figure of wisdom) is Basilius. (*Old Arcadia*, pp. 67–71; 146–52; 356; *Works*, i. 214, 226–37, 261–2, 329–38). The plot was used by Beaumont and Fletcher for the play *Cupid's Revenge* (1615). Some of the philosophical ideas are discussed by W. R. Elton in his book on *King Lear* (*King Lear and the Gods* (San Marino, Calif., 1966), pp. 34–62).

xv. 129.   *but a baiting-place is all our portion*: Cf. the description of Basilius consulting the Delphic Oracle at the beginning of the *Arcadia*, moved with 'the vanity which possesseth many who, making a perpetual mansion of this poor baiting place of man's life, are desirous to know the certainty of things to come' (*Old Arcadia*, p. 5). This image, as well as the foolishness of Basilius in general, makes the alteration of 'Boulon' to 'Basilius' in the *New Arcadia* rather unsatisfactory.

xv. 177.   *The ass did hurt, when he did think to kiss*: a reference to the fable of Aesop's in which an ass, trying to compete with a playful young dog, fawns on his master and kicks him (Aesop, *Fables*, trs. Caxton (?1550), fol. 62ᵛ).

xvi.   This echo poem is sung by Philisides (who in the *Old Arcadia* is clearly based on Sidney himself; cf. OA xxxi) in the Second Eclogues in both versions of the *Arcadia* (*Works*, iv. 152–4; i. 352–3). There were a few earlier English echo poems, for instance one by Gascoigne in Leicester's entertainment of the Queen at Kenilworth in 1575, which Sidney saw, but there were none in hexameters. (J. G. Nichols, *Progresses of Queen Elizabeth I* (1823), i. 494–6; John Grange, *The Golden Aphroditis* (1577), sigs. J1–J2; Henry Wotton, *A Courtly Controversy of Cupid's Cartels* (1578), p. 238.) The irregularity of the quantitative metre here suggests that the poem is one of Sidney's earlier experiments.

xvii.   Pyrocles sings to Philoclea, in the Second Eclogues from the *Old Arcadia*, in 'Anacreon's kind of verses' (*Old Arcadia*, pp. 163–4); the poem does not appear in the *New Arcadia*. Possibly this may confirm Thomas Moffett's statement that Sidney on his death-bed 'blushed at even the most casual mention of his own Anacreontics, and begged his brother . . . that not any of this sort of poems should come forth into the light' (Moffett, *Nobilis*, edd. Heltzel and Hudson (San Marino, Calif., 1940), p. 91); though it is more likely that the word 'Anacreontics' refers to secular verse in general. The Greek poems attributed to Anacreon were printed in 1554 by Sidney's friend Henri Estienne (Stephanus); Ronsard also uses metres which approximate to Anacreon's. As in the Greek poems themselves, the metre is felt as accentual as much as quantitative, the accent almost always corresponding with the long syllables.

xviii.   Pyrocles follows the Anacreontics, at the request of Basilius in the Second Eclogues, with these 'Phaleuciacs', to which he accompanies himself on a lyre. The metre is taken from Catullus, and is rather difficult to sustain. The last syllable can be either short or long. Like the Anacreontics, this poem does not appear in the *New Arcadia*.

xix.   Musidorus concludes the Second Eclogues with this, the most complex of the poems in quantitative verse. The metre, which is taken from Horace, is very imperfectly executed, according to Sidney's own rules, and the theme of woods does not seem especially appropriate to this section of the *Arcadia*. Ringler suggests that the poem is an early experiment, like OA xvi. The theme is comparable to Rixus's speech in praise of the life of a forester in *The Lady of May* (1578 or 9; *Misc. Prose*, p. 29). A poem with the same opening lines, but in accentual verse, was set by Dowland (*Second Book of Songs or Ayres* (1600)).

xx.   Phoebus is the deity of Arcadia, referred to at times by the characters— though more in the *New Arcadia* than the *Old*—as if he were equivalent to the Christian God. Basilius reads these verses to Pyrocles to assure him that he bears greater devotion to him 'than to any unseen deity' (*Old Arcadia*, p. 177). The poem does not appear in the *New Arcadia*.

xxi.   Pyrocles discovers these verses by Gynecia set in his cave under 'a little wax light' (*Old Arcadia*, p. 181). The sonnet reflects her painful dilemmas; she is in love with her daughter's suitor, Pyrocles, whose transvestite disguise she has penetrated. The imagery of darkness suits the fact that she is writing inside a cave. The phrase 'mangled mind' (line 5) occurs also in the farewell to love at the end of *Certain Sonnets* (CS xxii):

> Desire, desire, I have too dearly bought,
> With price of mangled mind, thy worthless ware.

The use of a single rhyme throughout reinforces the painful repetitiveness of Gynecia's reflections.

xxii.   This famous sonnet is set in a curious context in the *Old Arcadia*, where Musidorus is trying for his own ends to make the shrewish Miso jealous of her husband, Dametas. He tells Miso that on a hill near Mantinea he saw a beautiful shepherdess; 'in her lap lay a shepherd so wrapped up in that well liked place, that I could discern no piece of his face, but as mine eyes were attent in that, her angel-like voice strake mine ears with this song'. The shepherdess, Charita, is purely Musidorus's invention; the shepherd (in his story) is Dametas (*Old Arcadia*, pp. 189–91).

xxiii.   Musidorus quotes this poem, Dametas's (invented) reply to Charita (see preceding note), to Miso: 'as if the shepherd that lay before her had been organs which were only to be blown by her breath, she had no sooner ended with the joining her sweet lips together, but that he recorded to her music this rural poesy' (*Old Arcadia*, p. 191). The rhetorical structure of the poem is complex, as befits Musidorus, who is the most accomplished singer in the *Arcadia*: a neat use of *correlatio*, with four elements in each of the first two verses, and two, representing consummation (skin and flesh), in the final one, drawn together in the last two lines. But the imagery is rural—even agricultural, as in 'two fair ox's eyes'—as befits the supposed speaker, Dametas.

xxiv.   This is probably the first English madrigal. It is sung by Basilius in the *Old Arcadia* as he sits on the grass with his daughter Philoclea, 'seeing the sun, what speed he made to leave our West, to do his office in the other hemisphere' (*Old Arcadia*, p. 207).

xxv.   Basilius also sings this madrigal (see previous note), looking at the disguised Pyrocles, 'whom now the moon did beautify with her shining most at the full' (*Old Arcadia*, p. 213). In both madrigals Pyrocles is praised as a second sun, appropriately, since in an earlier song (OA xx) Basilius has asserted that he worships him rather than Phoebus.

xxvi.   This *blason*, or catalogue of beauties, is attributed to Philisides in the *Old Arcadia*: Pyrocles has heard it, and remembers it when he sees Philoclea lying on her bed, just before the consummation of their love; though Sidney says, 'Do not think (fair ladies) his thoughts had such leisure as to run over so long a ditty; the only general fancy of it came into his mind, fixed upon the sense of the sweet subject' (*Old Arcadia*, pp. 237–42). The attribution of the song to Philisides suggests that it was probably written quite early, though Sidney revised it carefully (Ringler). In the *New Arcadia* the song is given more dramatic plausibility: Pyrocles himself composes it, accompanying himself with a lute, as he watches Philoclea bathing.

xxvi. 25–6.   Cf. Suckling's *At a Wedding*:

> For streaks of red were mingled there,
> Such as are on a Katherine pear
>   The side that's next the sun.

xxvi. 98. *Like cunning painter shadowing white*: perhaps a recollection of Sidney's conversation with Nicholas Hilliard, recounted in the latter's *Art of Limning* (Nicholas Hilliard . 'The Arte of Limning', ed. P. Norman, Walpole Society, vol. i (1912), pp. 27, 29–30). Miniaturists represented roundness by whitening the highlights for brilliance, rather than darkening the shadows (Edward Norgate, *Miniatura*, ed. Martin Hardie (1919), p. 22).

xxvi. 116. *the hate-spot ermelin*: The ermine was believed to die rather than allow her skin to become dirty; cf. note on AS 86.

xxvii. This is one of the earliest English epithalamiums, based on Gil Polo's epithalamium for the marriage of Diana and Sireno in the continuation of Montemayor's *Diana*, though only the first line and the eighth and tenth stanzas are closely related to it (*Diana*, pp. 378–9). The epithalamium, as suits the discussion of marriage in the Third Eclogues, has a more didactic tone than most examples of the form (Cf. Virginia Tufte, *The Poetry of Marriage* (Los Angeles . Calif., 1970), pp. 152–6).

xxvii. 3. Cupid is identified with inordinate desire or lust, which is inimica ι to marriage, both here and in lines 55–63. Cf. the cruel Cupid depicted in Spenser's House of Busirane (*Faerie Queene*, iii, xi). Sidney consistently identifies Cupid with a bad kind of love, though not always in such an extreme way as in Dicus's description of him as a monster (OA iv).

xxvii. 16. The traditional elm and vine image is derived from one of the epithalamia of Catullus, number lxii.

xxvii. 57. Cf. the imagery of Sidney's 'Farewell to Love', CS xxii. 3: 'Grow rich in that which never taketh rust'.

xxviii. This poem belongs to the medieval tradition of the fabliau, though it is perhaps not a very successful example. The touches of archaism suggest that Sidney deliberately attributes to the ill-bred Nico a poem which is old-fashioned in form and style. Greville wrote a more successful fabliau, also on the subject of a poor man's wife courted by a nobleman, in *Caelica*, l, giving it the form of a pair of sonnets. Sidney's fabliau amply demonstrates the dangers of jealousy, condemned in the epithalamium which precedes it (xxvii. 82–98).

xxviii. 14. *Who yet was good, because she knew none ill*: Cf. Sidney's description of Philoclea, 'who was in their degree of well doing, to whom the not knowing of evil serveth for a ground of virtue' (*Works*, i. 169); but cf. also Philanax's advice to Basilius: 'he can not be good, that knows not why he is good' (*Old Arcadia*, p. 8).

xxx. This poem forms a tribute to the wisdom in statecraft of Sidney's friend Hubert Languet, the Protestant statesman whom he met when he was French ambassador in Vienna in 1573, and with whom he maintained a correspondence until his death in 1581. (The correspondence, which is in Latin, was edited and translated by S. A. Pears (1845), selected from the original edition of 1633) Sidney and Languet had been together 'on Ister bank', i.e. in Vienna, in August 1573 and 1574. In spite of Sidney's condemnation of Spenser in *The Defence of Poetry* for 'that same framing of his style to an old rustic language' (*Misc. Prose*, p. 110), this poem is written in archaic diction of a courtly kind, distinguishable from the rather 'Drab' diction of Nico's fabliau which precedes it (xxviii). The theme (that a strong aristocracy is better than tyranny) and the stanza-form link this poem with many of Greville's. It has only a very general relevance to the discussion of marriage in the Third Eclogues, in that it concerns harmony in society.

xxx. 28. The reading 'our wits', from the 1613 and later editions and some of the MSS., has been preferred to 'your'. Philisides does not appear to be addressing a strongly imagined audience in this poem, nor is it likely that he would think that God was not beyond his own wit.

xxx. 40. *worthy Coredens*: Coredens, evidently one of Sidney's friends, occurs also in the prose of the Third Eclogues (p. 82), and is mentioned in the Fourth Eclogues (*Old Arcadia*, p. 340). He is described as also in love with Mira and melancholy, like Philisides. He has not been identified with certainty; the likeliest possibilities are Greville, Dyer, and Edward Wotton. The last, the only one who was with Sidney in Vienna (see opening of *The Defence of Poetry*) seems the likeliest candidate. He was six years older than Sidney, so might have served him as a mentor in place of Languet.

xxx. 58. *envy harboureth most in feeble hearts*: perhaps a parody of the Chaucerian tag, 'Pity runneth soon in gentle heart'.

xxx. 89. Cf. OA xxvi. 116, and AS 86.

xxx. 109. Cf. Ovid's description of the vegetarian life of men in the Golden Age, and their descent to butchery (*Metamorphoses*, xv. 75–142).

xxx. 152. *A plaint of guiltless hurt doth pierce the sky*: perhaps a reference to Abel's blood crying out for vengeance (Genesis 4:10), especially as this too is a creation story.

xxxi. This poem, like its predecessor, may bear some relation to Sidney's friendship with Languet, since Languet urged Sidney to marry and seems to have felt that he was slow in doing so (*Sidney–Languet Correspondence*, ed. S. A. Pears (1845), p. 102).

xxxi. 75. Cf. Shakespeare's Sonnet xiii. 14: 'You had a father; let your son say so.'

xxxi. 98. A reference to Histor's account of the troubles of Erona, who condemned Cupid, in the First Eclogues; cf. note on OA xv.

xxxi. 118–20. These lines were omitted in the 1590 *Arcadia*, where the poem appeared in the First Eclogues, separate from Kala's marriage.

xxxii. This poem is sung in the Fourth Eclogues of the *Old Arcadia*, when the Arcadian shepherds lament the (supposed) death of their king Basilius, and others use the occasion 'to record their own private sorrows' (*Old Arcadia*, pp. 328–30). In the *New Arcadia*, where the figures of Strephon and Klaius are developed much further, the poem is recited by a friend of theirs called Lamon as part of the First Eclogues. Strephon and Klaius are two shepherds both in love, but without rivalry, with a mysterious shepherdess called Urania, who may be equivalent to divine love. This and the following poem lament her departure from Arcadia, which in the *New Arcadia* occurs at the very beginning of the romance. (*Works*, i. 5–8; cf. K. Duncan-Jones, 'Sidney's Urania', *RES* xvii (1966), 123–32.) The sestina form used by Sidney is identical to that used by Petrarch (*Canzoniere*, cccxxxii) and Sannazaro (*Ecloga* 4); it is different from Montemayor's (*Diana*, pp. 191–3). Sannazaro's sestina resembles Sidney's in being a despairing dialogue between two shepherds, with some links in style and imagery. Sidney's poem has been discussed by Empson (*Seven Types of Ambiguity* (1930), pp. 45–50) and John Crowe Ransom (*The New Criticism* (1941), pp. 108–14).

xxxii. 75. The reading of the 1590 and 1593 Folios, 'is this', has been preferred on grounds of metre to the MSS. reading 'this is'.

xxxiii. After their double sestina (see preceding poem), 'as though all this had been but the taking of a taste to their wailings, Strephon again began this dizain; which was answered unto him in that kind of verse which is called the crown' (*Old Arcadia*, pp. 331–4). The word 'crown', equivalent to the Latin *corona* = wreath or garland, is used in a technical sense to describe a circular sequence of linked poems; cf. Donne's *La Corona*. In the *New Arcadia* the poem is recited by Lamon in the Second Eclogues (*Works*, i. 348–52). Like its predecessor, the poem is a consistent use of paradox and hyperbole, but it lacks the formal and rhetorical tension of the double sestina.

xxxiii. 63.   Cf. the *impresa* borne by Amphialus in the *New Arcadia* of the torpedo fish, representing the fact that the object of his pursuit (Philoclea) is, once caught, his destroyer. The properties of the torpedo fish are described by Pliny (*Natural History*, 32. ii).

xxxiv.   This poem follows on Philisides's account of his own upbringing and youth in Samothea, which is patently an account of Sidney's own life (Introduction, p. ix; *Old Arcadia*, pp. 335–40). In the *New Arcadia* the poem is rather unconvincingly transferred to Amphialus, who has it sung to Philoclea by 'a fine boy' (*Works*, i. 394–9). Sidney wrote a handful of poems about Philisides and Mira (cf. Additional Poem, p. 191) of which this is the most elaborate. It may well have some biographical reference. In the prose of the Fourth Eclogues Philisides goes on to say that his friend Coredens was also in love with Mira, also hopelessly. The situation of two friends in love with one lady recurs repeatedly in Sidney's poetry; cf. also Dyer's *Amaryllis*. The fact that Mira is a waiting woman of Diana suggests an allusion to one of Queen Elizabeth's ladies; but this would not get us very far in identification. Sidney's sister Mary was summoned to the court by the Queen in 1575, soon after Sidney's return from his travels, and attended the Queen for the next two years. It is possible that both Mira and Urania belong to amorous fictions invented by Sidney for her before he had the idea of the *Arcadia*. It certainly seems probable that the name of Mira's original was Mary. Some sort of Petrarchan game played by Sidney and his sister would suit their literary interests and the little we know of their relationship (mainly the fact that he composed the *Arcadia* for her). The poem can however stand by itself as an adaptation of the theme of the Judgement of Paris, given a satirical twist by the peevishness of the two goddesses.

xxxiv. 36.   Samothea was believed to be the original name of Britain, so called after Samothes, one of the sons of Japhet (William Harrison, 'Description of Britaine' in Holinshed, *First volume of Chronicles* (1572), sig. A1). The fact that Samothea is an old name for England indicates the autobiographical character of Philisides in the *Old Arcadia*; Sidney is otherwise careful to maintain the Greek fiction in his place-names.

xxiv. 141.   The amber crown probably corresponds with amber-coloured hair.

xxxv.   Agelastus, in the *Old Arcadia* Fourth Eclogues, 'rather cried out than sang' this pastoral elegy in grief for Basilius; in the *New Arcadia* it is 'roared out' in lamentation for the death of Amphialus, near the end of the revised fragment (*Old Arcadia*, pp. 334–8; *Works*, i. 498–502). It belongs to the Greek tradition of the pastoral elegy, deriving originally from Moschus's lament for Bion; cf. also Theocritus, Idyll I; Virgil, Eclogue 5. Spenser's November Eclogue (based on Marot) is probably the earliest English example. Sidney's immediate model, as so often, is Sannazaro: Ecloga II, in which Ergasto laments his dead mistress Massilia, with which there are a good many correspondences. Sidney's elegy is unusual in that the 'shepherd' whom it laments is a king rather than a poet; his questionings of nature and providence are more coherent and philosophical than in most examples of the form; and there is no apotheosis or heavenly consolation at the end. If there were, it would turn out to be rather absurd, since Basilius proves not to be dead at all. It is probable that Amphialus in the *New Arcadia* would also have been restored to life.

xxxv. 29.   A reference to the legend of Hyacinthus, loved by Phoebus, from whose blood the flower sprung, the petals of which were supposed to spell the Greek capital letters 'AI', a cry of lamentation (Ovid, *Metamorphoses*, x. 162–219).

xxxvi.   This poem was chosen by C. S. Lewis to exemplify what he called 'Golden' poetry, though his use of a poor text made nonsense of line 4 (*English Literature in the Sixteenth Century* (1954), pp. 326–7). It is sung by Agelastus in grief for Basilius immediately after the preceding pastoral elegy. The sestina-form here is that used by Petrarch (*Canzoniere*, clxii, ccxiv, ccxxxvii, and ccxxxix) and Montemayor (*Diana*, pp. 191–3), except that the end-words rhyme. Pontus de Tyard wrote two rhyming sestinas (*Erreurs amoureuses*, 1549). Agelastus had sung another sestina, with the same pattern of end-words but without rhyme, in Book 4 (Ringler, OA 70; *Old Arcadia*, pp. 284–5). He is there described as 'one notably noted among them, as well for his skill in their poetry as for an austerely maintained sorrowfulness, wherewith he seemed to despise the works of nature'.

xxxvii.   This sonnet against the fear of death is sung by Musidorus in Book 5 of the *Old Arcadia*, when he and Pyrocles are in prison, expecting to be condemned to death in their trial the next morning (*Old Arcadia*, pp. 373–4).

Certain Sonnets: Commentary

i.   This sonnet and the following one appear to form a deliberate opening to the *Certain Sonnets*, balanced by the two farewells to love with which the collection ends.

iii.   Title from printed text. This song was later used by Sidney in the *New Arcadia*, where Amphialus causes it to be sung to the imprisoned Philoclea from the lake; the music is 'five viols and as many voices' (*Works*, i. 441–2). On the evidence of MS. circulation, this poem, an elaborate use of *correlatio*, was one of the most popular of Sidney's in the sixteenth century. The Italian tune on which this and the following poem are based has recently been discovered by F. J. Fabry in a MS. at Winchester College. He points out the skill with which Sidney adapts the metre to its polyphonic setting (F. J. Fabry, 'Sidney's verse adaptations to two Italian art-songs', *Renaissance Quarterly* xxiii (1970), 237–55).

iv.   Title from printed text. The theme of this song is the nightingale into which Philomela was metamorphosed after being raped by her brother-in-law Tereus (Ovid, *Metamorphoses*, vi. 438f.); according to a later tradition she was believed to have a thorn at her breast with which she pricked herself to keep herself awake. Cf., among many other Elizabethan poems on the theme, the poem in *The Passionate Pilgrim*, probably by Barnfield, 'As it fell upon a day'. The idea in line 20 that rape is a manifestation of excess of love—'too much having'—is a characteristic piece of Sidneian sophistry.

v.   These are Sidney's only rhymed quantitative verses; cf. Greville's rhymed sapphics, probably written in emulation, *Caelica*, vi. The repeated 'my my' to fill out the line is reminiscent of similar filling devices in Sidney's translation of the first forty-three Psalms.

vi.   Title from printed text. There are many settings of the Italian song '*Basciami vita mia*', and it is impossible to tell which one Sidney had in mind.

vii.   Title from printed text. The tune of this Spanish *villancico* has not been traced. The meaning of the title is 'If you, lady, have no pity on me'.

vii. 8.   *though tongue to roof be cleaved*: Cf. Psalm 31:15, which Sidney translated as 'My cleaving tongue close to my roofe doth bide.'

viii.   Title from printed text. The poem is a close translation of Horace's *Carmina*, II. x. It consists of a catalogue of prudent commonplaces many of which had acquired proverbial force by the Renaissance; for instance Horace's version of Sidney's line 9, *Feriuntque summos fulgura montes*, was used for an emblem which Sidney knew (Paolo Giovio, *Dialogo dell'Imprese* (Lyons, 1574), p. 13, copied by Abraham Fraunce in a MS. dedicated to Sidney, Bodleian MS. Rawl. D. 345, fol. 19).

ix. 16–20. The 'knotted straw' refers to a classical proverb, *nodum in scirpo quaerere*—to seek a knot in a bulrush—which does not seem to have gained wide currency in English. The wooden horse led to the destruction of Troy. The tripod from which the Delphic priestess pronounced the oracle determined the course of wars; and Demosthenes, to prove the triviality of the interest the Athenians took in his speeches, told of a man who, trying to sit in the shade of an ass that he had hired, was told that he had hired the ass only, not its shadow (Plutarch, *Moralia*, 848 A; Tilley, *Proverbs*, K168).

ix. 45. *Think Hannibal did laugh when Carthage lost*: Cf. Petrarch's *Canzoniere*, cii. 5–8, translated by Wyatt as:

> And Hanniball eke, when fortune him shitt
> Clene from his reign and from all his intent,
> Laught to his folke, whom sorrow did torment.
> (Wyatt, *Poems*, ed. K. Muir and P. Thomson, 1969, p. 2.)

x. Cf. the sonnet attributed to Sannazaro, imitated by Marot, and translated by Wyatt as 'Like to these unmesurable montayns'; though there are many other Petrarchan sonnets which allegorize landscape.

xi. Title from printed text. The sonnet is an extended use of paronomasia in which the syllable 'part' is used in a wide variety of senses.

xii. Title from printed text. The poem resembles Petrarch's *canzone* cv, in which he describes his love in six exotic similes; but the formula was also imitated by sixteenth-century followers. (Cf. for instance the sonnet by Serafino in which he compares his mistress to a monster with seven heads, translated by Desportes, *Amours de Diane*, I. lxvii.)

xii. 4. Stonehenge is about eight miles from Wilton, where Sidney's sister, the Countess of Pembroke, lived. The question of how the stones were transported is still unanswered. William Harrison in his *Description of Britain* says that they are 'very difficult to be numbered', because of their position. (Holinshed, *First Volume of Chronicles* (1577), fol. 97; Camden, *Britannia*, tr. Holland (1610), pp. 251–3.)

xii. 14. The story that the lake at Brereton, in Cheshire, sends up dead trees when the lord is about to die is told by Camden in his *Britannia*. (tr. Holland (1610), p. 609).

xii. 24. This attribute of the pike is described by Drayton in his *Polyolbion*, iii. 261–72, which is a recapitulation of Sidney's seven wonders. Cf. also the final version of Harrison's 'Description of Britain', Holinshed, *First and second volumes of Chronicles* (1587), p. 224.

xii. 34. This may be a reference to the cave near Buxton called Poole's Hole, which has a small entrance and large caverns within; though there are many other caves in the Peak District with stalactites and stalagmites. Buxton was a favourite Elizabethan watering-place, which Sidney's uncle, the Earl of Leicester, often visited.

xii. 44. A reference to the ruins of Winburn monastery, near Bath; the phenomenon is described by William Harrison in the latest version of his *Description of Britain* (Holinshed, *First and second volumes of Chronicles* (1587), p. 130).

xii. 54. The barnacle goose, thought to be hatched from barnacles clinging to shipwrecks, is a wonder credited by travellers from Mandeville to Raleigh.

xiii. Title from printed text. The tune to which the poem is set was originally that of a French Catholic song composed in mockery of the Huguenot Prince Louis de Condé in 1568; it was adopted by the Prince de Condé's own troops, became the song of the House of Orange, and is now the tune of the Dutch National Anthem. The theme of the poem appears to be some kind of Platonic love.

xiv. Title from printed text. The tune, perhaps a folk melody, has not been traced.

xv. The metre is one used by Horace in alternate lines of his *Carmina*, I. viii.

xvi. Title from printed text. The Italian tune has recently been discovered by F. J. Fabry in a MS. at Winchester College. (See note on CS iii.)

xvii. Title from printed text. The tune has not been traced.

xviii. Title from printed text. This is a translation of the first song in Montemayor's *Diana*. The green silk, which might have stood for Hope, turns out to signify Fickleness; see following note. The poem was also translated by Bartholomew Yong, Thomas Wilson, and Southey (*Diana*, pp. 12–13, 423).

xviii. 4. Sidney in the *Arcadia* makes great use of the various Renaissance systems of colour symbolism. These systems were by no means consistent, and green could represent fickleness, or the supernatural; however, its association with spring made its identification with hope a natural one. Thomas Wilson, who translated Montemayor's *Diana* and dedicated it to Greville, had the manuscript bound in green, perhaps in token of his hope that it would be favourably accepted. (H. Thomas ed., '*Diana* de Monte Mayor done out of Spanish by Thomas Wilson (1596)', *Revue Hispanique*, cxvii (Oct. 1920), 367–418).

xviii. 35. This motto from Montemayor, '*Antes muerta que mudada*', was used (altered to the masculine gender) as the epigraph to the portrait of Donne prefaced to his poems in 1635.

xviii. 40. The idea of words written in sand as an image of fragile promises is a traditional one. Cf. Spenser's *Amoretti*, lxxv.

xix. Title from printed text. This poem occurs in the *Diana* of Montemayor soon after 'What changes here, O hair'. It is recalled by Silvano, friend of the forsaken Sireno, who recites it (*Diana*, pp. 19–20).

xx. One of Sidney's most popular poems, both among his contemporaries (on the evidence of MS. circulation) and in modern times. Tennyson, protesting at source-hunters, complained that 'They will not allow one to say "Ring the bell" without finding that we have taken it from Sir P. Sidney' (Hallam Tennyson, *Alfred Lord Tennyson: A Memoir*, (1897), i. 258).

xxii. 6. The image of the 'sweet yoke' identifies the alternative to the 'love which reachest but to dust' as divine love, since it refers to Christ's words 'my yoke is easy, and my burden is light' (Matthew, 11:30). Sidney knew the emblem consisting of a picture of a yoke with the motto *Suave* used by Pope Leo X (Paolo Giovio, *Dialogo dell'Imprese* (Lyons, 1574), p. 45; Bodleian MS. Rawl. D. 345, fol. 28).

xxii. *Splendidis longum valedico nugis*: The source of this motto, 'I bid a long farewell to splendid trifles', has not been traced.

Astrophil and Stella

1. Sidney opens his sequence with a metrical innovation: a sonnet in alexandrines, or twelve-syllabled lines.

1. 2. *she* (*dear she*): Metre, and Sidney's compulsive use of parenthesis, support this reading from the 1598 folio, rather than 'the dear she', the reading of the quartos and MSS., adopted by Ringler.

1. 14. *look in thy heart*: C. S. Lewis says of the final line of this sonnet, which has been made much of as a profession of sincerity: 'When a poet looks in his heart, he finds many things there besides the actual' (*English Literature in the Sixteenth Century* (1954), p. 328). Such professions of sincerity are in any case in themselves conventional.

2. The theme of this sonnet is genuinely unconventional. Dante, Petrarch, and most of the French Petrarchizers did claim to have loved at first sight. The assertion is consistent with what we know of Sidney's relationship with Penelope Devereux: he seems to have shown no interest in the dying wish of Penelope's father, the Earl of Essex, in 1576, for a match between his daughter and Sir Henry Sidney's son. Penelope was at that time only thirteen (Wallace, *Life*, pp. 169, 244–5; cf. sonnet 33).

2. 9. *like slave-born Muscovite*: The Russians—Slavs—were believed by the Elizabethans to enjoy the oppressive rule of their Tsar, at this time Ivan the Terrible. They were also thought of as comically clumsy and barbaric, as in the Muscovite disguise of the four lovers in *Love's Labour's Lost*, v. ii; cf. also Francesca Wilson, *Muscovy: Russia through Foreign Eyes* (1970), pp. 60–2. Cf. also sonnet 30. 3–4.

3. 1–8. Sidney catalogues four current ways of ornamenting or elaborating verse: invocation of the Muses; imitation of Pindar and other Greek lyric poets, as professed by Ronsard and the other Pléiade writers; logical and rhetorical elaboration, introduced about this time into English poetry by Thomas Watson in his *Hekatompathia* (1582); and the use of exotic similes from natural history initiated in English prose by Lyly, but already employed in poetry by Petrarch and his sixteenth-century followers. Sidney himself uses all four forms of elaboration in poems in the *Arcadia*; rhetorical and logical complexity is the only one which he employs persistently in *Astrophil and Stella*.

5. 11. *Which elements with mortal mixture breed*: a reference to the Platonic theory that mortal beauty, clothed in the physical elements, is only a shadow of absolute virtue; the elements combine in a perishable way (e.g. *Republic*, ch. x).

6. Like sonnet 3, this is a catalogue of current ways of ornamenting love poetry; its allusions are both more specific and more difficult to explain with confidence. Like sonnet 1, it is in alexandrines.

6. 4. The reference is to Petrarchan paradox and oxymoron; 'wot not what' refers to his phrase '*non so che*', which became the French '*je ne sais quoi*'. The 'freezing fires' are the most often quoted Petrarchan oxymoron; cf. Leonard Forster's study of Petrarchanism, *The Icy Fire* (Cambridge, 1969).

6. 6. Ronsard also uses the metamorphoses of Jove—into a bull for the love of Europa, swan for Leda, and shower of gold for Danäe—as metaphors for his love; e.g. in the sonnet translated by Raleigh as 'Would I were changed into that golden shower' (Ronsard, *Amours*, xx; Raleigh, *Poems*, ed. Agnes Latham (1951), pp. 81–2). But many other poets of the period used them too.

6. 11. The reference seems again to be to Petrarchan devices; the phrase 'sweetest style' suggests the *dolce stil nuovo* poets of the fourteenth century.

6. 12. *I can speak what I feel*: The metrical awkwardness of this may be intended to reinforce Sidney's assertion of poetic spontaneity and casualness.

7. Penelope Devereux is known to have had dark eyes and fair hair; but there is also a tradition of praise of a dark mistress.

8. 2. *Turkish hardened heart*: Sidney is thinking of Cupid in contemporary Greece, which was part of the Ottoman empire, and sees him as a refugee from the proverbially cruel Turks; cf. sonnet 30. Cyprus was taken by the Greeks in 1573.

8. 5. *too coldly*: The quartos' reading 'too' has been preferred here, on grounds of metre and sense, to the 1598 folio's 'do'.

9. 12–14. This elaborate punning metaphor, in which Sidney may be attempting to imitate recent Spanish poets, plays on three or four senses of 'touch': Stella's eyes are of touch-stone (black marble) which without physical contact has an emotive effect. The last line either sustains the 'touch-stone' metaphor, or introduces yet another reference, to touch-paper or touch-wood, which sets the straw alight. The new image in the last line would be typical of the many sonnets in which Sidney introduces a surprise or twist in the last line.

13. 6. All the coats of arms refer to amorous exploits; Mars's, to his affair with Venus.

13. 11. *Where roses gules are borne in silver field*: possibly a reference to the Devereux arms—*argent, a fesse, gules in chief three torteaux*, or three red discs on a silver ground—as well as to Stella's rosy cheeks. Cf. Sidney's reference to his own arms in sonnet 65.

13. 13. *blaze*: a pun; 'blaze' is the technical term for spelling out or describing heraldic accoutrements, but is also an appropriate word for the activity of Phoebus in illuminating Stella.

14. The first of many sonnets showing Astrophil in a social context, with a single uncomprehending or disapproving friend; cf. sonnets 20, 21, 23, 27, 51, 88, 92, and 104.

15. A third sonnet on contemporary poetic styles; cf. 3 and 6. The references here appear to be general ones, rather than allusions to specific poets.

15. 1–4. Presumably a reference to those who rifle classical poets for phrases and images, and those who borrow from other poets who have done the same.

15. 5–6. A reference to poets who use alliteration, mimicked in the phrase 'running in rattling rows'. The poets C. S. Lewis calls Drab, who overlap with Sidney in time, habitually use alliteration.

15. 8–9. A reference to the imitators of Petrarch, in French, Italian, Spanish, and to a smaller extent English.

16. 9. *while I thus with this young lion played*: a reference to the Greek fable of the shepherd who brought a pet lion cub into his family which when it grew up destroyed his flocks; the story was applied by Aeschylus to Helen of Troy (*Agamemnon*, 717–36).

18. 14. *Than that I lose no more for Stella's sake*: This is the first sonnet which makes explicit the wholly secular nature of Astrophil's love for Stella, which in many other sonnets he uses sophistry to disguise. A comparison with Milton's sonnet on his wasted youth, 'How soon hath time, the subtle thief of youth', underlines by contrast Astrophil's bold urge for self-destruction.

19. 10–11. *him that . . . in a ditch doth fall*: a commonplace comment on astronomers, deriving from an anecdote about the Greek scientist Thales who fell into a well while gazing at the stars; Sidney also used it in the *Defence of Poetry*: 'The astronomer looking to the stars might fall in a ditch' (*Misc. Prose*, p. 80; Tilley, *Proverbs*, S827).

21. 6. *coltish gyres*: probably a reference to Plato's image of reason as charioteer to the passions, identified with horses.

21. 9. *mad March great promise made of me*: a reference to the extraordinary success of Sidney's three years of foreign travel, in which he impressed scholars and politicians with his wit, charm, learning, and promise as a possible leader of Protestant Europe against Spain. His youth at the time—nineteen to twenty-two —might have led his friends to expect something more of the sowing of wild oats suggested by 'mad March'. Surviving letters to Sidney from his continental friends are printed in translation by James M. Osborn, *Young Philip Sidney* (New Haven, Conn., and London, 1972).

24.   This characterization of jealousy or selfish lust is a cryptic satire on Penelope Devereux's husband, Lord Rich, whose name is used also in sonnets 35 and 37.

25. 1.   Plato, the wisest scholar of Socrates, who had been adjudged wisest of men by the Delphic oracle (Plato, *Apology*, 21), did indeed say that if we could see the true form of virtue we should instinctively love it. But Sidney is probably deriving Plato's idea from Cicero (*De Officiis*, 1. 15), as is suggested by his reference in the *Defence of Poetry* to 'the saying of Plato and Tully . . . that who could see virtue would be wonderfully ravished with the love of her beauty' (*Misc. Prose*, p. 96).

26. 10.   *know those bodies high reign on the low*: This sonnet is a deliberately light treatment of a weighty Renaissance topic: the question of whether the stars were placed simply for delight, or, as in the medieval view, as pervasive influences on human character and behaviour. Sidney's acceptance of astral influence, though flippantly expressed here, is consistent with what we know of him elsewhere: his friendship with John Dee; his having a horoscope cast (Bodleian MS. Ashmole 356(v), printed by James M. Osborn, *TLS*, I January 1971, pp. 17–18; cf. also *Young Philip Sidney*, pp. 517–22); and passages in his writings such as Musidorus's description of the birth of Pyrocles in the *New Arcadia*: 'The senate house of the planets was at no time so set, for the decreeing of perfection in a man' (*Works*, i. 189). But Sidney's delight, as a poet, in images drawn from the heavens (Thomas Moffett describes him as worshipping the new moon at the age of three) makes it unwise to attribute to him any serious belief in medieval astrology (Moffett, *Nobilis*, pp. 70–1).

29.   The strategic and military metaphors in this sonnet are complex and perhaps not wholly successful. The initial idea is that Stella allows love to keep arms in every part of her body except her heart, so that her heart itself may be free; this is succeeded—and confused—by the idea that Astrophil, simply because he has looked at her outward beauty, has been taken captive by her love.

30.   The seven topical questions to which Astrophil is indifferent place this sonnet in the summer of 1582.

30. 1–2.   The Turks were a constant threat to Europe well into the seventeenth century; and in the early summer of 1582 an attack on Spain was expected.

30. 3–4.   Stephen Bathory, the elected king of Poland, invaded Muscovy (Russia) in 1580 and besieged Pskov until December 1581. By the summer of 1582 a treaty had been signed, but Sidney may not have heard of this.

30. 5.   The three parts are the Catholics, the Huguenots, and the moderate Politiques, who struggled for control of France until the accession of Henry of Navarre in 1589.

30. 6.   A reference to the Germans (Deutsch), not the Dutch (who come in the next line); the Diet of the Holy Roman Empire was held at Augsburg from early July to September 1582.

30. 7–8.   The towns of Breda, Tournay, Oudenarde, Lier, and Ninove were won by the Spaniards during 1581–2; the hope of the Dutch lay in William of Orange.

30. 9–10.   Sir Henry Sidney subdued the province of Ulster during his third term of office as Lord Deputy Governor of Ireland, in 1576–8, partly by dividing it into shires under the government of sheriffs, and partly by imposing a 'cess', or land-tax, on the great lords; this may be the meaning of the 'golden bit'.

30. 11.   The extreme confusion of the political situation in Scotland is suggested by the word 'weltering' (editions of *Astrophil and Stella* in James I's reign emend

it tactfully to 'no welt'ring'); during the summer of 1582 there were complex intrigues leading up to the Raid of Ruthven on 22 August.

31. 14. *Do they call virtue there ungratefulness?*: Sidney's constant inversion of the order of subject and object makes it impossible to tell whether this line means: 'Do ladies in heaven call their own ungratefulness virtue?', or 'Do ladies there call their lovers' virtue unpleasing?' Given Sidney's habitual inversion, the first sense is probably the likelier; many analogous constructions could be found, e.g. in the Second Song, line 16: 'Cowards love with loss rewardeth', meaning 'love rewards cowards with loss'.

32. 1–2. Morpheus, the son of Somnus, had the special function of bringing human images to dreamers (Ovid, *Metamorphoses*, xi. 735). Sidney may be particularly recalling here the opening of Chaucer's *Book of the Duchess*, in which the dreamer reads of Morpheus bringing the drowned king Ceyx to his wife Alcyone, and subsequently himself has a dream of death and living death.

33. This is unusual among the sonnets of *Astrophil and Stella* in being almost inexplicable without reference to Sidney's biography. The allusion is presumably to the fact that Sidney, when he was offered the thirteen-year-old Penelope Devereux in marriage (see note on sonnet 2) rejected the proposal, failing to anticipate the love he was later to feel for her. He was too wise to fall in love with her when she was a child; and so their love must be frustrated in maturity (lines 10–11). The meaning of the last line is probably: 'Would that I had been foolish enough to fall in love when I first saw Penelope, or wise enough never to fall in love at all.'

34. 4. *Oft cruel fights well pictured forth do please*: a reference to Aristotle's *Poetics*, which Sidney made also in the *Defence of Poetry*: 'As Aristotle saith, those things which in themselves are horrible, as cruel battles, unnatural monsters, are made in poetical imitation delightful' (Aristotle, *Poetics*, iv; *Misc. Prose*, p. 90).

36. 14. *By sense's privilege, can 'scape from thee*: Not only Astrophil's soul, which *has* sense, but stones and trees, which *lack* sense, are enchanted by Stella's voice and face; cf. the opening lines of the Third Song. Sidney plays on the word 'sense' elsewhere, as in the account of the whipping of Philoclea in Book 3 of the *New Arcadia*: 'the very stone walls did yield drops of sweat for agony of such a mischief; each senseless thing had sense of pity; only they that had sense, were senseless' (*Works*, i. 471).

37. This sonnet appears in only one MS. of *Astrophil and Stella*, and in neither of the quarto editions; it was first printed in the 1598 folio *Arcadia*. It was probably suppressed from the copy which gained MS. circulation because the attack on Lord Rich was too explicit. Though the language is deliberately distanced and romance-like—as in the word 'lordings'—the allusion is inescapable. The seat of the Riches was in eastern England—at Leighs, in Essex—so that the fairytale-like phrase 'Towards Aurora's court' has a direct reference; there may also be a sense of 'near Queen Elizabeth's court', though Aurora was not one of the deities commonly identified with the Queen. The 'riddle' posed by the nymph's 'misfortune' could hardly give a moment's difficulty to any contemporary who knew of Penelope Devereux's unhappy marriage.

39. 9–14. The offer of gifts to Morpheus is conventional; but a specific source here may be Chaucer's *Book of the Duchess*, 240–69; cf. note on sonnet 32. The 'rosy garland' probably means a garland of silence or secrecy, as in the phrase *sub rosa*.

41. 4. This probably refers to the *Triumph of the Four Foster Children of Desire*, an allegorical tournament in which Sidney, Greville, the Earl of Arundel, and the Baron of Windsor took part in May 1581, in the presence of the French commissioners, led by Simier, sent to negotiate the marriage of Elizabeth with the Duke of Alençon. The contemporary account of the tournament, by Henry Goldwell, is printed in J. G. Nichols's *Progresses of Queen Elizabeth I* (1823), ii. 310–29. Though Sidney took part in other tournaments in 1581–2, this was much the most striking one at which a French delegation was present.

41. 11.   *nature me a man of arms did make*: Sidney's father and grandfather, Sir Henry and Sir William Sidney, were both tilters in their youth; and so were his mother's illustrious brothers, the Earls of Leicester and Warwick. The phrase 'man of arms' refers specifically to one who fought in the heavy semi-medieval armour of the tournament; cf. the description of Phalantus, who organizes the first tournament in the *New Arcadia*, as 'the fair man of arms' (*Works*, i. 97).

42. 14.   *Wracks triumphs be, which love (high set) doth breed*: The last line of this, one of the few sonnets in *Astrophil and Stella* which appears to be largely a rhetorical display, recalls the last line of Petrarch's *Canzoniere*, cxl, a sonnet translated by both Wyatt and Surrey; Surrey's version of the last line is 'Sweet is his death, that takes his end by love.'

44. 1–6.   An unusually simple use of a rhetorical schema, climax, a device used obsessively by many of Sidney's contemporaries; e.g. by Kyd in *The Spanish Tragedy* (ii. i. 119–29 and *passim*).

45. 14.   *I am not I, pity the tale of me*: Sidney is exploiting the Aristotelian paradox that objects represented in art may have an emotive effect that they lack in life; Astrophil, metamorphosed by love, is no longer himself, and claims to have become himself an artefact; the suggestion may be also that the sonnets of *Astrophil and Stella* constitute the 'tale of me'.

46. 12–14.   The meaning of these lines is rather obscure: perhaps it is that Astrophil begs to be excused from being schooled in virtue until Stella can learn how to feed love without satisfying desire.

50.   The ingenuity of this sonnet lies in opening with the name 'Stella', which supposedly preserves the whole sonnet from destruction; the poem thus depends upon itself. The fancy may be imitated by Shakespeare in *The Two Gentlemen of Verona*, i. ii, where Julia shows her tenderness to the name 'Proteus' written on a letter she has just torn up.

51.   One of the more obscure of the sonnets putting Astrophil in a social setting: the person addressed is presumably a fellow-courtier gossiping about court intrigues and quests for favour ('cunning'st fishers in most troubled streams'), whose conversation, according to the literary theory of *decorum*, Astrophil finds incongruous with his pleasant reflexions on Stella.

53.   Contrast with sonnet 41. Whether Astrophil does well or badly in the tilt-yard, he attributes the outcome to Stella.

54. 13.   *Dumb swans, not chattering pies, do lovers prove*: quoted by Nashe in *Will Summer's Last Will and Testament:*

> Well sung a shepherd that now sleeps in skies:
> 'Dumb swans do love, and not vain chattering pies'.
> (Nashe, *Works*, ed. McKerrow, iii. 271, line 1173.)

Cf. also OA iii. 7.

55. 8.   *How their black banner might be best displayed*: A military metaphor is employed to express an idea analogous to that of the last line of sonnet 2—'while with a feeling skill I paint my hell'; Astrophil employs poetic artifice to set off to advantage what is fundamentally a painful and unpleasing subject. The image of the 'black banner' is reminiscent both of the last major combat in the *New Arcadia*, in which Musidorus and Amphialus are both dressed entirely in black (*Works*, i. 453–63), and of the tradition, used by Marlowe, that Tamburlaine the

Great marched with black banners on his enemies when he meant to destroy them utterly (1 *Tamburlaine*, IV. i, and *passim*).

57. 10.   *most sweetly sing*: The suggestion is probably that the actual sonnets of the sequence we are reading are sung by Stella (who sweetens them and drains them of pathos). The Petrarchan sonnet-form was originally designed for a musical setting, though few Elizabethan composers set sonnets. Hallett Smith's suggestion that there is a whole second sonnet-sequence which we are to imagine Astrophil as having composed seems over-elaborate. (Hallett Smith, *Elizabethan Poetry* (Cambridge, Mass., 1952), p. 151.) The actuality of Sidney's friends' singing his poems is borne out by the allusion to his 'songs', which Denny is to remember to sing, at the end of the newly discovered letter of advice to Edward Denny (John Buxton, 'An Unpublished letter from Sir Philip Sidney', *TLS*, 24 March 1972).

58. 1–8.   This refers to a controversy in classical oratory about whether the words or the manner of delivery have more influence on the audience (Cicero, *De Oratore*, ii. 223; Quintilian, XI. xii. 2–4). The opening image of the golden chain of rhetoric is a traditional one, employed for instance in the emblem books, where Hercules is shown leading crowds by golden chains from his mouth (Alciati, *Emblemata* (Antwerp, 1574), p. 458).

60. 1.   *my good angel*: a reference to the classical theory that every human being is accompanied by two spirits, one good and one bad, which prompt him accordingly; cf. Shakespeare's sonnet cxliv, and the Good and Bad Angels in Marlowe's *Faustus*.

62. 6.   *a love not blind*: a reference to the neo-Platonic theory of two Venuses and two Cupids, earthly and heavenly (Ficino). The earthly Cupid, or Desire, is blind; the spiritual, or Platonic, one is sighted. The divine Cupid is shown in the emblem books (e.g. Alciati, *Emblemata* (Antwerp, 1574), p. 291, emb. cix).

63. 14.   *two negatives affirm*: this rule applies to Latin rather than to English grammar, but Astrophil is taking advantage of it for his own sophistical ends. The impudent 'to grammar who says nay?' neatly repeats the idea of a negative reply. The refrain of the Fourth Song ('No, no, no, no, my dear, let be') shows that doubled negatives do *not* necessarily affirm in English.

First song. 4.   Though in its setting in *Astrophil and Stella* we assume that the 'you' of this song is Stella, the poem could well have been written earlier, as an exercise or in relation to some other lady.

64.   Cf. Shakespeare, sonnets xc and xci.

65. 14.   *Thou bear'st the arrow, I the arrow head*: a reference to Sidney's own arms, *or, a pheon azure*—a blue arrow head on a gold background. The arrow head, borne also by Sidney's uncle Ambrose Dudley, Earl of Warwick, who was Master of the Ordnance, became the crest of the Ordnance Office, stamped on its property, for instance the traditional convict's uniform, now seen only in comic cartoons.

67. 8.   *What blushing notes dost thou in margin see*: The 'text' is Stella's eyes, the 'margin' her cheeks, blushing as in the preceding sonnet. Cf. the image used of Pyrocles in the *Arcadia*, where he sets Philoclea's hand close to his lips, 'as if it should stand there like a hand in a margin of a book, to note some saying worthy to be marked' (*Works*, i. 119).

69. 14.   *No kings be crowned, but they some covenants make*: Like many of the gnomic last lines in the middle parts of *Astrophil and Stella* this apparent platitude is a cloak for Astrophil's attempt to 'make [himself] believe that all is well'; the 'covenant' to which he has agreed, that he should take a 'virtuous course' in loving Stella, proves in succeeding sonnets to make the treaty an impossible one.

70. 4. *since I Jove's cup do keep*: possibly an allusion to Sidney's tenure of the very minor office of cup-bearer to the Queen, as well as an identification of Astrophil with Ganymede, who mixed nectar for Jove. He received the office in 1576 (Wallace, *Life*, p. 165).

72. 8. *Virtue's gold now must head my Cupid's dart*: a reference back to sonnet 65, where Astrophil exchanges roles with Cupid, and to the allusion there to Sidney's arms, a blue arrow head on a gold ground.

Second song. 28. This song makes Astrophil's desire more explicit than the sonnets, in which he cloaks it in sophistical justifications. He blames himself, not for breaking Stella's injunction of virtue, but for not breaking it more completely. The dramatically abrupt ending is comparable with the final line of the Eighth song.

74. 5. *Some do I hear of poet's fury tell*: the idea is consistent with *The Defence of Poetry*, where Sidney dismisses the idea of poetic inspiration. The clumsiness of '(God wot) wot not', in the following line, is probably intended to suggest Astrophil's plainness of speech. Giordano Bruno's work, *De Gl'Heroici Furori*, which to some extent concerns artistic inspiration, was dedicated to Sidney in 1585, but it probably did not meet with his full comprehension or sympathy, although Bruno, an Italian philosopher who developed the theories of Copernicus, received kindness from Sidney during his stay in England in 1583–5 (Wallace, *Life*, pp. 298–302).

75. 6–7. Edward IV usurped the throne in 1461, after his father, the Duke of York, was killed while fighting against the Lancastrians.

75. 9–11. In 1474 Edward invaded France, and was persuaded by Louis XI to withdraw with a payment of 75,000 crowns. Scotland was not at this time in league with France against England. (The 'bloody lion' is the red lion of Scotland.)

75. 12–14. In 1464 Edward married Lady Elizabeth Grey, widow of Sir Richard Grey. Warwick, the 'king-maker', who had been negotiating a French match for him at the time, drove Edward into exile in 1470, though he recovered his throne in the following year. (The episode is treated by Shakespeare, *3 Henry VI*, III. ii, and *passim*.)

76 and 77. Two more sonnets in alexandrines.

78. This characterization of the monster jealousy is evidently also a portrait of Lord Rich, as the final wish that he might be cuckolded, which would not really make sense as applied solely to the abstract quality, makes explicit. Cf. the composite monster in Dicus's poem about Cupid in the *Arcadia* (OA iv, (8)).

79. 14. *Cease we to praise, now pray we for a kiss*: The rhetorical device of interruption here has a strongly dramatic effect, as the formal exercise of praising Stella's kiss gives way to an immediate demand; cf. the three preceding sonnets.

83. 1. *Good brother Philip*: Stella's sparrow is brother to Astrophil both because they are rivals for her affection and because, in one aspect, they have the same Christian name. The sparrow, traditionally identified with lechery, may be partly an image for Astrophil's own desire (cf. Campion's song 'Of all the birds that I do see', where the innuendo is inescapable); but also belongs to a tradition of sparrows in love poetry, as in Catullus and Skelton.

Third song. 7–10. Allusions to two anecdotes in Pliny's *Natural History*: the story of Thoas, an Arcadian, who was rescued from robbers by a dragon (lizard) to whom he had been kind; and that of a maiden of Sestos who nurtured an eagle which flew into her funeral pyre and was consumed (Pliny, *Natural History*, viii. 61 and x. 18).

84. 2. *to some ears not unsweet*: one of the few hints in *Astrophil and Stella* that the sonnets may reach, or even be intended for, an audience larger than Stella

herself. This sonnet was criticized adversely by Yvor Winters, who seems to have misunderstood its meaning ('The Sixteenth-century lyric in England', *Poetry*, liii (1939), 258–72, 320–72).

85. 5–8. Sidney's concern with the need for a ruler to delegate duties to suitable underlings is shown in the passage in the *New Arcadia* about Amphialus's skill in 'the art of men' (*Works*, i. 373–4).

86. 5. *like spotless ermine*: The ermine was believed to die rather than allow its skin to become sullied; it could therefore be captured by being surrounded by a wall of dung. It is used in Renaissance emblem books to represent chastity or constancy of purpose; the ermine is also so used in Hilliard's 'ermine' portrait of Queen Elizabeth at Hatfield; and Clitophon, in the *New Arcadia*, carries an *impresa* of an ermine with the motto 'Rather dead than spotted' (Luca Contile, *Regionamento sopra imprese* (Pavia, 1574), f. 40b; *Works*, i. 108). Cf. OA xxvi. 116.

Fifth song. Both in its style, which is rather clumsy and tedious, and its theme— curses on the cruel mistress—this song seems out of place in *Astrophil and Stella*. It may have been written earlier by Sidney and inserted here by an early editor. Ringler suggests that it belongs with Sidney's Philisides–Mira poems. It does not appear in any of the MS. texts.

Fifth song. 42. *Ungrateful who is called, the worst of evils is spoken*: a confusing ellipsis for 'She who has been called ungrateful has had the worst of evils spoken of her.' The notion of the lady being ungrateful may reinforce the idea that the 'ungratefulness' in the last line of sonnet 31 is Stella's rather than Astrophil's.

Seventh song. Quoted by Abraham Fraunce (*Arcadian Rhetorike*, i. 23) as an example of *epanodos*, or repetition in parts of a whole spoken earlier.

Eighth song. This song, the only one to employ a third person narrative, is by far the most explicit account of the relationship of the lovers in the whole sequence. It is distanced, however, by being set in the traditional form of the *reverdie*, or encounter of lovers in spring. Stella's reply, lines 69–100, was omitted in the 1591 editions. The poem was imitated well into the seventeenth century, and may have influenced such Metaphysica l lovers' meetings as Lord Herbert of Cherbury's 'Ode upon a Question Moved, Whether Love should continue for ever?'. One of the earliest imitations is Greville's *Caelica*, lxxv.

Eighth song. 1. *most rich of shade*: presumably a reference to Lady Rich, as the habitual puns on 'rich' alert one to every use of the word. In so far as there is any biographical reference, the suggestion may be that the shade is made rich by Lady Rich's presence, and not necessarily that the meeting occurs in the garden of one of Lord Rich's houses.

Eighth song. 104. *That therewith my song is broken*: The shift from third to first person in the last line suggests vividly that Astrophil has attempted in this poem to give an objective account of a crisis in his relationship with Stella, which breaks down at the end so that he forgets to mask his identity. Cf. the shift from first to third person in the sixth stanza of the following song, lines 26–30, where Astrophil is clearly the speaker throughout.

87. 4. This, the first of the 'absence' sonnets, makes it clear that the lovers' physical separation is brought about by Astrophil's responsibilities elsewhere— 'iron laws of duty'– and not by Stella's wish. It is thus consistent with the early sonnets in the sequence which show Astrophil amid the pressures and demands of court life.

89. 14. *I feel the flames of hottest summer day*: This sonnet, in which only two 'rhyme' words are used, 'night' and 'day', but in a pattern approximating to the Petrarchan form, ends in a complete reversal of normal relationships; cf. one of

Sidney's other stylistic *tours de force*, the double sestina of Strephon and Klaius, at the end of which mountains become valleys and music harsh cries (OA xxxii. 71).

90. 14. *love doth hold my hand, and makes me write*: Thematically this sonnet might seem to belong with the group early in the sequence on the motives for writing poetry and the problems of originality of style (cf. 1, 3, 6, 15); but in its context here it suggests Astrophil's increasing concern with the conflict between private emotions and public responsibilities. There may be an implication that Stella has been encouraging him to circulate his poems more widely.

91. 11. *such be wood-globes of glistering skies*: The 'sphere' is one of the main subjects studied by Sidney during his year in Italy, and he recommended its study to his brother Robert and to his friend Edward Denny, both in 1580. (*Works*, iii. 80, 132; John Buxton, 'An unpublished letter from Sir Philip Sidney', *TLS*, 24 March 1972.)

92. 1. A reference to a proverbial expression, 'Indian ware' being scarce and expensive; the proverbial remoteness of the Indies (rather than India) is also suggested by the passage in *The Defence of Leicester* where Sidney says that, given his noble ancestry, Leicester's want of gentility 'would seem as great news as if they came from the Indies' (*Misc. Prose*, p. 133).

93. Astrophil's 'foul stumbling' against Stella is as obscure as the 'fault' of the young man in Shakespeare's Sonnets.

97. The narrative meaning of this sonnet appears to be that another, unidentified lady (the moon) is attempting to console Astrophil for the absence of Stella (the sun). The paradox of Stella (Star) being equated with sun rather than moon would not exist for a sixteenth-century reader, accustomed to referring to the sun as the 'day-star'. Stella is also referred to as 'my sun' in sonnet 76.

100. 1. *O tears, no tears*: Cf. Kyd, *The Spanish Tragedy*, Act III. ii, 'O eyes, no eyes, but fountains fraught with tears', a speech mocked by Jonson in *Everyman in his Humour*, I. v. 57–8; but Sidney's model is probably Petrarch or one of the Pléiade poets who used the device.

102. Another sonnet (cf. 1, 6, 8, 76, and 77) in alexandrines.

103. 2. *with many a smiling line*: Sidney is fond of conceits in which water has a human face; cf. the images in the *New Arcadia* of blood filling 'the wrinkles of the sea's visage', and of the river Ladon 'smiling' as the princesses strike his face (*Works*, i. 10, 218).

104. 10. *If I but stars upon my armour bear*: Sidney may really have worn star-spangled armour in tournaments; a star-engraved banner is shown in Lant's *Funeral Roll* (5). A knight in the *New Arcadia*—possibly the shepherd Klaius in disguise—wears accoutrements 'all cut in stars' (*Works*, i. 462).

Eleventh song. 43. *unjust is*: The folio's reading has been preferred to 'unjustest', the reading of the two MSS. in which the song appears; Sidney rarely leaves a phrase without a main verb, particularly at the end of a poem.

105. On a narrative level this is perhaps the obscurest sonnet in the sequence. The general sense is clear, however: Astrophil has missed an opportunity of seeing Stella. The 'Dead glass' has been variously identified as Astrophil's eye, a telescope, or his tears. The phrase 'dazzling race' might suggest a lantern or torch, as in line 11; or the glass of window pane, or a mirror. But the likeliest interpretation (Ringler's) is that the 'glass' is Astrophil's eyes, which were not to blame for not seeing Stella: the page, darkness, and the coachman were responsible. 'Dazzling' would then be intransitive, as in Webster's 'Cover her face; mine eyes dazzle; she died young' (*Duchess of Malfi*, IV. ii. 281).

107. 8. *this great cause*: The allusion was probably identifiable by the sonnet's immediate audience. It could be referring either to some public duty—though there is no major one that suits the date of *Astrophil and Stella*—or to the composition of the *Arcadia*, which Stella herself wishes for ('what thine own will attends'). The fact that it is his 'wit', rather than his physical presence, which he wishes to be excused, would reinforce the second interpretation; but the idea that neglect of the duty will make him an object of scorn suggests rather the first.

108. The final sonnet appears—after the adieu of its predecessor—to be a reversion to Astrophil's old confused absorption in his sufferings. But in the context of the sequence as a whole it is appropriate that it should come at the end, if we take as authoritative the conclusion of the *Eighth song*, 'That therewith my song is broken'—a conclusion in which nothing is concluded.

Additional Poem

This poem (Ringler OP4) though probably written in 1577–80, when Sidney composed other poems about Mira and Philisides, was only printed in 1593, in the second edition of the *Arcadia*; it was inserted in the Third Eclogues, but does not seem altogether appropriate to the theme of marriage. It is the first *canzone* to be written in English, and is loosely based on Sannazaro's Ecloga 3.

45. Probably referring to the idea that bees were born from the dew on flowers.

126. The poem appears to be located somewhere in Eastern England—perhaps at Wanstead in Essex, one of the Earl of Leicester's houses; Mira is somewhere to the west of Philisides. Sannazaro's *canzone* is sung on 3 March; Sidney's appears to belong to high spring, and could have been written in 1578 or 9, when Sidney wrote *The Lady of May* for the entertainment of the Queen at Wanstead. But Penshurst is also in Eastern England, and closer to the coast.

The Psalms of David

29:18. *Sirion like young unicorn*: Cf. Sidney's praise in *The Defence of Poetry* of the Psalms as 'a divine poem': 'what else is . . . his telling of the beasts' joyfulness and hills leaping, but a heavenly poesy, wherein he showeth himself a passionate lover of that unspeakable and everlasting beauty to be seen by the eyes of the mind, only cleared by faith' (*Misc. Prose*, p. 75).

First Line Index

Errata

p. 5, line 47 Deck yourselves with *should be* Deck yours with your
p. 6, line 53 own; wool's *should be* own; me thinks wool's
p. 7, line 89 rich *should be* dear
line 111 hold *should be* holds
p. 10, line 28 large long *should be* long large
p. 16, line 14 into *should be* unto
p. 17, line 13 spheres senseless *should be* senseless spheres
p. 18, line 5 to a beggar *should be* to beggar
line 21 the sore *should be* a sore
p. 20, line 90 so small rest *should be* so small rest rests
p. 21, line 116 shown *should be* showed
line 120 I burn, I burn *should be* I burn, yet I burn
p. 22, line 140 all things *should be* each thing
line 148 fame by thy *should be* fame be thy
p. 23, line 164 be hopes *should be* be my hopes
line 164 lies *should be* lives
p. 33, line 43 whence *should be* where
p. 34, *three lines have been omitted, and the lineation is wrong as a result: line 51 onwards should run:*

> Plangus must live, to see Erona's death.
> Plangus must live some help for her to try
>> Though in despair, for love so forceth me;
>> Plangus doth live, and shall Erona die?
> Erona die? . . . &c.

p. 38, line 22 Can fancy *should be* Can fancies
p. 39, line 33 Then what *should be* Then then what
line 34 Wind, tempest *should be* Wind, tempests
p. 40, line 48 What odds *should be* What an odds
p. 42, line 12 thy reason? *should be* thy counsel?
p. 43, line 5 the heavenly *should be* heavenly
line 9 to the stars *should be* unto the stars
p. 46, line 9 two fair *should be* fair great
p. 48, line 39 cherries, roses *should be* cherries, and roses
p. 50, line 94 that *should be* what
p. 57, line 28 water *should be* waters
line 30 too *should be* to
line 48 the head *should be* her head
p. 60, line 10 were but absent *should be* absent were but
p. 68, line 125 What *should be* That
p. 86, line 43 good men *should be* good men,
p. 99, line 20 And ass's *should be* An ass's
p. 124, stanza 15, line 4 thereabouts *should be* thereabout
p. 136, stanza 39, line 9 sweet pillows *should be* smooth pillows

p. 145, stanza 57, line 10 she is *should be* is she
p. 162, line 13 can no man *should be* no wit can
p. 165, line 29 we both *should be* both we
line 34 to swell *should be* doth swell
p. 173, line 5 my eyes *should be* mine eyes
p. 197, Psalm 13, line 7 foes *should be* foes'